PIMLICO

15

THE PRIVATE LIFE OF ISLAM

Ian Young was educated in London and Paris. He qualified as a doctor in London and apart from a few interruptions has worked there ever since.

THE PRIVATE LIFE OF ISLAM

An Algerian Diary

IAN YOUNG

PIMLICO

Published by Pimlico 2002

2 4 6 8 10 9 7 5 3

First published in Great Britain by Allen Lane 1974
First Pimlico edition 1991
Reissued 2002

Pimlico
Random House, 20 Vauxhall Bridge Road,
London SW1V 2SA

Random House Australia (Pty) Limited
20 Alfred Street, Milsons Point, Sydney,
New South Wales 2061, Australia

Random House New Zealand Limited
18 Poland Road, Glenfield,
Auckland 10, New Zealand

Random House (Pty) Limited
Endulini, 5A Jubilee Road, Parktown 2193, South Africa

The Random House Group Limited Reg. No. 954009
www.randomhouse.co.uk

A CIP catalogue record for this book
is available from the British Library

ISBN 0-7126-5037-7

Papers used by Random House UK Limited are natural,
recyclable products made from wood grown in sustainable forests.
The manufacturing processes conform to the environmental
regulations of the country of origin.

Printed and bound in Great Britain by
Mackays of Chatham PLC

Introduction and Epilogue

Students at some London medical schools may take their midwifery training in the country of their choice. I decided on Algeria, and wrote to the Departments of Obstetrics and Gynaecology at various hospitals in the Algerian provinces – Kabylia, the Aurès Mountains, the Sahara, the districts of Oran and Constantine – asking if they could take me for two months in the summer of 1970. I heard nothing for a long while. Then a letter came from a senior official in the Ministry of Health in Algiers, to whom one of my requests had been forwarded for approval. He was happy to grant it, he said, and he was writing to the Director of the hospital concerned, to ensure I received the best possible welcome. I was all the more grateful in that it was the hospital of my first choice, the one in the province of Kabylia.

I heard next from the Director. He was glad I was coming, and he was having a room made available for me in the hospital. He didn't say how much this would cost. When I got there, I was to find there was no question of my being expected to pay for anything, either for board and lodging, or for any tuition I might receive. The Econome was even to offer me money if I needed it.

I heard finally from Dr Vasilev himself. He was the man in charge of Maternity and his letter was the longest. He recalled the surprise – and the pleasure – that he'd felt on first hearing from me. He spoke of the number of deliveries I would do, the amount of pathology I would see. He mentioned there was no point trying to learn any Arabic before I came. The language of the province was Kabyl, an unwritten Berber dialect that was quite different. Neither he nor his wife could speak either. French was sufficient. He wrote of the climate of

Kabylia, and its beauty. Oranges and lemons, grapes and figs. Mediterranean Sea and Djurdjura Mountains. He enclosed a postcard of the town hall. There was blue sky in the background, and a hill studded with olive trees. If I let him know the time of my arrival, he said, he'd come and fetch me from Algiers.

I was very proud of my choice. I sent back some happy thank-you letters. I'd never been so excited by the idea of a new country. I was determined to please. I read some books on Algeria. I even read some medicine.

This book is taken from the diary which I began shortly after I arrived. I began it as an alibi, as a way of saying: 'I might appear to be collaborating, but I'm not really.'

Of course, I could have left. But I did believe that something could be achieved by staying. Only gradually did I realize my mistake. The foreign doctors had seemed the first cause of the misfortunes of Kabyl women. But I had conversations with Algerians of both sexes, I read articles in the national newspaper and declarations by a variety of Government officials which greatly diminished the doctors' role, though doing nothing to lessen their guilt. These men were the unhappy executors, working in blood, excrement and death, of the most respected attitudes in Algeria.

The diary became a means of revenge. An eye for an eye, to hurt back at those who hurt. At the time, this motive was very strong. It even sustained me. What stopped me from using my fist on one occasion was the hope that I might hurt more with the diary. But now the personal feeling's gone. It's served its purpose. I got down what they said and did. I no longer feel the frustration I felt then, when I was actually confronted by their vastly superior powers. I've concealed their names and made the hospital unrecognizable. It shouldn't be thought that sending some home or dismissing others would improve the situation in any way. None are misfits in the society in which they live.

Baya still writes, and keeps me in touch. She despairs of ever getting married, and she prays in every PS for a nice young man to bring an end to her misfortune. At the opposite extreme, Zora has been turning away her suitors one after the other. She's neither married nor engaged, and she's still working in Maternity. There's no news of Djamila – predictably. Malika married her gendarme and has stayed on as *chef de service*. Dr Nikolenko left six months after me, and was replaced by a Hungarian. Tamara's still there. Dr Kostov too, though not for long – his contract runs out at the end of the year. His temper's as short as ever. 'He hits the women', writes Baya, 'and pinches them inside.' This summer he's gone to Munich, to collect his BMW. The Econome's still the Econome. But the Director's been dismissed, and his place has been taken by 'Monsieur Chameau – Mr Camel', Baya's nickname for the tempestuous Supervisor.

Dr Vasilev left in June last year and was replaced by another Bulgarian. He had a little holiday in Italy before going home. He even tried to come to London that summer, but the British Embassy in Algiers wouldn't grant him a visa. They were afraid he was coming for asylum, he told me. He sent me regular postcards when he got back to Bulgaria. He'd choose views of his home town that he hoped I'd like – and that he trusted one day I would see – solemn statues in empty squares, huge white apartment buildings with blue sea in the background. His messages were always enthusiastic, thoughtful and kind. He'd end each card with: 'Je vous embrasse.' I wasn't as assiduous. I had a lot of work to do, and the postcards stopped. When exams were over, I sent him a newsy letter on the backs of four giant views of London. I had an answer by return of post, in unfamiliar handwriting. It was from a family friend, with a sad duty to perform. A heart attack had struck 'like a thunderbolt', and frail Dr Vasilev was dead.

The engines that brought us hum in our ears, muffling voices. Children stir in mothers' arms, over fathers' shoulders. Parents gather things, raffia bags from the racks above their heads, cardboard boxes from beneath their seats. A man in airline clothes and another in overalls beckon us down on to the tarmac. We file towards the airport building, small and white under the full moon. 'El Biar', it says, repeated in Arabic.

The air's warm, and a gentle wind carries the smell of roasting nuts, faintly sweet. Three in the morning. What better time to land. A provincial airport, with one runway. A closed control tower, in the dead of night. Smuggled into Algeria.

I

I wasn't sure what to expect – something small, something decrepit, a few beds, no more. But the taxi turned into a dual carriageway, lit along the centre island by soaring steel lampposts. Down one side, there were blocks of new apartment buildings, and opposite was the hospital. A magnificent building, vast, modern and clean, that stretched out of sight down the hill. In front, a long stone wall, broken by two gates. At each one, there was a man in a cabin, with a pole painted red and white that wound up to let the traffic through. Frontier posts of medicine.

I asked the driver to turn back to the last café we passed. I felt suddenly unequal to the privilege of working in such a place, and I didn't want to insult them further by arriving as I was. In the café I threw away my shoes and put on new ones, new trousers and a new shirt. I tried to wash and shave away the effects of two days without sleep. But about the heat there was nothing I could do. I walked off to the hospital with a wad of tissues to keep my face dry.

There was a fountain in the courtyard behind the main gate. I followed an empty trolley, pushed by a little woman in blue with swinging plaits. We came to some doors with flaking paint, and above them was the word MATERNITÉ. She beckoned for me to follow. We left the main building, and took a corridor that ran like a bridge over the hospital roadway. Painters hung outside, working on the windows. We reached a landing, and a door marked DELIVERY ROOM. I saw a corridor, and women standing in coloured robes at the doors to their rooms.

Downstairs, the doctors' office was open. There were two men in white coats inside, seated round a desk. They hadn't noticed me, and I had to knock. I was unhappy about making myself known. Not only had I invited myself, but I was bringing them nothing, neither knowledge nor practical experience, and I was late into the bargain. The man behind the desk cried a jubilant: 'Welcome!' He shook my hand very warmly, and declared himself enchanted: Dr Vasilev. He'd been expecting me earlier in the week. What happened? I began to tell him – about Marseille, about the boat and the plane, about how lucky I was to have arrived at all. It was such a complicated business. 'Never mind,' he said, cutting me short, 'what matters is that you're here.' He introduced me to his assistant, Dr Kostov, a heavier, jovial man, a closer fit to the ideas I had about people from Eastern Europe. He was reading a newspaper from home. I asked if they were Russians. He told me they were Bulgarians. I said: 'You're the first Bulgarians I've ever met.' Dr Vasilev smiled and put his hand on my shoulder: 'You'll find we're human beings like everyone else.' Dr Kostov said: 'You're a capitalist and we're communists,' and roared with laughter.

Dr Vasilev introduced me to his wife, a former theatre sister in Bulgaria and now the chief nurse in Maternity. She invited me for dinner that evening. They welcomed me like an old friend. I remembered how, in his first letter to me, before he'd known I'd be making my own way here, Dr Vasilev had actually offered to fetch me himself from Algiers airport.

The hospital workman wouldn't let me carry anything except the keys. With my bags under each arm, he led the way down a corridor thick with dust. We came to a door that was marked EAR, NOSE and THROAT. He waited until I'd opened it, and then set the bags down the other side. He shook my hand, and wished me a happy stay.

I was in another corridor, dustier than the first, and darker, with more doors that gave off on either side. I switched on the light. There was a notice-board next to me, with rusty drawing pins, and curling yellow circulars dating from 1965. I opened the door to the TREATMENT ROOM. On the table inside, there was a metal tray with a crust of dried food, and in the corner, a bin with rubbish round its feet. Next, there was the DOCTORS' OFFICE and, beyond that, four small wards, blinds drawn, of a dozen beds each. Mattresses lay in different poses across the frames. Some were thin, tattered and flat, others were abandoned, split by great gashes into arms and legs that dangled over the side, their stuff spilling on to the floor.

I'd been promised a room. I'd been given an entire floor. 48 beds, 10 washbasins, 4 lavatories and 2 baths.

I wound up the blinds. I chose to occupy a ward facing east, with a view of the Djurdjura Mountains. It was conveniently situated opposite Maternity and the building where the doctors lived. I cleared out all the beds except one, and put them in the other wards. I swept the dust and dead birds from the floor, and brought in a table and two chairs from the doctors' office. I stuck maps of Kabylia on the walls, scrubbed my baths and excavated all four lavatories from the area that lay behind the door marked TOILETS at the end of the corridor. That afternoon, the painter asked me if I was in the Scouts.

I turned up at the Vasilevs' apartment as arranged. I brought with me a litre of Mascara wine. They introduced me to a cat with a milky eye, and warned me not to get too close. It never allowed anyone but them to touch it, and besides, it had just had kittens. 'She's a very intelligent cat,' explained Dr Vasilev, 'she came to an obstetrician to have her babies.'

We talked a great deal, about medicine and our respective countries, about the summer heat and the food of Algeria. Dr Vasilev seemed delighted with his visitor. His hands flew, and his French frequently left me behind. He'd been the director of a maternity unit on the Black Sea, he told me. His work there was done. Enough young doctors were ready to take over. He'd accept no credit for having come out to Algeria. He disclaimed any political motives, any 'call' from the Third World. He'd admit to no enthusiasm for Algeria's war against the French. Even his medicine appeared untechnical. He was neither a Communist saint, nor a doctor with a social conscience. He was totally unassuming, and I felt drawn to him all the more.

But as the evening wore on, I remember, he became established in my mind as a man who'd been seriously overworked. Helping Algeria to its feet had sapped his strength. He was small, brown and wasted. He told me that for the first eighteen months he'd been entirely on his own. He used to operate day and night. It was only when he threatened to go home that they found him an assistant. Things had improved since Dr Kostov came out here. But Vasileva, who'd got up to fetch in the food, stopped by her husband and put her hand on his shoulder: 'The Doctor still suffers from that time.'

'It's all in the past,' said Dr Vasilev, shaking the sympathy off, 'let's eat.' But he scarcely touched his food. Cool yoghurt soup, chicken and fried potatoes, Balkan salads, and cold beer. I beamed at countless views of the Black Sea, exclaimed over the golden sands and the rows of hotels, and became familiar with the map of the country I was to feel so close to over the next few weeks. It became an evening of Anglo-Bulgarian solidarity, of extravagant promises, cemented after the chicken by the Caesarean section that Dr Vasilev performed, and at which I assisted, on a nameless Algerian woman in Theatre. We stumbled back to the doctors' building. There were grapes and melon, and more beer. Vasileva had gone to bed, but she'd left out a bundle of magazines, *Life* and *Paris-Match*, for me to carry back to my room.

2

I wake in the hollow ward before it's light, step down from the high hospital bed and sit at the open window. Swallows flit insanely about in the space between my room and Maternity – over the garden silently, up to their nests in the roof, in bare concrete corners, and down again. Vests and pants flutter on wooden struts from the Vasilevs' kitchen window. Beyond, pitchblack countryside stretches upwards, walls of a crater, to the rim of hills. The sun rises very fast, you feel it's going to pour down towards you. The theme of 2001 resounds through my head, as if the sunrise itself wasn't enough. The country between the hospital and the hills comes quickly into view. White mosque spotlighted on a nearby ridge. Four cows, and a boy with a stick, on the grassy slope between the hospital and the cork dépôt. I run a bath, and the water echoes through the deserted floor.

There are three people in the consulting room downstairs in Maternity: Dr Vasilev, Vasileva and a patient, a Kabyl woman in a coloured robe that Dr Vasilev catches and lifts up. Underneath, there's a pair of pants that stretch down below her knees. Dr Vasilev goes to the door and calls down the corridor: 'Madame Fatma!' The cleaner with the swinging plaits comes running. 'Tell this woman to take off her pants.' Fatma translates into Kabyl. The woman looks away, and steps out of her pants. They're dark, and heavy with blood. Without needing to be told, Fatma takes the woman's arm and guides her up the steps on to the table. The woman lies back, allows her knees to be folded over the stirrups and turns her eyes away, to the nearest wall. Fatma takes her robe and pulls it back off her thighs, on to her stomach. 'Ai, ma,' says the woman, and brings a knee out of its stirrup to join the other knee and

7

conceal what has just been bared. Fatma the cleaner puts it back.

Dr Vasilev unscrews the lid of a tin that says 'Sterile Gloves'. He picks out a two-fingered rubber gauntlet and fits it over the index and middle fingers of his right hand. He puts his right foot on the steps between the woman's knees, and slips his fingers through the dark hair into her vagina. They come out with strands of blood between them. Fatma opens the cupboard by the woman's head and brings down a long metal box, that she puts on the trolley next to Dr Vasilev.

She comes round the front and holds the handle of an instrument that Dr Vasilev has just introduced into the vagina. It's wide, with a gutter down the centre. Dr Vasilev peers up the cavity, with a long pair of pincers that have little teeth at the end. They grip the cervix, with a series of clicks as they slot into position. The woman cries 'ai, ma!' sharply, and tries to throw down her robe. But Fatma the cleaner restrains her and talks to her in Kabyl.

Dr Vasilev pulls the cervix down into the vagina. It's open, by a centimetre or two. He takes an instrument with a loop at the end and pushes it through into the womb. He uses it to scrape the back, the front and the sides. Blood-clot and pieces of placenta run down the gutter into the enamel bowl that waits on the top step. The woman's cries fill the room and she'd close her thighs to stop the operation if Fatma didn't hold them apart. Dr Vasilev changes instruments, taking a curette with a smaller loop. Nothing more comes. The womb's been cleared. He unfastens the teeth, and Vasileva shakes iodine on to a cotton wool swab for him. He wipes the inside of the vagina clean and drops the swab into the enamel basin.

'Dayin! – All over!' cries Fatma. Vasileva taps the woman's bottom, and she rolls on her side for her injection. It's Methergin, to help her womb contract. The woman sits up, and shakes her head. She comes down the steps, leaning on the stirrups like crutches. She collects her dirty pants from the floor and Fatma helps her down the corridor to her room.

Dr Vasilev tells me: 'Medicine here is very different from England and Bulgaria'.

He lights a cigarette as we wait for Fatma to prepare a second woman for curettage. The pants come down with a struggle. The woman says she's about forty. She has six children and she's been bleeding for a week. Dr Vasilev extinguishes his cigarette under the tap and assisted this time by his wife, he scrapes the womb clean. The woman's in great pain and she holds on to my hand for dear life, clenching my arm in time with the scrapes. When it's over she asks me, and Fatma translates, if she's going to have a baby. I shake my head. She kisses my hand several times and struggles upright to try and kiss Vasileva, who smiles briefly and gives her an injection of Methergin instead.

There's a razor in the cupboard, and antiseptic. There's local anaesthetic in the same small bottles as in London. The equipment is there, plain to see. Why don't they use it? The answer must be obvious to everyone but me. I stay numb, and Dr Vasilev invites no questions.

He's telling me that there's a lot of miscarriage in Kabylia. Bits of placenta stay inside the womb and if the women aren't scraped out, they go on bleeding till they die. He asks the Postmaster if that isn't true, the man says: 'Eh oui,' and limps off to deliver more mail on his surgical boots. He's brought El Moudjahid, the Algerian national newspaper, and a postcard from the oasis town of Ghardaïa, sent by some Bulgarian friends.

Dr Vasilev stands close to show me the card. He points out 'the palm trees, here', 'the minarets, there', and 'the camels'. Then he puts his hand on my arm and bends very close, so that he becomes shorter than he's been before. He directs his words to my heart. 'One day,' he says in a voice that has an odd nursery-rhyme lilt, full of excitement and promise, 'when it's cooler,' he pauses to swallow, 'in the car of these very sympathetic friends who sent us the card,' he glances up to see if I'm following, 'you,' with an emphatic nod into my chest, 'Vasileva and . . .', very strongly, 'myself, of course! We'll all drive . . .' He straightens up and stands away from me. He waves the postcard in the air, sending the minarets plunging into a blue floor, he looks up at me and when the surprise that he's kept till the end breaks over his face, it's more than the name of a place, it's the name of a feeling – expectation of joy in my comradeship – that leaves me at a loss for a reply. 'We'll drive . . . ,' he's crying, 'to the SAHARA!'

A massive sixteen-year-old girl from a village in the Djurdjura Mountains wears a blue scarf and a beautiful yellow robe. Her legs are thick and hairy, and she's never seen a gynaecological table before. She doesn't know what she's supposed to do on it. She gets up with her pants on. 'What's this, Madame?' cries Dr Vasilev. The girl tumbles off the table and looks at us, the Vasilevs from Bulgaria, me from England, and Fatma who's running the instruments from the last curettage under the tap. Fatma confirms: 'Eksesserwell – off with your pants.' Dr Vasilev sits on the stool, with a sigh and a cigarette, waiting. The girl reaches up under her robe and pulls down her pants. They're attached with elastic bands just below her knees. Their crotch is soaked in blood.

She gets back on to the table and lies there flat, knees tightly together, and as far from the edge as she can. 'Sob! – Down!' cries Fatma the cleaner, and the girl consents to shift towards the end of the table, and even to have her knees separated and put over the stirrups. But she won't let go of her yellow robe. She holds it clamped between her legs. Dr Vasilev doesn't move from his stool. He shakes his cigarette at her: 'Back home, Madame.'

She relents. She lets Fatma hold her robe back over her stomach. She clutches my hand. Dr Vasilev's cigarette fizzles out among the products of the last curettage in the enamel bowl, and he doesn't bother this time to put on the rubber apron. The operation takes about three minutes. Towards the end, the curette is fairly bubbling in the womb. 'It's called "the song of the curette",' says Dr Vasilev, and he invites me round to see the pink, frothy blood in the vagina. 'It's the sign it's nearly finished,' he says, An iodine swab and: 'Dayin! – All over!' The girl's eyes are rolling. Her forehead's damp. She's a little shocked. She's been bleeding for two weeks, Fatma tells us. Her husband works in France, and she had to wait for his permission before she could come to hospital.

'Eh,' goes Dr Vasilev, a weary Italian sort of 'é', that may once have been an exclamation but that's now routine, and that's accompanied by a fresh cigarette in his uplifted hand.

Chaos: station wagon braking in the courtyard in a cloud of dust, taxi-driver shouting in Kabyl and French, anxious male relatives and a heavy cortège of tattooed women. Stretcher hoisted out of the back of the taxi, arms falling off the side, woman's head thrown back, lips snarling. Hurrying with her down the Maternity path, lifting her on to the table in the curettage room quickly vacated. Her pants drop with a splash into the enamel bowl. Her pulse is fast and weak. There are great beads of sweat on her forehead. Kabyl cries from Fatma as she sweeps the robed women back into the hallway.

We close the door. Vasileva switches on the spotlight, and her husband performs the curettage. There's no sound from the woman. She doesn't react in any way. When it's over, the pulse at the wrist I'm holding has completely disappeared. 'A drip!' cries Dr Vasilev. A pint bottle of saline, ampoules of hydrocortisone, a stimulant called Coramine, and Vitamin C. We saw and snap the ampoules as fast as we can while Dr Vasilev hunts for a vein on the woman's arm. 'Why Vitamin C?', I ask Vasileva. 'It's for shock,' she says.

Fatma has both hands tightly clasped round the woman's arm, but no veins stand up. Dr Vasilev flicks the skin. It's cold and wet. Still nothing. The woman's too shocked, her veins have all collapsed. Dr Vasilev tries three times at an elbow, where a vein should be. Then he hands the needle to me, to try my side. I fumble it, the needle falls to the floor. Fatma fetches it, wipes it with a swab soaked in alcohol, and hands it back. Dr Vasilev comes round my side. He gets into a vein. The fluid goes through, drop by drop. The needle's the size you use for giving injections. There's nothing wider. Vasileva clears up while we wait for the woman to come round.

Dr Vasilev lights a cigarette in the office. I ask him the same question, about the Vitamin C. 'It's for shock,' he says.

He asks me if I know what is meant by hysterography. He draws a diagram on a piece of prescription paper, and shows me how you can inject a dye into the womb and then follow it up the tubes with X-rays, to see if the tubes are open. It's one of the things you must know if you're treating a woman who can't have a child. He's an excited teacher, but his French is shaky and I can't follow all he says.

Fatma brings the woman to the office door. She's been married seven years, and she's not had a baby. We walk across the courtyard with her to the X-ray department. The glare of the sun is so intense that I take my first steps with my eyes closed. Dr Vasilev's immediately concerned. 'You must be careful!' he cries.

The X-ray room is vast, and well equipped with machines from France. The radiographer is from Oran, on the other side of Algeria. She's an Arab girl who can speak no Kabyl. She's reading a Jean Bruce thriller behind her screen. The woman looks around her, bewildered. Fatma can't explain to her what's going to be done, she doesn't know herself. She says some words in Kabyl. The woman stares at us, and nods.

Dr Vasilev fills a long syringe with dye and draws up his chair to the table. Then he raises one foot after the other an inch or so off the floor, in a curious sort of dance, holding the nozzle of the syringe high in the air and crying to himself in anticipation, exploiting each syllable like a small boy in front of his favourite dessert: 'Hy-ster-o-gra-PHY!'

The woman lies on the table, knees up and apart. The X-ray plates slot into the table beneath her. The radiographer swivels the gun over her pelvis. Dr Vasilev catches her cervix in the pincers. 'Pa . . . pa . . . pa', says the woman, and Fatma takes her hand. Dr Vasilev pushes the nozzle of the syringe through into the womb and presses the plunger. But the thick, oily dye won't flow. It begins coming out the wrong way, through the attachments of the syringe itself. He screws up his face in effort and pushes harder. The plunger begins to move and he thinks that some of the liquid must be getting into the womb. 'Take!'

The girl from Oran flicks switches behind her screen and comes out to put the plates through the hatch. We go next door to the darkroom. When they're developed, the radiographer clips the films up against the light. They're bare. There's nothing on them at all, not even a picture of the woman's pelvis. 'I must have turned the wrong switch,' says the girl from Oran, and she yawns goodbye.

We walk back across the courtyard in silence. Dr Vasilev appears overcome by the anticlimax. I'm too embarrassed to mention it. We say nothing to the Kabyl woman. She walks behind us, and she's sick by the little fir-tree outside Maternity. But it's only a clear liquid, and she smiles. 'We'll ask her to come back another day,' says Dr. Vasilev hoarsely.

After lunch I go into town, to give in some letters at the Post Office. I come back quickly, down the main street, afraid I might be late for the afternoon – I am. There are already noises from behind the opaque glass door of the curettage room. I slip inside. It's the assistant, Dr Kostov. There's excitement in the air. He's a larger presence than Dr Vasilev, he takes up more room. His face is fleshy, his forearms thick and muscular. I tell him I'm sorry to be late, I was out at the Post Office. Dr Kostov blows through his lips, as if to say that's no concern of his.

'Sob! Sob! – Down! Down!' he's crying like a herdsman to the woman on the table. His style is vigorous, outdoor. The woman inches down until her vagina's just over the edge of the table, a foot or so above the enamel bowl that's ready on the top step. Her robe is rolled back over her breasts. Her belly's large, she's six months pregnant. She came into hospital ten days ago, says Dr Kostov, to keep the baby she was in danger of losing. She went home only this morning, and already she's back again. Her legs are stained with blood. There's a mattress of clot and pubic hair across the entrance to her vagina. And the already familiar smell.

Dr Kostov leaves her to find the rickety stirrups with her knees. He twists off the top of the sterile glove tin, with a look of displeasure on his face. He pulls on the heavy-duty rubber glove, made in Poland and sterilized by Vasileva in tap water and talc. Her back is turned, she's busy at the sink.

A small purple foot has fallen through the vagina. Dr Kostov touches it, and his face says it feels like warm excrement. The baby's been dead for days and days. 'She wanted to go,' says Vasileva without turning round. 'It wasn't me who sent her out,' says Dr Kostov. The rest of the body falls through, but the head gets caught at the cervix. Dr Kostov pulls on the shoulders, too hard. The neck comes apart, and the body falls the length of its cord towards the basin below, a broken headless alpinist swinging on his rope. Dr Kostov shoves a large-looped curette past the head into the womb. The placenta comes away followed by the head, a soft sack like a rotten pear.

'You were out at the Bank?', asks Dr Kostov. I remind him that I was at the Post Office, sending letters. 'Ah!', he remembers.

A French girl arrives outside the door of the curettage room. She's a newly qualified doctor, doing a month's voluntary work in a fishing village east along the coast from Dellys. She's brought along one of her patients. I invite her inside to watch. She wonders if she should. After all, she says, she has nothing to wear. She has no mask or gown, and nothing to even cover her hair. Nervously, she comes inside. She sees the table, Dr Kostov, Vasileva and me. It's small, she says, there'll hardly be room for the anaesthetist. She doesn't believe me when I tell her there is no anaesthetist.

Dr Kostov brings no modification to his style for her benefit. He doesn't linger over the vaginal examination. He brings out a black clot between his fingers, and flicks it off into the enamel bowl. 'Cervix open,' he intones, 'miscarriage . . . curettage.' The French girl's patient shakes her head, flutters her hands and goes 'pa . . . pa . . . pa' at the prospect. Kabyl women seem to know what 'curettage' means. 'Yes,' says Dr Kostov knowingly, and without sympathy, as he dons the rubber apron that hangs by the cupboard door. The French girl takes the woman's hand. Fatma arrives with her mop, and adjusts the position of the enamel bowl.

The woman makes a final attempt to throw down her robe between her legs. 'What's this thing?' shouts Dr Kostov already seated between her knees, pincers and curette in hand, the knife and fork of a vampire diner. He throws the robe

back to her face. He wastes as little time with me. I'm already
assisting. Into the vagina sideways with the wide-lipped gutter.
Once it's in, turn it flat and hold it down – 'harder', says Dr
Kostov's hand on mine. The gutter's cold steel and the woman
shudders. Dr Kostov searches upwards with the pincers.
The spiked teeth bite through the front rim of the cervix.
'Pa . . . pa . . . pa.' He pulls the cervix down, and pushes the
curette through. He begins to scrape. Big, energetic scrapes at
first, down the back wall of the womb. The loop rasps on the
muscle and bloody débris spills through the vagina into the
bowl below. It runs over my hand on the way. But I'm ready
for the feeling, and when it comes it's strangely distant, as
if the hand's not mine.

Finer scrapes next, higher-pitched, with a smaller-looped
curette. It's for the corners, explains Dr Kostov, for the en-
trances to the tubes. 'Pa . . . pa . . . pa.' He pulls on my hand
and I take the gutter out. He releases the pincers and clips
them over a dry swab, which he forces through the closed
vagina and swirls around inside, bread for a salad bowl.
Followed by a second swab soaked in iodine. 'Pa . . . pa . . .pa.'
He throws the instruments back in the box with a clatter.
Vasileva takes them to the sink. It's been less than three minutes. The muscles along the woman's thighs are trembling.
The French girl leaves immediately. 'You're in a madhouse,'
she tells me.

We're crossing the courtyard, over to the X-ray department,
with a second woman for hysterography. The air is hot and
still. The sun is all-powerful. I could sense its strength from
inside Maternity. And now it strikes from every angle, from
below, off the white gravel, from the side, off the white hospital walls. My eyes are watering. 'You don't have weather
like this in England,' says Dr Kostov. No, I say, we don't. In
the same tone of voice, he asks me if it is true that there are
many banks in England. Yes, I say, it is.

The woman behind us is nearly forty, but she doesn't look it.
She's small and slim, like a little girl, with a red scarf round
her hair and a brightly coloured gypsy robe. Her husband has
been working for years in France. She stayed at home in the

mountains. She's never had a baby, and it's the first time she's been to a doctor. When we arrive in the X-ray room, she stands absolutely still.

Dr Kostov thumps the black table in invitation. She climbs the steps and crawls along the table on hands and knees, with no idea what way to face or where to go. I fold her into the right position, on her back, legs drawn up and apart, robe back over her chest. She consents, with perfect docility. Down his end, Dr Kostov inserts an instrument that allows him to look up the vagina. When the radiographer from Oran comes close, to slip the plates under the table, the woman reaches for her hand, believing that she was coming for her. But the girl pushes the hand away without a word, and adjusts the X-ray gun over the woman's hips.

Dr Kostov pushes the pincers through the open vagina and closes the teeth round her cervix. The woman's hand shoots out towards me, fingers taut and splayed. She pulls my hand down on to her chest, I've never been held so hard, it's painful. Dr Kostov's cursing in Bulgarian. He's having the same trouble with the apparatus that Dr Vasilev had this morning. But Dr Kostov's stronger by far. He forces the plunger down, with a strength that makes you pray nothing's going to slip.

When it's over, and the plates have been passed through the hatch to the darkroom, the woman sits up. She doesn't know what's happened. Maybe she thought she was going to have an operation. She doesn't seem able to get down off the table. The others have gone away, they're washing the greasy liquid off their hands, throwing the empty ampoules into the bin, going next door to have a look at the films. I move the steps up to the table and put my arm round the woman to help her off. I only get her half-way down when she begins shaking like a leaf. She won't come any further. I turn to see what's the matter, and she's kissing the collar of my white coat.

We walk back to Maternity in the sun. It's incredibly hot. The woman walks behind, barefoot. She vomits twice on the way, and that's only 50 yards. The first time, we stand by her. I say to Dr Kostov that I could carry her the rest of the way.

He laughs, and says she'll manage. He goes on ahead. The
woman manages.

Dr Kostov invites me into the doctors' office. He sits in
Dr Vasilev's chair, I sit in his. 'Are there Swiss banks in
London?' he asks. Yes, I say, they have branches there. He
asks after their reputation. It's excellent, I say, but ordinary
people don't use them. There are so many English banks. Dr
Kostov nods, and gives me the feeling that I've not answered
his question.

'How will you be sending money home?' he asks. I've none
to send, I tell him. He doesn't understand. I've only got the
money I came with, I say, and that isn't very much. 'Aren't
they paying you anything here?' he asks. Of course not, I tell
him. I'm a student, I've just come to learn. 'To learn!' – Dr
Kostov roars with laughter.

He slips the wrapper off his Bulgarian paper and grins at me
almost sheepishly. I feel I've become a bit of a character for
him, in the tradition of English eccentrics.

A taxi from the mountains stops outside. Two men in dusty
trousers help a woman down the path, into the hall, up to the
door of the doctors' office. 'Fatma!' shouts Dr Kostov without
rising from his seat, 'get her ready!' He looks out the window,
into the blue Algerian sky. 'Ai, ai, ai,' he says to me, 'two and
a half more years.'

We go next door. The woman's ready, and two others follow her in quick succession. We deal with all three in under
twenty minutes. Off with the sodden pants, back with the
bloody robe, up with the stained thighs, through the matted
black hair to the vagina, to scoop out the dark clots that
wobble like jelly in your hand, to feel for the soft open cervix
that you know is going to be there. Metallic clatter of the
curettage box, and before I know it (but that's not honest, I
did know it, I was shutting that future out of my mind), Dr
Kostov's strong hands are on my shoulders, pressing me down
between the legs into the operator's seat. 'In' goes his hand
on mine with the gutter, 'bite' goes his hand on mine with the
pincers through the cervix, 'pa . . . pa . . . pa' from far away,

17

'through' with the curette till we reach the roof of the womb, and then 'back, back, back' unrelentingly, scraping hard on all sides down to the cervix. The placenta comes through in bits over Dr Kostov's left hand. He takes the small curette and finishes off the corners.

The third woman I do on my own, swabbing the whole area with antiseptic soap, cleaning the hair as best I can, asking Vasileva for needle, syringe and local anaesthetic. She says they're all in the sterilizer. Dr Kostov says that anaesthetic can be dangerous just for a curettage, it isn't worth the risks He's watching me with my soap and swabs: 'That's a nurse's job.' Vasileva is a nurse, and she says: 'It's an orderly's job. The orderly's upstairs.

'Why bother?', says Dr Kostov. He's right. Why clean one Kabyl woman? I'm doing it for myself, not for her. I'm falling back on what I've been taught in London. Infection, inflammation, septicemia – the reasons were sound, and I repeat them to myself. It's what I know, it's what I must do. But the words are a poor support. I swab on, and feel like a blackleg in a strike.

Sweat pours off me into the enamel bowl. Like Dr Kostov, like Dr Vasilev, I haven't looked at the woman, and I haven't heard her cries. She's the first woman I'll ever have curetted and I won't recognize her in the morning. Dr Kostov is impatient for me to finish. I get up and feel ashamed before everyone.

3

It's Djamila's day in the delivery room. I like her face. It's grossly, uncompromisingly Arab. Her lips are almost negroid. Harsh, flashing eyes that look at you out of the corners, eyes made for the veil that her mother still wears in Oran. Her languages are French and Arabic. Her Kabyl's no better than mine. She's been away from home for two years. She's been a midwife in the Sahara, and in the Djurdjura Mountains. She's small and strong and independent. She's not impressed by a medical student from England.

On the delivery bed a huge woman from the hills heaves and strains and groans in a language I'm beginning to make some sense of. Her orange and black robe is up around her chest. There are great drops of sweat on her face and a sodden handkerchief in her hand. Her thighs are enormous, with earth in the creases. Her feet and hands are stained with henna.

It's her eighth delivery, and her first in a hospital. This time, she says, she felt 'tired'. She's been in labour all night. Her cervix is fully open and the baby's head is where it should be, ready to come down. But something's wrong. Her contractions are short and weak. She doesn't seem to have her heart in the whole business. Djamila wags a finger and threatens the woman in French, which she doesn't understand: 'If you're not careful, Dr Kostov will come and give you a big spanking.' She gets up on the bed and kneels beside the woman, pressing down on her belly with both hands, arms stiff and straight, trying to push the baby out. To no avail. We go out on to the landing to rest.

We come back to find the woman squatting on the floor, holding herself upright by the bedpost. Fatma the Kabyl cleaner screams. Djamila spits Arab war-cries. They shoo the woman back on to the bed. Djamila won't hear of delivering her on the floor. She's scandalized. She's never seen it done, but she knows there must be a good reason against it. Women deliver on their backs, all else is primitive.

On the bed, the woman looks sullenly at Djamila. Then she flicks her thumb nail against her front teeth at her. Djamila's wounded, and she falls on to the chair in the corner. She'll have nothing more to do with the woman, who's telling Fatma that she won't go anywhere else but the floor. She always squatted before, and that's what she's going to do now. If they won't let her, she's going to sleep. She stretches out her legs, throws down her robe and closes her eyes.

Fatma takes her cue. She's the cleaner. But that's only officially. She's older than the woman on the bed. She's been through it all before. She's got grandchildren, and golden cartwheel earrings, and hair parted down the middle, brushed fiercely against her scalp and tied in a single plait behind. She climbs up the steps beside the bed, takes hold of the enormous oxygen cylinder like some kind of lectern and launches into folklore – folklore twisted to serve the purposes of European obstetric morality, of course, but you forget that in the exchange that follows. There are rapid excited moments, slow dramatic pauses, ritual insults from woman to woman, touchings of chests, flickings of teeth, exclamations and imprecations – all of which Djamila and I understand not a single word. Gradually, Fatma comes out on top. The woman on the bed follows her hands as they fly through the air, she's becoming mesmerized by the argument. Eventually, she begins to nod her agreement. She'll do it. Fatma pats her head and returns to work.

The woman from the mountains is true to her word. She stays on her back with the best will in the world. The baby comes into Djamila's hands nice and easily a few minutes later. A boy – 'Akshish'. There's no response from the woman. I look at her, smile and am totally unable to get a smile back. She's saying something to Fatma. She wants an injection to stop her having more babies.

Two of the three beds in the delivery room are occupied. One woman is expecting her first, the other her fifth. They both slapped their robes between their legs as soon as I came in. I'm nervous in there on my own and I'm on my way out when I meet Djamila arriving from the midwife's room next door. She asks me to keep the women company for a moment, while she runs over to the Econome's office.

Keeping company is difficult. I can't talk their language, and they're not pleased to have me there. I need something to do if I'm to stay. I decide to do what's never been done yet. I take their blood pressures. Then I hunt for a thermometer, but I've not seen one yet and I don't find one now. I decide to assert myself, on the older woman first since she must be used to it. I've got antiseptic soap and a supply of swabs, to clean her the way you should. She lets me ease the robe off her knees and back over her belly. Her hands grip the head of the bed and her face strains. Her womb is hard, she's in the middle of a contraction and I can hear nothing through the stethoscope.

Then I look below and see the vagina bulging. I'm caught, in the classic situation. I've not touched a baby yet, let alone delivered one. I've only been watching. I want to shout for Djamila, to run and get her from the Econome's office. But that's the other side of the hospital and I can't leave now.

I put on a pair of the Polish gloves, collect some cotton wool and alcohol. Then I remember, and get one of the delivery boxes from the cupboard with clamps and scissors checked. My hands move towards the vagina and then stop, because I have no idea what to do with them. The vagina opens and I can see the wet black hair on the back of the baby's head. I swab furiously, it's something to do, and I clean the earth from the thighs with antiseptic soap.

'Pa . . . pa . . . pa,' and I know this must be it. The next contraction's coming. The head comes out almost with a pop, face down, and then turns to the side. All I have to do now is pull it out, and I put my hands round its head. But how do you hold it? I'd never paid attention. Palms above the ears, fingers round the jaw? I try, but the skull feels so fragile, I'm sure there's something wrong. I daren't pull. I'd only stretch its neck.

I do nothing. I just stand there. Everything comes to a halt.

I stare into the bedpan between the woman's legs, that's full of fluid, excrement and blood. What must she be thinking of me? And what about the woman in the next bed, what's she thinking, all ready with her first? I haven't the courage to run away. Djamila arrives back. I'm weak with relief. Hands on her hips at the end of the bed, she's laughing at me down her Barbra Streisand nose.

'But what do I do?' She's laughing too much to tell me. 'Eh bien', she said, 'you just pull . . . down . . . harder . . . up There's nothing to it.' I follow everything she says. The baby comes, slipping out of my hands into the pan and the cord's wriggling like a snake. 'Sob! – Down!' shouts Djamila, and the woman pushes herself further down on to the bedpan, allowing me to retrieve the baby without pulling too hard on the cord. Djamila holds the baby while I clamp the cord, and then cut it between the clamps. The actual cutting is something so definitive that the moment I've done it, I'm winded by horror and remorse, convinced I've made a mistake. 'But that's right,' cries Djamila, lifting the baby away. The cord's tough and strange. It's stranger than the baby. It has a sinewy feel through the scissors. It's blue, white and metallic, it glistens with a life of its own.

Djamila wraps the baby in one of the cloths, tightly, arms to its sides, the way the women like it. The mother's silent. I want to say something to her. I'm elated. I ask the word for congratulations. Djamila doesn't know it, and she calls the cleaner. Fatma laughs, and says they have no such word in Kabyl. Instead, she explains to the woman that we're glad she's had a baby. When the woman answers, I want to know her every word. 'She's rid of it,' says Fatma. Is that all? Isn't she pleased? Fatma doesn't ask her. 'Perhaps,' she says, 'you can't really tell.'

The reply doesn't dampen things for me. I'm full of confidence now, and I take the next girl in my stride, Djamila aiding me. For her first baby, it's easy. The head's not too big and she doesn't tear. It's a live boy, and he cries the moment he's out. The cord beats. It's an extraordinary feeling. The placenta too – you massage the womb a little, and then you squeeze from the top. The placenta comes out like the stone

22

from a fruit. I'm pleased with myself. I tell Dr Vasilev before he goes off to lunch that I've delivered my first baby. He cries happily: 'Bravo!'

During the siesta, when Maternity's quiet as night, I hear the demon shrieks of an ultimate panic that sends me rushing inside the delivery room to find a thin and sickly girl utterly berserk on the centre table, losing her head over her first labour pains, arching backwards, falling forwards on to hands and knees, swinging off the bed, crawling on the floor, stumbling in tears from post to post. I touch her to tell her someone's there. I hold her and stroke her and talk to her in French. She doesn't understand a word, I'm only calming myself. I look for her chart, but she doesn't have one. There's nothing that even bears her name. I put on a glove and feel inside. She doesn't resist, she's not able to. The head's on its way down.

I rush out to fetch Djamila. The midwife's room is empty. Her transistor's playing on the table, next to her sunglasses and the detective story she's reading. I run back for the birth. Djamila arrives as I'm clamping the cord. All's gone well. Fatma comes in and reproaches her. 'Shut your mouth,' says Djamila, 'and anyway, where were you?' She ties the twisted strip of gauze round the cord with extra severity.

4

Zora the Kabyl midwife is the first Algerian woman, Kabyl or Arab, that I ever spoke to. It was she, the dark girl in the white coat and bare feet, who I found on the landing of Maternity the day I arrived (as if she'd been waiting there specially), the girl who clapped her hands and spun for joy when she found out I was English. 'At last!' she'd cried, 'somebody civilized!' She'd exclaimed over my collection of disposable plastic syringes, she'd borrowed my Kleenex, she'd even tried out her English on me.

Zora's very pretty. She's the nicest thing in Maternity by far.

Midwives aren't supposed to, but Zora does a forceps quickly before Dr Vasilev arrives. She tells the woman not to worry, it isn't going to hurt. She places the blades either side of the baby's head, the way she's seen the doctors do. Then she screws them together and pulls. But she slips on the wet floor and calls in Kabyl for Fatma to be her anchor. The head comes down, Zora unscrews the forceps and pulls the baby out. He's breathing well, and he doesn't look damaged at all. 'Aren't I clever?', cries Zora triumphantly.

Dr Vasilev arrives as she's tying the cord. He must have been sleeping. 'Eh!' he goes, blinking in the bright light, 'so there was no need for a forceps after all.' As he leaves the room, Zora bursts out laughing on Fatma's shoulder. The open forceps box, the instruments themselves in the basin, the way the woman's ankles are strapped in the stirrups – the delivery room has forceps written all over it. 'Of course he saw,' says Zora, 'he's too afraid to say anything.'

Fatma invites us, Zora and me, to share her midnight meal. It's fried sardines from Dellys, bread and wizened oranges.

Washed down by a non-alcoholic drink called L'Antésite. It's flavoured with aniseed. 'Only those who worked with the French know it,' Fatma tells me proudly. She kept house for a French colonel and his wife in the years before Independence. She spreads a Kabyl blanket on the landing and we sit down, she matter-of-fact, Zora gracefully, demurely, legs together.

Zora's out of place. It's how they eat up in the mountains, she tells me uncertainly. 'Yes it is,' says Fatma, 'and I prefer it this way: I digest better.' Zora laughs and takes a sardine. She's happy when Fatma lifts up a corner of her scarf and admires her hair: 'Oh là, là!' They talk for a while in Kabyl. Zora's enjoying the outing. In a way, she's as far from the mountains as me.

In the morning, Zora goes home to her parents in town. Tamara the Russian midwife takes over. She arrives on the landing at 7.30, punctual and huge, wielding her handbag like a discus. Then she sits alone in an empty delivery room, sorting swabs and chatting to herself in Russian. 'Niet,' she says with a tumbling laugh, and I hurry away.

Zora's back in the evening. She comes by at 7.30 to see how I'm getting on. Then she disappears to the doctor's building, where Djamila has a room. She takes me for a doctor already. She won't believe that I've no experience at all. While she's away, I busy myself with nursing duties. I listen to babies' hearts, take blood pressures, smother vulvas in antiseptic soap. A woman waves, and says 'Saha – Thank you.'

A taxi brings in a girl from the fishing village of Dellys. A man and two shrivelled women arrive with her. The man stays down in the hall, the two women come up the stairs and sit on the landing outside the delivery room. They're very old and, like the very young, they don't wear veils. They have crisscross tattoos on their face and arms, and long silver teeth. They're natural officiators at any Kabyl birth. But we're in a hospital, and Fatma the cleaner hustles them away.

I call Zora in Djamila's room. She doesn't sound pleased, as if I'm failing in my role. I should be doing all this for her, coping with the deliveries, even the forceps, like a doctor and a man, instead of interrupting her while she's working on her hair with her girl-friend. She comes over with her hair still wet under her scarf. She's anxious to deliver the girl and she punctures the membranes with a pair of scissors. The fluid that comes out is tinged with green. It's a bad sign for the baby, and its heart is beating much too fast. 'Come, my little girl, hurry,' says Zora in Kabyl, 'push! harder!' The girl grips her knees and strains. 'As if you were going to the lavatory, my little girl!' cries Zora, 'it's kif-kif, it's the same thing.' She gives vigorous massage to the vagina, the two fingers of either hand in up to the hilt, with great sweeps to either side, wider each time. Hand playing over the girl's belly, tickling it, pinching it, till the muscle of the womb hardens again: 'N'ki! Ernu!' The contraction wave recedes, the womb becomes soft once more: 'Now rest, my little girl, rest.' The girl pants, her tongue flitting from side to side.

She tries again, a huge effort. Zora grabs some cotton wool to block off the anus, catches the baby's chin through the skin underneath, and tilts it upwards. The rim of the vagina looks dangerously white. Zora could get the scissors and do the sideways cut that would stop the girl getting torn right through. But she decides not to. She's going to take a chance and pray. 'I can't stand stitching,' she tells me.

Anxiously, she works the baby through. She's doing it very well, she couldn't be doing it better. She smoothes down the rim over the baby's head, like the neck of a very tight sweater, but the skin's at full stretch and she loses. It tears as the head jumps out, a split that flashes in a zig-zag downwards, and wells with blood. 'Merde!'

The baby boy doesn't breathe. The tap's broken on the oxygen cylinder and the gas escapes under such pressure that it blows up the baby's chest like a balloon. Zora holds him by the ankles to drain his lungs. Fatma flicks the soles of his feet and rubs alcohol on his chest. At last he begins to whimper. He loses the screwed-up old-man appearance of impending death and he begins to look like a baby.

We break the table under the girl and get her legs into the stirrups ready for stitching. Her placenta comes through

26

smoothly, riding out without a sound, and drops three feet into the pan on the floor that's full of blood, urine and faeces. We're drenched and the floor's awash. 'Fatma! Come and clean!' Teetering on her silver shoes, Zora pulls a sheet off the next bed and throws it down to absorb some of the mess. The woman on that bed watches with wide brown eyes, then winces at the beginning of another contraction. Zora attends to her and entrusts me with the stitching of the girl's tear.

The split vagina's a mystery to me. Its edges are ragged and swollen. The field's obscured by blood. I pack it with swabs and put the sides of the tear together, trying to identify the different layers, muscle, mucosa and skin. I keep the hazy picture in my mind, then inject the local anaesthetic that produces pale balloons over anything recognizable. The sterile catgut in its glass tube is the only ingredient of this scene that has the right to be here. But it loses the privilege immediately, as I unravel it with my hands, trail it from the end of the needle across the girl's filthy thighs and through the débris in the bed pan. Stitches through the muscle – perhaps. I'm surer of the ones through the skin. The misery of doing an important job badly. I offer to bring the girl her baby. She shakes her head, she doesn't want it near her. She says it hurt her too much. Instead, she asks me to pick up her raffia bag from the floor. She takes out two wild pears, one each for Zora and me.

We eat our pears outside, under the hospital lights. We go walking in the courtyard, past the bins and the refuse lorry with the cats on top, past the dogs on the mound of rubble that keeps the heat of the day. Zora tells me the Bulgarians are brutes, as well as bad doctors. She asks me about my hospital in London. The doctors there must be very different. She'd love to come and work with them. Zora's enthusiastic over England, and over me. She isn't Djamila, who seems to have her own life to lead, who's shown no curiosity over mine. Zora's different, she's eager to be let inside.

5

A difficulty with a first pregnancy and Zora decides to call on Dr Kostov. He's in one of his better moods. There's almost a twinkle in his eye. He decides on a forceps. Zora begs him not to tear her. 'Algerians don't like work,' grunts Dr Kostov. Zora volunteers to help him with a 'Chris-Taylor' of her own, and she puts her manicured fists on the girl's belly and bears down with her. I'm pulling backwards on the thighs, Dr Kostov's pulling opposite me on the forceps. It's a tug-of-war, with the baby as the rope. The head's out in less than a minute, unscathed, and the baby's alive.

Zora examines the vagina. There's no tear. She spins round to Dr Kostov: 'Bravo, Doctor!' I think she could hug him. What has she said to me about Bulgarians? All's forgiven now. Dr Kostov grows younger under the praise. About the twinkle, there's no longer any doubt. 'Look at his fine smile!' Zora's crying, 'look at his fine eyes!' And Dr Kostov – still a candidate, though Dr Vasilev has long since retired – laughs, and beckons: 'Come nearer, Mademoiselle Zora!'

I'm on the landing outside when the 'ai, mas!' become high-pitched and hysterical, the unmistakable note reached by a woman delivering for the first time. I rush inside. But someone's already there: Tamara. I watch her stride up to the bed, wag her thick finger and say: 'Sussem!' After six months, her Kabyl consists of 'girl', 'boy', and 'keep quiet!' A word every two months. The woman stares, panting. Then her cries begin again. Tamara's hand comes up and I duck outside before the blow lands. For graduation in Moscow, they gave her a hysterectomy and a lifetime supply of androgens.

I flee into town. I have an orangeade and hot sausages with

a crowd of others, all young men, who've just come out of the cinema. There are two men in rags asleep on the Post Office steps. Others are asleep in front of the Town Hall. There are cats and dogs everywhere, starved, scavenging, emaciated. The side streets have ruts and holes and dust. All is quiet by 10.30. Everything's closed. But the night's alive with crickets, the bells I heard in the roof of the airport at Constantine. By the end of the walk, on my way back down the hospital avenue, I actually feel some of the excitement I'd thought would be inseparable from being here.

Zora runs a glove under the tap and examines the girl on the centre bed. The cord's dangling through the open cervix. There's no danger yet, the contractions are short and weak. But when they get stronger, they'll press the baby's head against the cord and stop the exchange between mother and baby. If nothing's done then, says Zora, it'll be dead before it can be born.

She goes out to fetch Dr Vasilev. He feels for himself. It's not only the cord, he says, the baby's hand is there as well. Two things there shouldn't be. Face contorted, he reaches inside to try and push them away so as to let the head come down. But the cervix isn't wide enough yet. Besides, the girl's in agony. She's screaming for her mother: 'Aiee, ma!' She knows something's wrong, she's surely going to die. She strains down and extrudes faeces into the bedpan. Their smell is particularly powerful. The whole room smells rotten. Dr Vasilev comes away, his face screwed up. 'We'll wait!' he decides. He lights a cigarette on the landing. Perhaps it might right itself spontaneously, he says. 'If not,' he cries from the stairs, 'I'll do a Caesarean . . . this evening . . . certainly!' His words float upwards, encircled by cigarette smoke.

Zora's doubtful. She thinks the Caesarean should be done right away. She goes out, and comes back with Dr Kostov. A completely different style and a more competent man, I feel, by far. He surveys the filthy room, the stained floor and the overflowing bedpans, he takes in the lingering smell of pungent faeces, he hears as if for the first time the frantic cries of the girl on the centre bed, and he asks surlily: 'What's the problem?' For the girl, whose body above the womb he doesn't acknowledge, he has a scowl. Zora outlines the case to him. Dr Kostov nods. It's a job to be dealt with quickly. He's got just over ten minutes before supper.

The girl is terrified. I go by her head to play my self-absolving role as a human anaesthetic. Dr Kostov snaps a worn glove off the sagging neck of the lampstand, and winds it over his right hand. He drops the second glove on the floor and gives it a kick that sends it slapping wetly against the wall. A shove on one knee, a shove on the other, each time with a growl in his throat. The girl's legs come apart. Whites of panic in saucer-wide eyes, she's screaming Kabyl. Dr Kostov's gloved fist punches through her vulva. I feel the impact in her hands. It's anybody's guess who's holding hardest.

I keep my eyes off her face, and look between her legs instead. Dr Kostov's deep inside. His glove is buried. 'A hand?' he says contemptuously, and shakes his head. It's a foot that he has in his grasp. But it keeps slipping. The girl twists her hips and won't keep her vagina straight. Dr Kostov shouts I can't tell what, he's beside himself too, and he delivers two crashing blows with his free hand, one to the inside of each thigh.

He asks Zora for a cloth and uses it to improve his grip. He pulls with a strength I could never use. He's pulling the baby out by its foot through a cervix that a few minutes ago was hardly wide enough for Dr Vasilev's hand. I look at Zora who shrugs. The sweat pours off him, he shouts to Zora to press down hard on the girl's belly, and the insane screams are weakening. The girl's muttering Kabyl, her grip's fading on my hand, her legs are going limp and they're falling, falling over Dr Kostov's arm, to get revived each time with a jab from his elbow.

The baby's hips are out, its shoulders follow, first one, then the other. But the cervix seems to grip the head, it won't let it through. The baby's now upside down and Dr Kostov's tugging it up to the ceiling with both hands. The girl's eyes are closed, one leg dangles over the side of the table and her grip's gone completely.

The head's out. Quick clamps from Zora and then the scissors. Dr Kostov flings the cord back on to the mother's chest, the handle of the clamp striking her chin without reviving her. The baby's head lolls brokenly. Its neck is thin and immensely long. It isn't breathing and I can't believe that any of its functions will be intact. A ten-second examination by Dr Kostov and all that's wrong is a broken thigh. And it's surprising how quickly that mends, he says, in a baby.

He's finished. My head's bursting, my heart's going like a bomb. Dr Kostov's smiling. He washes his hands in the basin, and demonstrates a little mistake he's seen me making with my left hand when I help a baby out.

I'm sitting alone in the delivery room. The air-conditioner's on and I've closed the door. It's mid-siesta and the room's empty. Stripped of its pot-bellied women, of its sounds and smells, what's it like? It has cupboards, three beds and an oxygen cylinder. It has a washbasin and a spotlight. It has cotton wool, and alcohol, and antiseptic soap. The elements are medical, but unconvincing. It remains a room, and these are only props, makeshift and much-travelled, for itinerant actors playing to peasant audiences.

The spotlight has a long and flexible neck, bent horizontal, so that gloves can be hung over it after they've been rinsed in the basin. As a light, it doesn't work. The basin's very small. It has no hot water, and no soap or towel. Two butcher's aprons hang beside it on a nail. They're rubber-fronted, frayed and stained with blood.

The oxygen cylinder's a rusty shell about 5 feet high. Today, as on most other days there's no oxygen inside it. The tap allows the gas to escape too quickly. But Dr Kostov will use the cylinder during a difficult delivery. No one ever summons Dr Vasilev for what the midwives call a 'Chris-Taylor' – I've asked them to write it for me, but they can't. It's Dr Kostov's prerogative, and there's something delicious about the way Zora welcomes him when he makes his sturdy, gold-toothed entrance to the delivery room. If the woman's not pushing as hard as she could, he'll help her by swinging up behind her like an agile butcher, one hand gripping the cylinder head, the other a clenched fist driving down on her womb. Both his feet are off the ground during the manœuvre, and the whole of his weight swings in with that fist till the veins stand out on his forehead. The chorus to the action goes: 'N'ki! Ernu! – Push! Harder!' It's shouted by Dr Kostov and the midwife in unison, an obstetric road gang.

The walls of the delivery room are blue, chipped like the frames of the beds. They're bare, except for two things: one is a picture of a European mother holding up a plump European baby. It's fixed to the wall with a drawing pin, and it's been cut out from a packet of detergent. The other's a painted card, dangling from a string, the only touch of sophistication in the room, It shows a smiling young doctor, hair en brosse, with a stethoscope round his neck.

I turn the card round. There's another young doctor the other side. He's smiling too.

It's Zora's turn to be on duty for the night. Bare feet and silver toes. Wiry black hair brushed flat against her head, with a central parting, held at the back by a comb, under tremendous tension so as to keep it straight. She's done it Kabyl-style, for a change. She's in a bra and shift under her white coat. She sings and she coos to the women, coaxing them in Kabyl and French. 'Come, my little girl, come.' Voluptuously, even licking her lips, she exclaims: 'How I love to see a woman giving birth!' It's nice, but there's something about her warmth that isn't genuine. It's a show, for Western man, not Kabyl woman.

An unforgetable sight. It's not this woman's age, though she's thirty at least, and that's very old for a Kabyl woman to be having her first baby. It isn't her single tooth, nor her frayed robe, nor the fact that she's already been in Maternity a whole day, lost in some room down the corridor (all the women are neglected in the same way). What's unforgettable about her is her body. It's puffy, soggy and numb. She's swollen all over. Take the stethoscope off her belly and it leaves deep lasting imprints, like a biscuit-cutter on dough. How long has she been like this? She can't tell us. She's not here, she's wild, perhaps her brain is swollen too.

The DOCTOR ON DUTY ... is Dr Kostov. He's come to collect his bottle of cold water from the Maternity fridge. He puts the bottle down and listens through the stethoscope. There's nothing there. The baby's dead.

The first step in the treatment of the mother's swelling is to get rid of her baby. It could be pulled out with forceps, but Dr Kostov puts a hand inside and finds that won't be possible. The head is too high up and besides, the cervix isn't wide enough yet. There's only one thing left.

Hardly a week gone, and I'm being treated to the ultimate obstetric experience, truly the ultimate, when it's Dr Kostov in his butcher's apron, with his septic technique, without an anaesthetic, on a wild Kabyl woman from the mountains, swollen like a sponge – an embryotomy, the cutting up of the baby while it's still inside the womb, its extraction in bits, beginning with the head, the widest part. Climbing at Dr Kostov's direction up the delivery room steps to the top shelf of the cupboard, fetching down the huge and ancient tin, eroded, discoloured, with the instruments inside named after their inventor, famous obstetricians of past centuries. Splitting the bed in half, laying out the instruments on the bottom half, getting the woman to the very edge, legs wide open and lashed to the stirrups. Whacks! – across her knuckles with the wooden stethoscope as she plunges her hands inside her vagina to see what's there. Angry cries from Dr Kostov, screams from the woman, and Fatma says she's going outside, embryotomies make her sick. That leaves Zora and me to hold the woman down.

First it's the cranial perforator of Blot (what a way to be remembered), with the arrowlike head designed to be pushed through the skull and then opened to let out brain and spinal fluid. Then it's the turn of the cranioclast, the skull-crusher of Braun, to compress the bones of the skull, and then Braun again, his inventiveness not exhausted, for the hook of Braun to pull the baby through the vagina. All nice in theory – but Dr Kostov misses time and again with the cranial perforator. It's a dangerous instrument in the wrong place and the wrong hands. If it can go through a skull, it can pierce the woman's bladder or rectum. Zora's on one thigh, I'm on the other, and we're trying hard to present Dr Kostov with a stationary target, but the woman writhes uncontrollably, shouting she's dying, she's dying, why did she marry. She pulls us away, her hands fly between her legs to grip the shaft of the perforator. Dr Kostov whacks them away, wood on bone, and shouts in Bulgarian and 'Sob! Sob! Sob!' as she runs from him up the table. His blows leave great dents in her thighs. To hold them makes you ill, they feel as though they've lain in water for weeks. The woman's eyes roll like a newborn baby's. They never focus on us. After each failure, Dr Kostov holds the perforator aloft, examining it with a scowl, seeing if its head opens as it should, before plunging it back in again.

He's through. Brain and spinal fluid pour down through the vagina, and he switches to the cranioclast, catching bits of skull in its serrated jaws and pulling back, staggering across the bloody floor as each piece comes away, the cranioclast all 5 pounds of it, its screws and powerful arms, waving in the air. 'Sob! Sob!' as the woman flees up the bed, 'Down! Down!' with her bottom on pieces of her dead baby's brain and splinters of its skull. It's a full-term baby, female. Its head looks like the worst kind of road traffic accident. It goes into a big Biotic-Algérie box, lined with grey cotton wool. The girl in the next bed – and then I remember, I'd wheeled her out before it all began and Dr Kostov had said: 'Why bother?' He spends five minutes at the sink, washing off the blood and pieces. He hasn't torn her, and he goes in afterwards with his arm to pull out her placenta.

I begin cleaning up the mess. But Fatma catches me and takes the mop from my hand. 'It's a woman's job,' she says. Zora turns round from washing at the basin. 'Let her do it,' she says, 'it's what they pay her for.'

Zora's said 'tu' to me for the first time. I follow her out, she's going down the path to the doctor's building to visit Djamila. What she's just said about Fatma, the 'tu' of complicity with me, her choice of the moment – there's nothing we have to say to each other. There's something I want to tell her, that I've needed to tell her for several days, a story I must establish and keep to. 'I got a letter today,' I say, 'from my wife. She'll be coming out here for three weeks.' 'I'd like to meet her,' says Zora without enthusiasm, and we bid each other goodnight.

6

I wasn't the only one to be disturbed in the night by the hospital dogs. Baya the Kabyl orderly, who lives in a room in the doctors' building, drags herself into Maternity, sandals flapping listlessly. She says she counted fifteen of them altogether. The hospital dogs are wild and starving. They run in packs, and their fights during the night are terrible.

Baya's state of fatigue is a Maternity fact of life. She has a red blood cell count of three million. And that's on her good days, she says. Otherwise it sinks nearer to two. The normal is five. But she's learned to live with her anaemia, she says, like many Kabyl women.

I follow her up the stairs to the first-floor landing. She pulls herself up on the banisters and flops into the chair at the desk, saying: 'I have no more strength.' The morning begins with a minor crisis. Strictly speaking, all crises are minor. In conditions such as these, when the drug cupboard is hardly fuller than the medicine chest at home, when the elementary rules are ignored by the doctors and unknown to the rest of the staff, in a situation where major crisis is the norm, anything else can only be an incident. Nonetheless, there's some dismay when Baya discovers that Maternity is out of Methergin. She sends a cleaner off to the Pharmacy, and the trolley comes back laden with supplies. We stack them away with pride, labels facing outwards, in neat little rows.

The wild woman with the waterlogged thighs stares into the wall and doesn't move when Dr Vasilev shuffles into her room on his ward round. Baya says she's 'mental'. The swelling's still there. Embryotomy hasn't improved her. Dr Vasilev puts her on a salt-free diet. Baya makes a note in her book. We pass on without examining her.

'Lebess? – Ça va?' Dr Vasilev's asking the next woman. 'Lebess', she answers, the way they all answer, neutrally, 'so-so'. She's to go home, he says, and he begins to write out a prescription for her to take with her. But then I show him the cot at the end of the bed. The baby has a long neck, and a swollen, misshapen thigh. It's the baby that Dr Kostov ripped out by its foot before going off to supper. A job for the Russian surgeon Ivanov, says Dr Vasilev. 'No one ever tells me anything,' he complains.

We see the mother of one of the babies born dead in the night. When Tamara writes anything on the charts, and to be fair to her, she usually does write something, it's in very poor French. For 'accouchement très difficile – a very difficult delivery', she's written 'acc. tre. deprecielle', or as near as makes no difference, given her problems with Latin script. Dr Vasilev corrects her French and rounds off her hand-writing, muttering: 'If it was difficult, why didn't she call me?' It's too late now. The baby's in a cardboard box, the woman's going home, and what we've just heard was the inquest.

Our Caesarean points to her belly: 'Ai, ma.' Dr Vasilev tugs back her robe, and prods gently round her bandage. Her womb is high under her ribs. Her bladder's enormous, it ought to have been drained. Baya the orderly says dully: 'It's not my responsibility.' Dr Vasilev jerks into life: 'Whose was it then?' Baya doesn't know. 'Was it "the Professor's"?' Baya grins. 'The Professor' must be a joke. There's a long silence. The Caesarean's sheets are crumpled, blood-stained, spotted with flies. Old melon slices are stacked on the table. Yogurt tops and more flies on the floor. Baya grins again, looking at me. I feel very bad for Dr Vasilev. He leads the way out, clicking the light switch on and off as he passes the door.

With Dr Vasilev, everything's changed. The first day or so, he really took me under his wing. The warm welcome, the meal that I know he really enjoyed, the Caesarean we did together. But the effort seems to have exhausted him. His shoulders appear more hunched every day, the lines on his

37

face deeper, his walk slower. He's on the verge of stopping altogether. There are times when he pauses to breathe, before lighting a cigarette. Things between us are waning fast. I don't feel wanted any more. Between him and me, it's like between him and everyone else. I'm part of a scene that weighs more heavily on him daily. The first days, I relieved the weight. Now I only add to it.

There's a fly perched on his shoulder blade during the ward round, during all fifteen minutes of it. He explains nothing to me unless I ask. And I ask less and less frequently. There's so little he's able to explain. The drugs he prescribes are for 'appetite', for 'blood' or, more vaguely still, for 'health'. Their detailed actions are quite unknown to him. He's been practising gynaecology as a speciality for twenty-three years. He took his exams before there was much talk of metabolism in medical schools. He's never tried to keep up. I remember asking him, during the meal that first evening, if he was carrying out any research. I asked him if he contributed to any of the Bulgarian journals. He told me he didn't, and Vasileva added that her husband wasn't interested in that kind of thing. He didn't even receive the journals, let alone contribute to them. The only printed matter in the apartment was a route map of Bulgaria (with a duplicate kept in the doctors' office), *Life*, *Paris-Match* and issues of the Italian weekly, *Oggi*.

We've come to the bed of a woman who's pleased. She's grateful: 'It's thanks to you, Doctor, and thanks to your injections.' She lifts her baby from the rotten sheets: 'Isn't he handsome, Doctor?' Dr Vasilev is a little overcome, but happy. 'Eh!' he cries as we leave the room, 'I should have been called for her delivery.'

We reach the high spot of the ward round. For three minutes we actually stop, at the bedside of the Supervisor's daughter. She has a room to herself, with net curtains clean and white. A flowered nightdress, a milk extractor from Germany, lemonade and petits fours. There are fresh mop-marks on the floor and the room smells of lavender. Dark grapes in a crystal bowl, a leather suitcase under the bed, and her baby's in a brand-new cot under a blanket with a powder-blue border. Only Turkish delight is missing. The Supervisor's daughter is a massive, white-skinned, totally useless twenty-year-old girl, an Oriental male's dream.

Medically, she's a slender problem. She had very low blood pressure during her pregnancy, so that she used to be seen by the Russian physician, Dr Ivanova, the surgeon's wife. Delivery went without a problem and the baby's fine. But her pressure's still low. Dr Vasilev advises her to keep to her bed: if she gets up, she might feel faint. She complains about her breasts being tender, and Dr Vasilev cries: 'You drink too much lemonade!' I'm sure he's right. She's been happy to see us. She's a contented patient. Sandals with petalled toes peep from beneath the covers.

Then back to the women with nothing on their charts but their names, and temperatures that are always marked as normal. 'Why bother to write them in?' asks Dr Vasilev, 'I know you never take them.' Baya, of course, says she does. Dr Vasilev picks up a chart and challenges a woman: 'Madame, you haven't delivered.' The woman laughs, her baby's next to her in the bed. Dr Vasilev insists, and shows her the chart: 'Where's your baby there, Madame?' The woman laughs again, pulling on his sleeve for him to stop. She's bashful from the attention he's giving her. What's embarrassing for me is not the midwife's indifference displayed on that empty chart – the indifference is no news – it's Dr Vasilev's impotent little ritual. Already I know how it has to end, and here he is, filling in the details of the delivery himself, saying: 'It's not for me to do.'

He goes: 'Ts . . . ts . . . ts,' takes a deep breath and moves on to the last room, with a shuffle of his sandals and a frail, tuneless little whistle. Baya and I trail behind. 'Lebess? – Ça va?' I hear him asking the last woman, a hoarse, kind 'Lebess,' delivered with a sudden access of energy and followed by an abrupt fall, during which he won't look at the woman or address her again. In this process, that's been repeated at twenty beds, I see the history of his relationship with me in miniature.

7

I'm up with the swallows, at the same time as the sun. The sounds of the hospital: from the street, which I can't see, there are the cars and trucks. From the little hill between the hospital and the cork depot come the shouts of the boy with the long stick and the four cows. There are cocks on his farm, and a donkey. The sound of the donkey breaks your heart. To me, it's crying: 'Help, help! There's a man in a turban, woollen hooded coat and baggy pants, who's coming towards me with a huge curved knife. Help! He's lifting the knife in the air, and ahhh . . .', that long-drawn-out wail at the end, as the blood pours into the dusty field.

Those are the nicer sounds. The others are truly terrible. There are two surgical wards on the floor above mine, one for woman and one for children. Both are under the care of the Russian surgeon, Ivanov. The children's cries seem to persist throughout the night. They always sound most acute in the morning because they fill my empty ward and there's little other activity going on in the hospital to mask them. It takes me a couple of hours each day to get used to them again. By midday, when I come back with my lunch, I hardly hear them. Yet the screams never stop. It's possible, if I try hard, to make out three or four different voices. But it's difficult to be sure, and I'm not keen to go upstairs and check. The noises range from simple crying to shrieks so piercing that you sit up in bed. Sometimes I can't tell if it's a child or one of the hospital cats. Too much concentration brings on a headache fast, and it's a poor way to start the day. Their echo is astonishing, the cries stay with me for hours. I'm constantly awake to them, hearing them for the rest of the day in the cries of the care-taker's children playing in the garden of Maternity.

Yesterday, I took the baby with the broken thigh to Theatre. I carried it over to the main part of the hospital, and up in the lift. It cried feebly all the way. Inside the main door, I looked for a mask, a gown and overshoes. But none were there. There was only a corridor with an operating theatre on either side, and an old man from the mountains squatting beside the wall. Then an orderly appeared with a piece of gauze round his neck, and invited me into the office. He began taking down the baby's details.

Suddenly there was an appalling shriek. The orderly continued his writing. The shriek came again. The old peasant beside the wall rubbed an eye. The shriek came a third time, and yet again, sustained and hysterical, enveloping us. It was impossible to tell what could be uttering it.

I laid the baby on the office table and peered into the Theatre next door. For a moment my view was totally blocked by the bare torso of a man well over six feet tall. His hair was close-cropped and his face, which I'm unable to remember in detail, remains in my mind only as the continuation upwards of his massive trunk.

Ivanov– sewn in red letters into his trousers belt – lumbered away towards the operating table, a scalpel and forceps in his bare hands. There beneath him, in the torn jeans and ancient shirt that are the uniform of children, was a small boy struggling in the grip of two orderlies. Ivanov went hunting in the small boy's elbow. He was trying to find a metal pin that had been inserted to mend a fracture. There was an X-ray picture of it on the wall, that Ivanov looked to for guidance. The pin was due to come out. But it was difficult to find, all overgrown with scar tissue. Ivanov cut and probed till he reached its metal head. Then he picked up a pair of pliers. But they slipped, and the elbow broke free of the orderlies' grasp, flying into Ivanov's face. The orderlies shouted in Kabyl. The small boy shrieked and spurted urine on to the table. But Ivanov betrayed no emotion. He stayed utterly silent. He didn't hate his elbows, the way that Dr Kostov can hate his wombs. His movements had none of that impatience and irritation. They had the grace and range of a factory press.

Ivanov took two sober steps to a glass cupboard, to fetch a

fresh set of pliers. His back glistened with sweat, like a stoker's in a boiler room. It was vast, and inviting. There was room for a thousand bullets.

The sights at 6.30: women flicking dark hair off their fingers on to the pathway that runs outside the ground floor windows of Maternity, the thin retriever that hangs head down by the kitchen path, waiting for the bit of meat or vegetable, but never coming nearer, the cats crawling under the refuse truck, springing away when the cleaners come across the courtyard from each department, carrying bins in twos. The hospital buildings have a pitted, honeycomb design, like a collection of giant white breeze-blocks, and they're already baking in the sun. Olive and fig trees on the slopes of the hills. A village on every hilltop. Vasileva has a nice way of describing it. She makes a fist with one hand and then points to the knuckles: 'A village on every knuckle!'

Relatives wait outside Maternity for the doors to open, the women in a line squatting against the wall, the men further out, squatting together in the garden, woollen coats slung over their shoulders, chewing on blades of grass. They arrive every morning, a few minutes after the first buses come down from the mountains. They arrive before the hospital painters and carpenters and kitchen workers, with long sticks and straw sombreros. Their faces are creased and brown, and they nod to me as I come back from the kitchen with my bottle of coffee. Later, when I meet them in the department near the end of the morning, I never hear them say they've been waiting four or five hours. They've been waiting all their lives.

At 7.30 the doors open and Maternity fills with people. A man wants his baby, born in the night two months premature. It's been left on the scales in front of the air-conditioner, because the incubators in Pediatrics are full. It's going to die. In fact, it's already officially dead. It's down in the Register as stillborn. In front of the father, I feel ashamed, at a loss for words. I'm afraid of the recrimination when I tell him his baby's too premature to live. But he seems to accept the news well. He tells me he's taking the baby to Algiers, he begins a new job there tomorrow. I suddenly realize he's taking it to

42

Algiers, literally. He's not taking it to a *hospital* in Algiers. I tell him it will probably die on the way. He smiles and shrugs, or rather he has a movement of the mouth you'd call a smile, a movement of the shoulders you'd call a shrug. I must be seeing it all wrong, it can't be as it sounds. His wife's veiled and shawled. She follows him to the car, a Renault 8, white and clean.

I remember an incident from the ward round yesterday: I knocked the cot at the end of a woman's bed. It slipped right off, turning the baby over and banging it against the wall. I caught the cot just in time to stop it from falling on the floor. My relief was enormous. The mother was seventeen, it was her first baby and a boy. She had every reason to be happy. Yet she never moved. Not even her eyes moved. Of the others only the Supervisor's daughter would have behaved any differently. I came away with the feeling you get from the films of the Indian reserves in the United States, a sort of racial depression.

Women sit on the benches and watch the men come forward to the desk on the first floor landing. If they're not taking away a relative, they're carrying food, or else social security papers they want signed, or else they're carrying nothing, in which case they've come for information. Frayed and dusty jackets, trousers falling over shoes with holes, lost and humble, infinitely patient. Humble with Baya, humbler still with me, but above all lost.

A man wants to see his wife, who might have delivered yesterday. Baya asks for her name. It means nothing to her. She has to consult the register to see if the woman has delivered or not. She has no idea what bed she's in. No one knows the names of the patients. The man goes past the desk, down the corridor and into each of the rooms, looking for his wife. Soon he's joined by other men, all doing the same. The cleaners stop their work and come forward too. They have friends and relatives among the visitors. They let them through to the rooms, or deliver their parcels of food for them.

'Eh!' goes Dr Vasilev, pushing his way through the crowd. Men clamour round his white coat. Dr Vasilev's submerged. To the men in their sombreros, to the women in their veils and shawls, he cries: 'Every day I say to your Econome:

43

"We can't work if Maternity's full of people"!' He pushes their forms aside, and plugs his ears to their requests. 'In Bulgaria . . .,' he begins telling them.

Gynaecology is at the very end of the Out-Patients' corridor. There's Medicine, Surgery and Paediatrics to pass before I get there. The faces of those waiting are so humble and depressed that it's painful. I walk through them with my head down. Snatches of faces carrying lumps the size of duck eggs, veiled mothers shaking babies that look at death's door – that might already be dead. Vast waiting rooms like barns, without chairs, people with their legs out leaning against the wall, others lying on the floor.

Our waiting room's only half-full. Dr Kostov must be galloping through the patients. He nods to me as I arrive and turns to run his glove under the tap. He looks his usual self, that combination of a light heart and heavy touch, the light heart always ready to burst into a flare of temper at the slightest pretext, of which there are an infinite number possible. I concern him very little. He's made no attempt to appropriate me. Dr Vasilev's the head of Maternity, he's the man who gave permission for me to come, he's my host. Dr Kostov's left me to him.

We see twenty-five women in the next hour and a half, one vagina after the other. Dr Kostov goes first, I follow. We have one glove each, which we keep on all the time. Dr Kostov writes prescriptions with it, opens the door with it, listens for babies' hearts with it. He may well rinse it under the tap between women, but that's only to avoid dirtying his biro. Unlike Dr Vasilev, he's preserved none of the old scruples. He's had the strength to break with tradition.

We use no lubricant or jelly. Heaven knows if it's necessary, especially with the women who haven't had children. We use force instead. Several times, even though I follow Dr Kostov immediately – my right foot's on the stool as soon as his has left it – I see the vagina closing hard, reflexly against further injury, and I have the greatest difficulty getting a single finger in. As he's rinsing his glove, he'll say: 'You'll feel an inflamed tube.' I say yes, withdrawing my finger with a pathetic attempt

44

at the doctor's benevolent smile across the woman's pubis –
always without effect, always unreturned – a smile to disculpate
myself, but doubly pathetic because I can't speak her language
and I haven't felt a thing.

'Baya!' shouts Dr Kostov, 'ask this woman how old she is.
Baya! Tell her to take off her pants. Baya! . . .' And so it goes
on. Baya is imperturbable. She does her duties at her normal
pace. 'This woman wants children,' she says. 'There are
plenty of children in Kabylia,' shouts Dr Kostov, 'why
doesn't she go and take one?' His face is contorted with
effort and disgust as he bends the woman's legs, one hand on
the thigh, the other on the shin, a circus strong man with an
iron bar, trying to fit them into the table. Whack! – across
the knuckles that try to hold the robe between the legs. Slam! –
with the feet that won't find the stirrups fast enough. The
woman winces as the metal hits her ankles, she glances up at
Baya and me. Baya holds her hand and strokes her head. I
try to be at the sink, running alcohol over my glove.

A girl comes in who doesn't know her age. Even when
Baya asks her to give a rough estimate, she still doesn't know.
Dr Kostov's gone dark, and I'm afraid for her. But she's not
yet within his grasp, she's not yet on the table. She goes out
to the waiting room and fetches her identity card. It says she's
twenty-three. She hasn't had a period since the birth of her
last child. When was that? Again, she can't say. Dr Kostov
shouts in Bulgarian, a word like: 'Prostate!' The girl senses
a storm, 'pa . . . pa . . . pa,' and flies out of the room to her
husband in the corridor. He comes in with the baby in his arms
and says it's eighteen months old.

Dr Kostov's mood has burst, he's laughing wearily: 'What
a country!' He's reminded of an occasion before I came, when
a woman had to go out to ask her husband what her name was.
He laughs at the memory, a great beer-hall laugh, and then
leans forward on his chair, clicking his fingers to an imaginary
animal: 'Even a dog knows its name.'

A woman approaches with a crouching, embarrassed walk.
Dr Kostov's writing: 'Miscarriage – curettage – hospitalization'
across her form even as she's coming over towards us. On

the table, her vagina's full of placenta. She gets down, as she got up, unaided. Legs tightly together, as she pulls on her baggy pants, to prevent it from all falling out. Then she stands up straight to take the form from Dr Kostov. Her hand's only halfway there when she sways back against the wall and slips to the floor. Dr Kostov throws the form down after her. It floats away from her. She gropes for it, misses and gives up, waving a hand in front of her to say she's dizzy. She's disgusted Dr Kostov. He wonders how long she must have been bleeding to have become so weak. His guess is three weeks. 'Do you call that culture?' he asks me.

Dr Kostov first became acquainted with Algerian culture in the early 1960s, just after Independence. He worked in Sétif. Algeria was in chaos and he was able to send out all the money he wanted, to a bank account in Zurich. He still remembers its number. When his three years were up, he journeyed to Zurich and collected his savings. From there, he made for Stuttgart and bought a Mercedes. He asks me if I know the make, giving it the full title, 'Mercedes-Benz'. He's not asking if I've heard the name, or if I could recognize one in the street. He takes that for granted. He wants the 'yes' of a connoisseur. I give it. He took his wife and son on a two-month motoring holiday. They saw Spain and Portugal, they visited France, Italy and Belgium: 'The only place we didn't go was England!' On his way home he bought a refrigerator, 'a Pontiac', and many other things.

No wonder he came back for a further three years. Besides, he had another reason for returning, even less to his credit, which I'm surprised he should be telling me (or does he feel so sure that I'll find out in the end from Vasileva? – as I did, during that meal on the very first evening): his son failed his exams in Bulgaria, and Dr Kostov managed to get him into medical school in Algiers instead. But he found a changed Algeria. The administration has tightened up. They won't let him send money out. He has to spend it all here. For a man with such a strong belief in free trade, Algeria's become little better than a prison. 'What do you expect me to buy in Algeria,' he asks me, 'cous-cous?'

There's integrity to Dr Kostov all the same. You'd never catch him giving after-dinner speeches on our duty to the patient. He has no time for medical ethics. Even my being here, a fresh young student from England, hasn't stirred the medical missionary that might have been in him. He's never tried to set me an example. On the contrary, he's only sought to emulate me. He knows: if I'm from England, I'm in it for the money too.

And thus we pursue our conversation, on the usual topic. The flow of women is no more than a series of interruptions, and sometimes not even that. I'm in the same business as Dr Kostov, and I come from a land of banks, from a city with a station called Bank and a street that's made up entirely of banks. Money is all we talk of outside medicine. We discuss it under its different appearances – the dinar (contemptuously), the peseta and the lira (little better), the French franc (ça va), the pound (good), the German mark and the Swiss franc (with a glow) and finally, most glamorous of all, the American dollar. There's both joy and humility in Dr Kostov's recognition of the dollar, it's the kind of tribute one pays to an outstanding world champion.

I'm excited by his envy of me, of my easy insertion in a civilization to which he's devoted, and I tell him everything. I tell him of what could be his were he practising his speciality in the West, I describe his climb from Rover to Rolls-Royce (he knows the makes) as he uses National Health facilities in his private practice, and he only pushes me further by crying: 'Of course! Half for the State, all for me!' He confesses that at home a doctor is not what he is in the West. There are labourers in Bulgaria who earn more than he does, whereas 'in England, a doctor earns a doctor's money'. Dr Kostov only gets one pound for an abortion in Bulgaria. I tell him that the same operation could fetch him 200 guineas in London. I tell him of a doctor in my teaching hospital, who runs a Jensen. Between patients, he asks me to write the man's name, and the make of his car. I do, and he pronounces them after me. These are his very first words in English.

But he says he's too old to start learning a new language, and, besides, English is very difficult. It's me who says: 'French-

speaking Canada!' It's Dr Kostov who finds: 'Montreal!'
And that is how, fingers in, fingers out, tap on, tap off, we
reach the solution to Dr Kostov's geld-lust. Across the pubis
of a Kabyl woman, he proposes this bond: 'You' – 'toi' – 'you
and I will open up a practice in Montreal when you qualify.'

8

Eight-thirty and the sun's shining into my room when I see Dr Kostov down below, on the steps of the doctors' building. White coat and trousers – white last Monday, at least – leather sandals. In his hand, a saline bottle. It's filled with drinking water, and it goes in the Maternity fridge, with 'KOSTOV' written on it in blue biro, to get cold for his lunch. He scowls at the sun. He crosses the gravel path, passes behind the little fir-tree, on to the stone walk that runs the length of Maternity, outside the ground-floor windows. He's in the shade. At the third window along, there's a patient. She wears dull silver bracelets round her forearms. Her black hair is parted down the middle and tied with a dark blue scarf. Her head rests side-ways on her hands. She's gazing into the garden. Dr Kostov strides by, and neither of them moves.

He's behind the second fir-tree that provides some shade for the one-eyed cat. He's level with me. I call out: 'Dr Kostov!' He looks up, bewildered. Thick-set, squat, bare-chested under his coat. He sees me, smiles. Big smile, with gold and silver teeth. 'Ward round!' He waves his bottle for me to join him.

I throw on my coat, trousers and shoes. I'd brought shirts and ties. I'd been taught in England that I could come to a ward round, in cardiology for example, without a stethoscope, without even the most basic idea of the heart, but on no account without a tie. With Dr Kostov, you don't even need the tie.

He begins the round with his customary vigour. Legs of the Caesarean, poked apart by the point of a biro. There's a rubber tube up her bladder, dribbling urine on to the sheet. She hasn't been washed since the day of the operation. There's fresh blood oozing from her vagina. 'In Bulgaria . . .,' begins Dr Kostov, then he stops: 'Why should I bother? It's not me who's head of the department.'

Pictures of dirt and fatigue, in stained robes and old sheets, the women stare up at us from their beds. Head to toe, taking turns on the pillow, a woman without a baby – strangled during delivery by its cord – shares with a woman who has no milk of her own. She's feeding her baby from an old yogurt carton, with cold mint tea brought in from home. The smell in the room is weeks old. Water-melon pips and flies, egg-shells in the corners, dry bread and broken vitamin ampoules, a half-finished packet of biscuits alive with red ants, newspaper soggy with meat juice on the floor. Dr Kostov's provoked. He points to each item: 'Look!' He grabs hold of the women and drives them to the window, to feel shame before the balcony thick with encrusted food and flies. 'Look!' he shakes their necks in French and Bulgarian, 'look!' The women climb back on to the bed. 'There's cholera in Libya!' he roars after them, 'and it'll soon be here! And bubonic plague, and typhus, and . . .' His medicine fails him. Djamila the midwife passes by, chewing gum. 'We Arabs always wash,' she tells me.

On to the next room: three women with nothing on their charts but their names and the month, both in Dr Vasilev's handwriting. He must have admitted them yesterday. 'What am I supposed to do with them?' Dr Kostov asks me, 'is that what you call a colleague?' Or at least, if he's not saying it to me, he's saying it in French, which amounts to the same thing because the nurse accompanying us on the round is Vasileva. It's the first time Dr Kostov's been so direct. Vasileva's embarrassed for her husband, she's anxious to get on. 'Why should I bother to examine them?' asks Dr Kostov again in French, 'he must know why he admitted them – let him look after them.'

On to the next, via the corridor where the one-eyed cat paces up and down, calling for its kittens. They're growing fast on the leftovers from the kitchen meals, the women bring in so much food of their own. 'Grrr . . .,' goes Dr Kostov and swings a threatening foot. The one-eyed cat slinks away. It's not that Dr Kostov objects to its presence on medical grounds.

He just doesn't like cats. Besides, the one-eyed cat is part of Dr Vasilev's image.

The Supervisor's daughter is doing fine. Her blood pressure's up. She's such a change from the other women. It's impossible not to feel cheered by her. She lives the life of the kept woman with gross satisfaction. The production of a male child at her first attempt only confirms her vocation. She's reading *Elle* and sipping coffee from a pink Thermos flask decorated with roses. Her breasts are gigantic – white cones of fat that reach down to her hips. The floor bears the traces of the phantom mop.

On to the next: 'What's she doing here?' asks Dr Kostov. Vasileva says the woman was due to go home yesterday, but no one came to collect her. Since she can't go home on her own, she'll have to wait till somebody comes. 'Nobody wants her,' laughs Dr Kostov, 'then we'll take her to the market: Woman for sale, one thousand dinars.'

Out of that room and into the next, still laughing. Finger pointing at the woman: 'Pain?' If she shakes her head, we'll pass on. We're already beyond her bed. But she nods, and starts off in Kabyl. Dr Kostov's impatient. Vasileva thinks the woman's ill. 'Ill?' echoes Dr Kostov, 'oh dear! Shame! The poor thing!' He rips the sheet down, and throws back the robe. She's well pregnant. Hand on her belly, and her womb's hard and contracted. Biro to the inside of each thigh, there's fluid on the sheet between her legs: 'Up to the delivery room with her!'

The baby with the broken thigh has had X-rays taken after his operation. Dr Kostov holds them up to the light. The broken ends are at right angles to each other, even further apart than they were to begin with. Ivanov will have to try again. We don't examine the baby. Like the others, it's all wrapped up, and it would take too long to undo.

The mother's in pain. Her robe's hurled back, and there's the reason – her belt, that's lashed tightly several times round her waist, the way the women insist on doing after delivery. Dr Vasilev's finger would point: 'Ah Madame! What's this?' Dr Kostov's fist is raised: 'Animal! Prostate! Is that culture?' He pronounces it 'Kultur', German-style.

Screams from further down the corridor, where all the women who can walk are standing at their doors. Dr Kostov walks sternly past them, to the room of a woman who had a stillborn baby in the night. She's clutching her belly. 'Pain?' She nods through her tears. Dr Kostov pulls the sheet off her. He doesn't bother with the tedious business of getting the pants off. He pushes through her robe, hard into her stomach. The woman writhes, cries out, spins towards the wall and before she's opened her eyes, Dr Kostov has left the room. I'm left standing there. The woman looks at me, and the eyes of all the other women at their doors are on me. They're not accusing me. They're not even accusing Dr Kostov. But I feel criminal and helpless. I follow Dr Kostov, in time to hear him telling Vasileva, with a 50 per cent chance of the order being carried out, to give the woman a pain-killer.

In the last room is a little girl of twelve, brought in yesterday by two veiled women because her periods had started and wouldn't stop. She's already lost a lot of blood, she's due for a transfusion when the laboratory can find a donor. She has cow eyes, she's brown and very pretty. She smiles a little as we come in. But she's wearing pants under her bloodstained robe. Dr Kostov shouts: 'Leave go this thing!' grips the pants and rips them off her hips down to her knees. The girl bends double to cover herself up. 'Why are you wearing them?' shouts Dr Kostov, 'it's supposed to be sterile in here.' He reaches down for the pants again, prises her knees apart, pulls them down off her feet and throws them on the floor. The girl bursts into tears. 'Why is she crying?' asks Dr Kostov.

I find Dr Vasilev in the doctors' office, back early from his siesta. He's buried in *El Moudjahid*. I tell him I'm sorry to be late, but over the top of the national newspaper he shakes his head. He doesn't want my deference, it only confuses him. Besides, nothing's happening. Afternoons are usually quiet, until about five o'clock, when husbands come home and their wives can travel with them to hospital.

I sit down in my usual chair, by the door. It's a small office, with a fine desk and chair for Dr Vasilev and a metal cupboard that's kept locked (it's where he stores his free samples from the drug firms). On the wall there's an old postcard of Timgad, and a large cardboard advertisement for a suppository that helps you to sleep, modelled by a heavily-lidded woman resembling Elizabeth Taylor.

Dr Vasilev's playing the game of the seven mistakes. He plays it every day. 'Our artist drew this picture,' says *El Moudjahid*'s back page, 'and then he copied it, making seven deliberate mistakes. Can you spot them?' Today's drawing is a goalkeeper saving a shot from a forward. Dr Vasilev finds a broken line in the net. 'One!' The forward has an extra quiff in his hair, and he's missing a stud from his left boot. That's 'three!' Then there's a crease in the forward's shirt at the elbow, where there isn't in the original. 'Four!' The goalkeeper's right eyebrow goes up instead of down. 'Five'. Number 'six!' is a goalpost that has an extra line down the side, giving it a whole extra dimension – easy once you've spotted it. The seventh mistake seems to escape Dr Vasilev. He could find out what it is by turning *El Moudjahid* upside down – but today, as on other days, he doesn't bother.

Dr Kostov strolls in with his water bottle. He has a curt word in Bulgarian for Dr Vasilev and sits down beside me. They have only the briefest of conversations together, and then always medicine, or rather their daily work.

They fill the afternoon in their particular ways. Dr Vasilev finishes his newspaper. Dr Kostov grips his saline bottle between his knees and fills in the fading letters of his name. Then he gets to his feet, stretches, and takes the bottle upstairs. He's less turned in upon himself than Dr Vasilev. He spends the rest of the afternoon defrosting the refrigerator, of which, after all, he's the principal beneficiary. It's done the way many things are done in Maternity. The door won't shut properly, so that the refrigerator frosts over very quickly. The sensible thing would be to get someone from the workshops to fix the handle. But no one's ever bothered. Defrosting has become Dr Kostov's job. It suits his temperament, as well as his interest. An embryotomy on ice. He's made a chisel out of the steel ruler from the desk on the landing. It's rudimentary, his blows aren't always accurate, and the cooling element gets badly shaken. He hacks away, chips of ice shower off and go skating across the room. Baya's assisting him. She chases after them with the enamel bowl and tips them into the sink. Then she turns round and there's more, more ice, pieces all over the floor.

Downstairs, Dr Vasilev's finished *El Moudjahid*. The paper's folded on his desk, ready for me. He sits hunched in his chair as I read. He smokes, and prises the silver paper off its lining from his packet of cigarettes. It's a strange ritual, accompanied by little 'ehs' and feebly whistled bars of a tune I can never catch. The first time I saw him do this, I imagined there was a point to it. I thought he was engaged in a contest with himself, trying to get off all the silver paper in one piece. I used to watch, to see if he'd succeed. But he'd always tear it, within a minute of beginning, and then instead of throwing it away and trying again with the next packet, he'd carry on until the desk was littered with silver scraps.

I've been seeing Dr Vasilev all wrong. I've been seeing him as a specialist, as the director of a hospital department. In the X-ray room that first morning, I saw him as a champion hysterographer, assassinated with a yawn by the girl from Oran. I've been making him into a seven-mistake spotter, a silver paper expert, and I've been seeing defeat each time, at his own hands, in a series of suicides. But he's never claimed to be any of these things. They've all been in my own mind. He's free of any notion of self-respect, and I'd failed to recognize it. I begin to feel better for him. I watch as he sits in the shade, alone on the little parapet outside the ground-floor entrance, stroking the one-eyed cat and whistling, in his Vasilev-whistle ... Delilah!, the song that Tom Jones sings with such rolling, torrential virility.

A man walks up to him with his wife. He'd like her examined. Dr Vasilev asks if she's an emergency. The man shakes his head. Then she must come to Out-Patients in the morning like everyone else, Dr Vasilev tells him. But they live in the mountains, says the man, and it's going to cost them so much to go back there and come down again in the morning. Dr Vasilev asks him what's wrong. They're desperate for a baby.

'Eh!' Is the woman ill? No, Doctor. Is there anything the matter with her at all? No, Doctor. Then she must come to Out-Patients in the morning, it's the hospital rule. 'Oh, but please, Doctor, please!'

Dr Vasilev puts the cat aside, as I always felt he would. He'll yield to pressure of any kind, even if it's against his own interests. He goes into the curettage room, calling upstairs for Baya to come and interpret. The woman tells them she wants a baby. She's never had one. Her husband spent seven years away in France.

All right, says Dr Vasilev kindly, we'll see what it is that's stopping you from having your baby. Down with the pants, and on to the table. Fingers in, he asks the routine questions via Baya. Are her periods regular? They are. Any pain with them? Not really. Any bowel trouble, any water trouble? None. Dr Vasilev withdraws his fingers. 'All's well, Madame,' he tells her. Then he asks her how long her husband has been back from France. When she says 'three days', Dr Vasilev falls back with a groan he can't control. He drops his glove in the sink, sits down, takes off his glasses and rubs his eyes.

'Eh,' he says at last. He begins writing a prescription. I ask him what it's for. He's too beaten to answer. I look over his shoulder. It's the usual salad of iron and vitamins.

We return to the office. The light's fading, it's drawing near to supper-time. Dr Vasilev gives me a little smile. 'You're seeing things that don't exist in England!' he cries contentedly. He wants to know if I'm happy over the way my first two weeks have gone. Of course, Algeria is not Bulgaria. Things there are very different.

We end our afternoon talking about Bulgaria. It's what I often talk about with Dr Vasilev. The health system, that's comprehensive and free. The foreigners holidaying on the Black Sea, who get the same treatment as Bulgarians – 'even better!' The way the system's divided into regions, sub-regions and local districts. The touring map, which allows Dr Vasilev to outline the regions for me. Sofia and Varna, and the mountain range that divides the country. Burgas, and Plovdiv further to the south, famous for its industrial production. The quality of its gas. The train times to and from these different cities. The choice of routes between Burgas and Sofia. The advantages of air travel, not least its cheapness. The account, in semi darkness, of an uneventful plane trip from Varna to Sofia in 1965. Dr Vasilev tires, he falls quiet.

9

I join Dr Kostov in Out-Patients. Something's wrong. I don't know what. A malaise of the Deutschmark? When I come in, his gloved hand is writing out prescriptions, the point of the cheap hospital biro digging into the cheap hospital paper, lips twisted as he writes a prescription of hate. The sudden exclamation and the swearing in Bulgarian as yet another biro refuses to work. He hurls the thing away from him. It ricochets off the desk, hits the wall and falls to the floor. And then I see the rubber glove on his right hand made of black leather instead, and his greying hair showing to advantage beneath the brim of a peaked cap, and the whole body at ease in the uniform that's essentially his.

A woman comes in with a boy of six. I suggest he could stay outside in the waiting room. 'Why bother?' says Dr Kostov, 'pants, Baya, pants!' The woman gets up on the table, puts her feet in the stirrups, lies back and listens to Baya. Dr Kostov arrives between her feet, forces her thighs open with his elbows and throws back her robe. You can feel his fingers going in. The boy stands against the wall, behind his mother's head. He screams and screams and screams.

Dr Kostov's examining a woman in her early forties, whose periods have suddenly stopped. It's her sixteenth pregnancy. She wants an injection, an operation. It's her sixteenth pregnancy. 'What's one more for her?' shouts Dr Kostov to the wall above the basin, 'and what could she give me for it?'

My heart's beating faster. Baya looks at me, and quickly away, the same look as Vasileva once gave me in the curettage room behind Dr Kostov's back. Dr Kostov writes on, with a new biro. Without looking up, he asks Baya what's wrong with the next patient. His voice is low and cold. It's a monotone under tremendous tension, ready to break into a shout at the slightest provocation. He won't look at the women, ever, ever. The woman says she's pregnant. Ominously patient, Dr Kostov asks – what – was – the – date – of – her – last – period. The woman smiles, she has no idea. She doesn't know dates. 'She wouldn't know what she had for breakfast,' says Dr Kostov, running alcohol over his glove at the sink. Even that remark is relief. The woman can't make head or tail of the table. At one point, she's kneeling on it. Baya tries to get her right before Dr Kostov comes back from the sink.

But she's too late. Dr Kostov grabs the woman's feet, hauls her down the table, to the edge and over. He grinds each foot into the stirrups with a growl to each one: 'Stay there.' One foot actually goes through the stirrup, and Dr Kostov wrenches it back. From the woman, fluttering hands and 'pa . . . pa . . . pa'. If this is what he's doing to my feet, what's he going to do with the rest of me? From Dr Kostov, hissing, spitting, cursing – 'Animal! Idiot!' the word that sounds like 'Prostate!' and more Bulgarian, much more. The woman's about five months pregnant. Her hands go down to stop Dr Kostov pressing so hard to find the baby's head, and they get the smartest whack yet from the wooden stethoscope. It takes the woman's breath away. Her eyes fill with tears and she grips my arm with both hands. 'Ai, ma,' goes Baya under her breath, and I think: we've arrived, we're here at last, we've been on our way a long time now, it's been like this for days, but not quite like this, not quite this bad. My heart's pounding, Baya's about to say something, and my hand's absolutely shaking because I'm about to hit Dr Kostov who I think has gone berserk.

But I don't and instead, in my notebook that's open on the desk, I write the word AUSCHWITZ. I needn't fear, though I'd been frightened at first. He won't look. He isn't curious about what I'm writing all the time. The very first day, he must have been aware, if he'd thought at all, that his teachings on obstetrics couldn't fill a single page. So what can it be that I'm writing? I couldn't believe he'd not guess. But he's never even asked himself the question. I want to hit him harder than he's ever hit anyone, I want to get it all down, absolutely irrefutably.

He puts the stethoscope the wrong way up on the woman's belly. He growls at it, swears, puts his ear to the baby's heart and scowls into the hills. He hates us all.

The worst thing possible happens. A woman I saw in Out-Patients with Dr Vasilev comes back, a tall, thin and intense Kabyl woman who works in the Post Office. European clothes, perfect French. Taut thighs, retreating genitals: 'Oh, mon Dieu.' But when Dr Vasilev's fingers were in: 'pa . . . pa . . . pa' like the others. Two months pregnant, her cervix was only a little open, and Dr Vasilev sent her home to rest, with hormones, iron and vitamins, to try and keep the baby. 'The one thing I'm afraid of is a curettage', she said as she left.

And now she's back, bleeding badly. It all came out in the night. She lies on the table as she should. Dr Kostov examines her with such viciousness that when his back's turned and he's washing her blood off his glove into the sink, she says he must be ill. I tell her she'll have to have a curettage. She covers her face with her hands: 'At least there's an anaesthetic?' I tell her I'll try to find something against the pain. 'You mean . . .?' she begins, and then she screams at me: 'I had a curettage before, in Algiers, I had an anaesthetic there!'

Dr Kostov strides back from the sink and shouts: 'That idiot Vasilev!' He ignores the woman's panic entirely, and paces back to the basin beside himself: 'Do you call that a colleague? He knew she would have had a curettage yesterday. "Let Kostov do it tomorrow"!' He switches to Bulgarian and Baya takes the woman to the door. She tells her to hurry. If she goes over to Maternity right away, Dr Vasilev should still be there and he'll do the curettage for her.

But she's one of the last patients. Only ten minutes after she's left, Dr Kostov's finished. When we get back to Maternity, we find her sitting with her husband on the bench in the hall. Dr Vasilev has already left. Dr Kostov tells her to come with him into the curettage room. She asks if she can lie down a little first. 'Do what you like, Madame,' says Dr Kostov, 'I'm nobody here, I'm only the doctor.' Her husband walks her to the first room. She lies down on the bed and he holds her hands.

I search the cupboard of the curettage room for something to relieve pain. The cupboard is Vasileva's, and it's against the rules. She asks me what I want, and I tell her. She says there's no need for such a thing. 'There are so many hysterical women in Kabylia.' But I fill a syringe with local anaesthetic nonetheless, and put it on the glass-topped table where the curettage box will go. I pass a sponge over the table where the woman will be lying, and I put the enamel bowl out of sight underneath.

'What's the matter with the doctor today?' asks Baya. Vasileva says there were a lot of mosquitoes in the doctor's building last night. Perhaps he didn't sleep well. She frowns severely when Baya laughs, head down on the curettage table. 'Does she think I'm mad?' Baya asks me as we go to fetch the woman.

Her husband accompanies her to the door, he's very gentle. She's shaking, crying, tearing at her handkerchief. She's in a far worse state before than the other women after. We lift her on to the table, and her husband goes to wait in the hall.

Dr Kostov comes in from the doctors' office where he's been reading the Bulgarian paper. The woman shakes when she sees him, and she shakes even more when he puts on the heavy rubber apron and sits down on the stool between her legs. He looks over at her with gold and silver teeth, heavy glasses, and steel instrument in either hand. She looks back, neck muscles standing out, eyes staring, and he listens as she moans 'oh, mon Dieu,' and 'je vous en prie, Docteur,' again and again. Then Dr Kostov asks her, in that same voice he'd had in Out-Patients: 'Have – you – a – child, Madame?' She falls for the words, she doesn't hear the tone, and she says eagerly: 'Yes, I have a little boy, he's seven months old, he's well . . .' Dr Kostov cuts her short: 'When you had your little boy, Madame, the whole town must have heard.' She grabs hold of me and screams: 'My God, he's going to kill me!'

Dr Kostov ignores the syringe of anaesthetic and picks up the gutter instead: 'This won't hurt her.' The woman manages an extraordinary feat. She grips my arm so tight – there are deep fingermarks afterwards through the coat – and stares into my eyes so intensely that she leaves her body behind her. And all the time she's asking questions and wanting answers. 'What's he doing now? Tell me, please. Tell me everything, exactly.' 'He's catching hold of your cervix.' She doesn't feel the pincers biting through. 'And now, what's he doing now?' 'He's putting in a big curette and he's scraping out your womb.' 'Where, where, oh tell me, please?' 'He's doing the back first, then the front, then the sides.' 'And now, what's that noise, what's he doing now?' 'He's changing curettes, he's putting in a small one for the corners.' 'Oh, how long will it be still? Has he nearly finished?' There's bright red blood frothing in the vagina, over Baya's glove, and Dr Kostov answers for me: 'No, Madame, I'm just beginning your curettage.' She believes him, of course, and when the instruments come out, she vomits on the floor.

IO

With Dr Vasilev's permission, given with indignation: 'Of course! You're not here just to work, you must enjoy yourself as well,' I'm off to collect the motorcycle. What it's doing in Skikda, a port more than 200 miles to the east, way outside Kabylia, is a long story, and too involved for Dr Vasilev. He accepts that it is there, and that it must be fetched. Besides, the mere mention of the motorcycle has revived the old Vasilev, the warm, excited, gesticulating Vasilev of the first day. He used to have a motorcycle too, with a Triumph gearbox! The Italian in him leaps to the fore, electrifying his fingertips, throwing life into expiring syllables, transforming a simple motorcycle into a magnificent 'motor-CYCLE!'

The Italian I sensed behind him was not in my imagination. There's mail for Dr Vasilev, left on the office desk by the Postmaster with the surgical boots. Brochures from the drug companies and, besides *El Moudjahid*, a glossy magazine with a pink Italian stamp: 'Repubblica Italiana!' Dr Vasilev pronounces well, and with satisfaction. He tells me he actually lived there for several years before the war, in Padua. It's where he got his medical degree. And he still keeps in touch with the country of his youth, with a subscription to *Oggi*.

The touring map again, and he pulls his chair round my side of the desk to show me the routes he used to take on his 'ex-cursIONÉS!' through the Bulgarian countryside. From the Black Sea, he'd take the motorcycle inland, to Vasileva's hometown in the mountains. How that little place has changed! He'd go bumping over the cobbled bridge, and everyone would be wearing peasant clothes. That's all gone, and today the town makes spare parts for cars. Dr Vasilev would drive on to Sofia, and back again. Sometimes he and Vasileva would drive up the coast to Varna, and sometimes they'd just go to Plovdiv, where they had friends. All that time, and they only had two accidents – both small, nothing serious. The tendons stand out on his forearms as he shows me how hard Vasileva used to hold on to him. Dr Vasilev laughs and sings – and drives again – through his memories of 'the time of the motor-CYCLE!'

I get up at four, while it's still dark. I hope to reach Skikda by the afternoon, and be back by night. I stand for two hours on the edge of town, trying for a lift. I have my windcheater and crash helmet with me, and the papers I need to collect the motorcycle. Among them is a form, duly signed by me, in which I promise to pay the shipping company, the Compagnie Générale Translantique, the sum of £12 on receipt of the motorcycle. But I'm determined to avoid it.

An old woman pushes two sheep, trucks unload cargoes of bark. Cars pass, and nothing stops. The town's taxi-drivers are hosing the dust off their cars, preparing them for the day. I recognize one of them who'd brought in a woman for curettage. He tells me the times of the buses, I take his advice and walk back into town. The painter waves from his moped, and there are a couple of others, from the hospital kitchen, going into work: 'Bonjour, Docteur!'

The bus leaves from the main square soon after seven. Boys run alongside, selling peanuts and orangeade. The bus is a Berliet, with notices in French. I have a window seat, but the other passengers insist on drawing the curtains to keep out the sun. It's a tortuous ride over the mountains. We're in the heart of Kabylia. Glimpses of brown villages on the hilltops, squares still visible in the vegetation of the slopes, cleared for helicopters to land. This was the maquis country.

The inside of the bus is concentrated folklore. Women shout at men from behind their veils, the gangway flows over into the seats. In front of me, there's a group of old men. They smell intensely of sheep or goat. They have white turbans and robes, and hooded coats in camel wool slung over their shoulders. They have white bristles, and deepset eyes. Some of the eyes are blue. They are the faces of wandering poets, all portrait. One of them's telling a story. It's not entirely unselfconscious. He knows he's an old man telling a story. It's bus theatre. It's all in Kabyl and I can't understand a word, except the numbers, which are in French. The passengers listen and laugh. Another of the old men takes over, rewinding his turban as he does so. The story lasts for hours.

The road seems unending. In 1956, after the battle of Algiers, when the rebellion was only two years old and all seemed lost, Belkacem Krim and Ben Tobbal came this way on foot. They came from Algiers and they crossed Kabylia, passed between Skikda and Constantine, and reached the Tunisian border. It took them six months. We stop at a cold-water spring. The passengers invite me to drink first. We're surrounded by magnificent country, country that belonged to the rebellion from the very outset, country in which the French couldn't have been anything but trespassers. There's a lonely ruin above the spring, the Hôtel-Restaurant de la Forêt, with these pathetic pleas fading on its walls: 'Come back to France – General de Gaulle offers you a hero's peace.'

A longer halt in a small town, sandwiches of sheep's liver and hot sausages. But most of all, bottles of orange. Then we're off again, climbing hairpin bends through plantations of cork, stopping to pick up passengers and to meet the bus that's coming in the opposite direction. The drivers chat in Kabyl. It's minutes before the bus has gathered speed again. Orangeade returns in a fluid vomit, and mothers come aboard prepared, with rusty powdered milk tins for the children.

A tree on the side of the road, in the middle of nowhere, with one old man standing, the others lying in the shade with their cloth-covered panniers. The driver hasn't seen them, he's been talking to a man in dark glasses in the front seat, a customs official from Skikda. The look-out realizes that the bus isn't going to stop. He hobbles towards us in his turban, the hood of his woollen coat flapping on his shoulders, waving his stick. The driver jerks the wheel to the side, swearing at the old man from behind his panoramic windows. The others under the tree haven't moved. What's one missed bus, one wasted day.

There's another old man, with a face like creased parchment, who gets on the driver's nerves. He has diarrhoea. The first time, fair enough. The driver rests on his wheel, and talks to the customs official from Skikda. The second time, there's trouble, especially as at every other stop in between, the old man's always first out and last back. With wet eyes, with his fingers twisting the corners of his moustache, the old man taps the driver on the shoulder. The driver gives a great blow to one of the arms of his wheel, and refuses to stop. The old man stands there, and the relatives plead. The driver pulls up in disgust. It's torture for the old man. He daren't go far, just off the bus and a couple of shaky steps up the side of the hill into the shade. He's in full view of everyone. The young people laugh, the old people pay no attention. He pulls his pants down and squats in the dry grass, steadying himself on a bush. He hasn't been there more than a few seconds when the driver starts to hoot. The old man waves. He hasn't finished. The driver revs up the engine. More frantic signalling from the old man. The driver edges the bus up the hill, and the customs official laughs. The old man comes running, pulling on his pants.

He's first out again at the next stop. It's another spring. Some are small waterfalls, coming down between the rocks and shrubs on the side of the hill, making a wet track across the road to the other side. This one's a pipe with cold water flowing into a huge stone trough, that has downy sides of moss. The name and the date of the construction are carved in its side in French. It's a full-length bath on the mountains, with half Kabylia below. I'd lie there for hours. And on the journey back, watching out for stray sheep as I'm being pulled by the nose round one bend after the other, climbing fast, ears popping, with a good view of the road ahead and having passed the last car an hour back, I'll jump into the trough and take my bath, washing off the dust and insects. It'll be nice, but it won't approach the fantasy on the bus.

We run downhill into the plain of Bejaïa, then climb steeply to the town square, built on rock several hundred feet up. It's as far as the bus goes. The connection to Skikda has already left, and the next bus isn't till tomorrow. A day will have gone, and I'll only have travelled a third of the distance.

I walk out to the city limit, over a steel bridge, to the fork to Skikda, trying again for a lift. I stand there for two hours, until I start to feel ill. It's noon, and the heat is colossal. Nothing stops, except a boy who walks past with a basket of prickly pears and peels one for me. The cars that ignore me take away my strength, and I walk back to the nearest café. The two miles or so seem much longer. I feel down, as much as I had done in Marseille, when everything was going wrong, in heat that was almost as great. I have one beer, a second, and a third. They have a telephone, and I get through to Dr Vasilev. Maybe it's just the line, but he sounds slighter than ever, the incredible shrinking man, agitating inside the receiver, an excited mascot for me. He cheers me up greatly. He won't listen to any long explanation. 'I am well,' he cries, 'and everything in Maternity is quiet!'

A man comes into the café, dressed like an advertisement for tropical fashion. Cool, light fresh clothes, dark glasses, the picture of how I'd like to be feeling at this moment. He orders a Spécial, the most expensive beer, the one with the silver wrapping round the top, and unfolds a fresh copy of *Paris-Match*. Quarter of an hour later, he drives away in a new white Citroën saloon, a DS 21 with yellow 'CT' plates. That stands for 'Co-opérant Technique', someone who's come from abroad to give technical assistance to Algeria. Was the man French, or did he come from Eastern Europe? I didn't hear him speak, and I'm trying to shut the loaded image of Dr Kostov out of my mind. But the man was all too conscious of his money. There was a newness, a naïvety in their relationship that you'd never have found in a doctor from France, for whom money is an old acquaintance.

It's become slightly cooler. I walk back, out to the fork, to try again. I've nothing to lose. A car stops, but it's only going to the beach, a mile further on. Then an old Peugeot station wagon pulls up past me, the driver waving. The car has a metal trunk and cardboard boxes tied to its roof, like so many others. The driver gets out and comes running back, with a great smile on his face. In a moment, he's shaking my hand and saying 'Marseille! The hotel!'.

I get in next to the cases on the back seat. Taleb is with his brother and they've just been to pick up his luggage in Algiers, where it was dumped by one of the company cargo boats. They'll take me to Djidjelli, the next big town along the coast, a hundred miles away. It's where they live, it's halfway, and there's a bus that goes on to Skikda at five in the morning. We drive on a long flat road by the sea, the bay of Bejaïa. Taleb's brother has a radio, and we hardly talk. It suits me. I'm exhausted from the hours of frustrated hitch-hiking, of fighting the nausea in the bus from those countless bends and brakings and restartings. I sit back and watch the sea go by. It's coast road all the way, miles of empty beaches. I couldn't be luckier.

It was nearly three weeks ago, on a Sunday, that I met Taleb in Marseille. Our boat was due to sail at six in the afternoon. I raced into that town along a smooth road from Nice, thinking I'd be riding in Algeria in twenty-four hours time, and trying to print the passing country on my mind so I'd know exactly what was different when I got to the other side of the Mediterranean. I arrived early at the port gates, rode along the cobbles to the quayside where the *Ville de Marseille* was moored, and watched the motorcycle being hoisted on board. Then I discovered that the ship wasn't sailing at all.

Upstairs, in the enormous concrete shed they called a departure hall, there was a blackboard on which a hand had chalked: 'The Compagnie Générale Transatlantique regrets to inform its passengers that, owing to a technical mishap independent of its will, the *Ville de Marseille* will not be sailing until 10 a.m. tomorrow'. I found myself wondering how I'd spend the night. Could I afford a hotel, or would I sleep here on the floor? There were a few hundred others, all Algerians, so far as I could see, with the same question on their minds. There was no one to help with the answer. The blackboard's total indifference only increased its authority. It occupied a space of its own in the departure hall. Algerians walked round it, they gathered before it, they deferred to it, as if it were the Compagnie itself.

On hand, there were four police vans, dark-blue priests to the blackboard oracle, with metal grilles over their side-windows. Twenty men were stationed at various points in the hall in pairs, watching Algerians establishing territories for the night on the grey concrete floor-space, Algerians shifting baggage to 'somewhere better', small men like donkeys twisted beneath huge cardboard boxes tied with string. The police looked on, unofficial foremen, overseers of a prison work-party.

I left and found a hotel, one of the many that were a stone's throw from the port, in a street that smelled of fish. I stumbled on it by mistake. It was not a hotel for me, and nor were any of its neighbours. My hotels were in town. I should have realized when the taxi-driver set me down. He'd been reluctant to enter the street at all. 'Careful of your bags, son,' he'd said, 'the place is full of Arabs.'

The room cost 8 francs. Two people were already in there. One was a Tunisian whose parents had found him a bride. He was going home to get married. The other was an Algerian my age called Taleb. He worked in a factory in Metz (it's not 'la grande vie,' he said), and he was going home to Djidjelli for his holidays. He had a motorcycle too, and we talked of that for a while, in semi-darkness. The light didn't work, and the shutters were closed to keep out the heat. We had our own beds, but the generosity stopped there. The sheets were grey and crumpled, Maternity sheets. There were no pillows. There was a basin but no water and, logically, no towel. The room gave on to a courtyard crossed at each floor by lines of washing, a well that reverberated to a football commentary from several radios.

Algerians came and went on the landing, small and frightened. The lavatory was all lavatory. It began from the moment you opened the door, and my sphincters closed like vices. I went to find the concierge. He came out of his room in slippers, he was watching the match on television. Thin arms, mean chest and a vest, the physique of the average patron of a Café des Sportifs. I asked if he had stars in the Michelin guide to Marseille. Up went the wretched arms: 'What do you expect? We only take Arabs here.' Back to the room, where Taleb too couldn't understand what was worrying me. He was comfortable, he was at home. Lying out on the faded bedspread, he told me he always stayed here when he came to Marseille. 'It's my hotel,' he said. He might have been a businessman at the bar of the Hilton.

Next morning the departure hall stank of a night's shame and humiliation. Urine and scattered excrement. Only the police were fresh, reinforcing the crash barriers, channelling people into a narrow line to pass through Customs. A vast triangle of struggling Algerians, with panic at the apex. Taleb joined in, it was 'his queue'. I stayed back and I lost him. Huge trunks and knotted cloths, cardboard boxes and screaming children passing from shoulder to shoulder, men staggering, others scrambling ahead, trying to answer the double demands of unwieldy baggage and ticket control, men falling back to sit dazedly on their cases before beginning again, refugee scenes.

For a few seconds the panic stopped and the crowd divided to let through a neat file of jolly campers bound for the boat to Corsica. Laughter and excitement, reminding us it was August, August the holiday month when everyone, but just everyone, leaves the towns for the country and the sea. They carried smart rucksacks – on their backs, where they were supposed to be – and in their map pockets, they carried maps. Water flasks and sleeping bags, eyes unafraid, faces open. They'd vanished in a second, and our flight from France resumed.

Passport control, impatient officials, and a long corridor to the gangway. There were three decks in the second class. They had no connexion with the rest of the ship. The only exit from below was upwards, via a narrow staircase. And the only exit from the top deck was the sea. It was a boat for Algerians.

Three deckfuls of refugees at rest. Every square inch was claimed. Mothers with babies at their breasts watched you step over their feet. The air below was stifling, but the direct sun made the top deck intolerable. People queued and requeued in front of the solitary tap of stale drinking water. Some were already asleep, drawn, unconscious faces on coloured blankets. Others had come on with plenty of food and bottles of lemonade, knowing there'd be nothing for them on board. Some passengers even sat in their own chairs, playing radios on their laps, under blankets they'd strung out from the winches as protection against the sun. They looked at home. They'd fought for a place on the *Ville de Marseille*, they'd laid claim to territories on its filthy decks, and they were resting. 'Here,' the Compagnie Générale Transatlantique had said, 'this boat is specially for you.' They'd taken it and they were making it theirs.

Ten o'clock came and went, and the *Ville de Marseille* stayed put. At one o'clock, the company chose to manifest itself, this time in the form of a loudspeaker announcement: 'The Compagnie Générale Transatlantique regrets to inform its passengers that, following a technical mishap independent of its will, sailing has had to be postponed until this evening'.

Not only did the Company regret nothing at all, not only was the technical mishap the result of an entirely conscious choice – the boats to Corsica ran like clockwork in comparison – but the *Ville de Marseille*, as it turned out, was not even going to make it that evening. The announcement was a triple lie.

And once more, the Company vanished. Couldn't we wait on shore, out of the sun? Couldn't we have water? Couldn't we send messages, telegrams? Men cupped their hands and shouted up to the bridge: 'Hey, Captain!' But there was no one behind those thick windows. We were cut off, and the Company had sunk back, to take on entirely the form of its property. Steel-wire stays, rivets, and panels and ropes. We pulled at the Company, we beat it with our fists, we kicked it and we attacked it with knives. All without success. There was nothing fragile except the bowls in the washroom downstairs, and these the Company was protecting in the form of a moat of excrement.

Someone on the lower decks managed to catch a dock-worker's attention. The gangway was replaced, and the Company doctor came on board, to see a woman who'd fallen ill with her child. He was a round little man in dark glasses, and he clutched his briefcase nervously – or perhaps that was just my wishful thinking. He went below, confident in his priestly immunity, and he left unharmed, his work of mercy done.

The gangway stayed in place, guarded by two Frontier Police. Once already that month, the boilers had burst on the *Ville de Marseille*. Passengers had camped for five days in the departure hall, they'd squandered precious money on the hospitality of Marseille hoteliers, and they'd wasted even more precious days. Some, it was said, hadn't even sailed at all. The atmosphere on board began to change. Those who'd got on first, those in the 'best' positions, in the collapsible chairs, with the blankets over their heads and the transistors on their knees – they were the last to be affected. The older men too hung back. But the rest had had enough. We went down the gangway and pushed past the two Frontier Police.

We went back the way we'd come in the morning. Chairs and wooden desks that had meant passport control a few hours before now stood forlorn and absurd. The blackboard spoke to no one. The departure hall was an empty stadium, a concrete wasteland still strewn with the débris of the night. We crossed the footbridge and went down into the Boulevard des Dames to the company offices. We went to the main window and asked for the free distribution of food and drink, immediate alternative transport to Algeria and compensation for the expenses already incurred. But the main window was not responsible. It was only a small cog in the Company. We started up a flight of spiral stairs. There was a shout from the main window of 'Where do you think you're going?' Upstairs, we said, to see the Company itself. 'There's no one upstairs.' But above us, further round the spiral, there was a wall of security corps uniforms.

We retreated to the ship and returned a few minutes later with reinforcements. But dark-blue vans with metal grilles over their side-windows had already drawn up on either side of the road. And the Company had risen once again, to fill 60 pairs of boots as feet, 60 dark-blue uniforms as muscle and bone, and 60 képi'd skulls as Bronze Age brain.

Feeble though it was, our demonstration must have been a

threat, for it produced results. A rumour began to spread that sounded pure fantasy, and to the majority it was to remain one: the Company was providing planes. How could it possibly? The planes were all booked for months. Besides, how many would be needed to transport hundreds of people and all their baggage? The Company was incapable of providing another boat, let alone a fleet of planes. Yet the insane rumour caught hold: 'Who told you?' – 'A man, someone.' – 'Will there be extra to pay?' – 'Perhaps, but it's our only chance.' – 'Yes, it's our only chance.'

Disembarkation: deck-chairs folded, positions abandoned, precious investments swept away by rumour. There came the tumult of the morning in reverse, three decks squeezing down the gangway, bouncing like a trampoline, everyone rushing to be first, suitcase handles snapping. There'd still been no announcement, nothing official. People crowded outside the ticket office in the departure hall. More vans of police arrived to contain the enormous queue, and they confirmed the rumour. There would be airline seats, they said. 'But only a few.'

First class passengers were served first, through a private and heavily guarded entrance to the ticket office. So, too, I quickly discovered, were Europeans, and it didn't matter what class they came from, their tickets were not even examined. Brown hands waved telegrams to Monsieur l'Agent about dying children. Monsieur l'Agent said 'merde'. The Algerians were driven away from the first class entrance with 'tus' of contempt.

The police hustled an Algerian woman through the first class entrance – they'd considered her an exception. She was travelling alone with eight children. The prospect of air tickets was bucking her up, until she was caught by a piece of bad luck. When she'd bought the boat fares, her smallest child had been young enough to travel free. But he'd had another birthday since then and by international air safety regulations, he required a separate seat which had to be paid for. The woman paid the money, went to a table and cried. Her breakdown was contagious and a blonde French woman, travelling first class, and for whom all was going smoothly, collapsed at the counter.

Midnight approached and despair mounted at the end of the

second class queue. They smashed the partition separating them from the ticket office: the sound of breaking glass, the sight of police running forward, weapons raised.

By early morning, the seats were all taken and the police locked the gates to the ticket office. They were anxious to disperse the remaining derelict Algerians, left in the departure hall with nowhere to go but back to the rooms and jobs that are theirs in France. The police swaggered between them: 'Allez, move on!' and told them they could come back at nine for a refund from the company offices. A man got up from the baggage where he'd been sitting, staring into the floor. He took out his knife and hacked the cardboard and string to shreds.

That's all over for Taleb now, until next year. We drive on, past Cape Aokas, through Ziama-Mansouria and Cavallo. We pass through villages in the dark, and smell skewered meat over charcoal fires. Crowds of children in the headlights, shining teeth and eyes. The tents of their summer camps out- lined among the trees. We stop for a mint tea, Taleb won't let me pay. The children make a circle, I help one with his English lesson, and another shows me a baby monkey, caught nearby in the Kerata gorge.

Djidjelli's a beautiful name. A mile or so before we get there I smell a tannery. In Djidjelli I smell fish. I've become used to being surrounded by mountains. Djidjelli is flat, open and cool. Wide pavements and men in the cafés, watching television in the open air. Taleb and his brother insist I spend the night in their home. Through a small green door into a square court- yard, with a lemon tree in the middle climbing two floors high. Up the whitewashed stairs to the terrace, where their mother and sister welcome them with kisses. The mother scuttles into the kitchen, aghast over her failure to sense a guest was coming. Water in a wooden bowl on the terrace, for my feet, another for my hands and face. The tree dangles lemons at arm's length, huge and yellow, the size of grapefruit, un- picked from last year. Minutes later, the table's laid, with shorba soup, fried fish, tomato salad and mint bread, cool buttermilk from a stone jug. Grapes and crisp water-melon. Offered with apologies.

We go out for a drink. We walk along the sea front to a luxury hotel-restaurant, built by the settlers for the settlers. It's still forbidding. Palatial and white, with a vast ballroom and a stage for the orchestra, an old world maître d'hôtel, and an expanse of cool terrace, with steps down to the beach. At one table there's a party of Russians, and at another there are two Algerians, whom Taleb identifies as the vice-prefect and the head of the gendarmerie. Like the Russians, they're drinking Spécial, and it's what we have too. Taleb won't let me pay.

I sleep in a bed with clean sheets, Taleb sleeps on a mattress on the floor. The alarm goes while it's still dark. He comes to the bus station, orders me a coffee at the bar and disappears. He's back with fried bread, hot and crisp, the first of the morning. Then he makes sure the driver will drop me outside the port gates at Skikda.

It's a Mercedes bus, and a happier driver. He clowns all the way for two deaf-mute children sitting next to him. Dawn is just breaking when we cross a dried-up river, and the bus laughs at a little man chasing his donkey over the vast bed of stones.

I I

Rails set in cobbled roads, fork-lift trucks, shipping offices and warehouses, against a background of cranes and masts: the port of Skikda is a port like another. The offices of the Compagnie Générale Transatlantique are the largest, and they're set a little way back from the quayside. They have a warehouse next door, and I look inside, but there's no sign of the motorcycle.

I walk on, to where a ship's being unloaded in front of Customs men in blue. The motorcycle's in the shed behind them. The mirror's not broken, and the pump hasn't been stolen. It's dusty but intact. Taped to the brake cable on the handlebar is a duplicate of the form I signed in Marseille. There's no one about. They're all busy unloading. I remove the form and put it in my pocket.

I wheel the motorcycle out, and prop it on its stand in front of the Customs office. The chief invites me inside. I show him my passport, my driving licence and my insurance. He doesn't ask to see anything else, and the only forms he wants me to sign are for Customs clearance.

Even these are in themselves a trifling matter. They're a pretext for an encounter on a diplomatic level. The chief takes his duties with touching seriousness. Englishmen, he tells me, are a rarity in Skikda. English doctors – I've promoted myself for the occasion – are rarer still. As a representative of Algeria, even though he knows I've already been here a fortnight, he gives me an official welcome. He even refers to the war between America and Algeria at the end of the eighteenth century, and declares that such times are definitely over. 'You'll find a new Algeria,' he tells me, 'an Algeria ready to cooperate with any people of good will. We harbour no bad feelings, not even against France.' The English doctor and the Algerian Customs official shake hands, across a desk thick with forms. A subordinate suggests I pass by the shipping company's offices, where there's a routine form for me to sign. 'Red tape!' his chief silences him, 'why bother the doctor with such bagatelles? He's come to see Algeria. Allez, et bonne route!'

He stands outside his office to watch me leave. He tells me that the Algerian police ride the same motorcycle. He even salutes me. I ride up to the port gates. They're guarded by Frontier Police, who don't move. I'm through, and I'm free. There are palm trees at the first roundabout, and grey posters of grey Boumediène on the arcades lining the main street. Slow – there are so many children. They stand in the road and wave, or come crouching towards me over imaginary handlebars.

Fast across the plain, taking risks in the hills, I'm in a hurry to get back. I'm returning via Algiers, where Calie's plane is due to land late in the afternoon. She'll be coming to work for three weeks in the laundry, and she'll be coming as my wife. Anything else wouldn't be possible. The Econome has seen to it all (the hospital Director is on holiday). He's been very helpful, except that he wouldn't hear of the wife of a future doctor working as a cleaner in Maternity. Work in the laundry was more suitable, he said, and besides, she'd be happier there. It was air-conditioned, and it was the only department in the hospital where the staff were all female. I didn't insist. I'm badly in need of her company.

Once I've crossed Kabylia, the road is virtually flat to Algiers. Miles of vineyards round white settler mansions, huge estates that are now managed by the veterans of the war against the French. It's very hot, and there's no wind. Children on the roadside sell prickly pears. Men in the fields load water-melon into wicker baskets on the backs of donkeys. Road workers sleep under trees.

I pass in front of the airport building, and a policeman whistles. He tells me to get dressed. Perhaps I can drive without a shirt in my own country, he says, 'but in Algeria, we have principles'.

Yet the airport's international. It appears centuries from Kabylia. Zoras everywhere, in airline uniform, Zoras realized. Even a pair of coyly bottomed men in velvet pants, holding a poodle.

The plane's on time. We drive away slowly, under stares, down an avenue of palms that continues westwards into Algiers. Calie's excited and for me, it's like arriving again. Not clandestinely this time, but ceremonially. No difficulty in imagining the French governor-generals riding down this triumphal avenue, under this sun and sky, to subdue a population of natives on donkeys, with a Legion at their command, neo-Romans.

It's dusk when we get back, and the lights are on down the hospital avenue. The day is over for the Vasilevs. We meet them as they're walking back to their apartment. Calie's recognized him immediately, and she fetches a carton of Kent cigarettes out of the saddle-bag for him, his favourite brand. She's kissed and hugged by Vasileva – mind the hot exhaust pipes! Dr Vasilev's excited and jubilant. We're promised a supper, and hand waving coastward in pure Italian: 'Un ex-curs-i-ONÉ alla mare!' in the car of the very sympathetic Bulgarian friends. At the sea, he assures Calie, who's still surrounded by Vasileva, she'll swim and sunbathe – and also rest, which she doesn't understand, so he tugs on her arm to get her attention, and puts his head on both hands, closing his eyes in 're-POS!'.

He helps wheel the motorcycle into the garage under the doctors' building. He's fussing and contented, clucking happy 'ehs'. He lifts a withered leg and can only move the kick-starter down a little. 'It's been many, many years!' he cries. We agree that another day I'll start the motorcycle for him and he'll take Vasileva for a ride.

Dr Kostov comes down, shakes Calie's hand and gives her one of his heartiest smiles. He bows a little, and even brings his heels together. He's almost shy. And then I remember, I'd told him about Calie's Canadian passport. As for the motorcycle, he wants to know if I paid for it in pounds, dollars or

Deutschmarks. He says he's in touch with the company in Munich for a new BMW car, to be paid for in French francs. But he's sure he could get it cheaper in dollars or pounds.

He's wearing his Theatre cap, that bit of old elastic stocking fixed with sticky tape. There's a Caesarean to do, he says, and there's no assistant but me. I don't want to go, not this evening. With a smile to Calie and something unmistakably masculine to me, Dr Kostov says it won't take long, three-quarters of an hour at the most, and I'll be quickly back to my wife. I leave Calie in my room, and say: 'With Dr Kostov, it might even be sooner.'

'In Bulgaria,' says Dr Kostov, 'doctors never wait.' I'm back in the world I was in before Calie arrived, sitting next to Dr Kostov on a Theatre stool. Neither of us wears a mask, neither of us wears overshoes. The hospital hasn't any. We're waiting for the instrument orderly to arrive. The girl on the table has nice veins. A second orderly is putting up a drip. He's the anaesthetist. The bottle contains normal saline, and comes from France. The giving-set is West German, and the needle's from Poland. With some tape and ingenuity, it can all be fitted together. The orderly's had plenty of practice. He'll be keeping the girl asleep with intravenous barbiturates. The hospital ran out of anaesthetic gas a month ago.

I ask Dr Kostov what the Caesarean is for. He tells me the girl's being looked after by one of the private doctors in town, the man with the diploma in obstetrics and gynaecology. The doctor sent her into hospital this afternoon because she'd started bleeding. In his note, he said she was eight months pregnant. He suspected a placenta previa. That means, says Dr Kostov, that instead of being at the back of her womb, the girl's placenta has taken root over her cervix. For the baby to be born, it would have to push its way through its own placenta. That's why she needs a Caesarean. I ask him if he could actually feel the placenta through the cervix. Probably, he says, but it was Djamila who examined the girl.

On the girl's chart, under the heading 'Examination', there's an empty space. The chart only gives her name and her age, eighteen. She's brown and slim and naked. For eight months, her belly's small. Her arms are strapped to a crosspiece that runs under her shoulders, and her thighs are held with clamps. She has a necklace, and bracelets round each wrist, from the jewellers of Beni Yenni in the mountains. Red and blue coral, set in silver. The soles of her feet are a deep orange, stained with henna. Her black hair has been brought back in two tight plaits, wound with green cloth. The Theatre light shines down on her belly, where the incision's to be made, and she groans a little as she breathes. 'Lebess?' cries Dr Kostov from his stool. 'Lebess,' she whispers back.

The instrument orderly arrives, and I go next door with Dr Kostov to scrub up. Coats off, we're barechested. Brushes in antiseptic soap, feet on the pedals that work a tap of sterile water. We wash for several minutes in silence. We come back into Theatre with our hands up, pushing the door open with our feet, and put on the sterile gowns that have the face masks incorporated. The gloves are sterile too, but they're the old Polish autopsy kind, deformed by over-use, curling back at the wrists so there's an inch of skin between the end of your gown and the beginning of your glove.

We're expecting Djamila any minute. A table's ready for the baby, laid with a cloth, next to the anaesthetic trolley. There's a rubber sucker for clearing fluid from its airway, and a little mask, in case oxygen's necessary. Djamila should also be bringing along the stethoscope, so that Dr Kostov can have a last listen to the baby's heart before going in. We're all gowned and ready to start. 'We won't wait for her,' decides Dr Kostov, 'on y va!' I ask him how the baby's heart sounded earlier. Probably good, he says, but it was Djamila who examined the girl.

He takes a swab and begins to clean the girl's belly with blue antiseptic. He suddenly realizes she hasn't been shaved. Whose responsibility? Djamila's or ours now? It's a detail, decides Dr Kostov, and we lay sterile cloths over her body. The orderly injects a syringeful of thiopentone into the drip, and seconds later the girl's unconscious.

Dr Kostov goes in via a midline incision. It's jagged, but that's the scalpel's fault more than his. We leave the bleeding points, Caesareans have got to be quick. Out of the corner of

79

my eye, I notice Djamila arrive, with a cloth for the baby.
Dr Kostov's reached the womb. I have two clamps and a pair
of scissors ready for the cord. He takes the scalpel again and
makes a cut an inch or two long across the womb. Two strong
forefingers pull the incision apart. His hand dives inside and
I'm holding my two clamps open, ready. But there's no baby
inside the womb. There's only a bunch of small red grapes – a
collection of bloody caviar.

'Mole!' gasps Dr Kostov, lifting it out. 'Oh là là,' says
Djamila, 'you won't be needing me any more.' The orderlies
mutter after her as she leaves: 'A girl who chews gum'.

There's a strange tumour that carries the old-fashioned name
of a 'mole'. The womb fills and the belly expands, as if there
was a real baby inside. But a mole pregnancy is more difficult
than a real one. The mother gets more tired and more sick.
Her belly's larger than it should be. After only three months,
a mole can look like an eight-month normal pregnancy. And
instead of increasing constantly, its size will often vary from
day to day. If you feel the womb, you won't find a baby's head.
If you listen to the belly, you won't hear a baby's heart. You
don't treat a mole. It miscarries, usually around the third or
fourth month, and the woman's soon back to normal. The one
thing you never do is operate. You run the risk of spreading
the tumour cells to the rest of the mother's body, allowing
them to grow and multiply in her lungs and brain.

Dr Kostov pushes aside my fingers with a growl. I can't do
anything right. I stay away, just swabbing blood here and there
on the edge of the field. Dr Kostov's beyond help from any
quarter. The error he's made is so grotesque that even in his
own eyes it must have expelled him from twentieth century
obstetrics. Instruments lie neglected on the tray beside him.
He's forfeited the right to their use. He stares into his incision,
as if paralysed.

It's the blood that stirs him into action. 'Djamila!' he cries.
But she's already out of earshot. He despatches the orderly
instead, to fetch the laboratory technician. The girl's going to
need transfusing. Then Dr Kostov reaches in with both hands
and scoops the rest of the mole from the womb. He drops it
into the basin on the floor and comes back, to pack the womb

with cotton swabs. The blood swells up over them. He wrings
them out over the basin and stuffs them back in again. They
drown again in blood.

The womb's not contracting fast enough. As the orderly
leans over and puts a double shot of Methergin directly into it,
Dr Kostov begins stitching its torn edges together. They're
strange edges – fine, flaky, spidery, more like mousse than
solid muscle. 'Ai, ai,' mutters Dr Kostov. An extra layer of
stitches, for safety's sake. He stands back, and waits to see if
they've held.

The laboratory technician comes and goes. Dr Kostov passes
a swab over his stitches, to see if they're dry. But they're not.
The womb's oozing blood fast between them. He cries for
more catgut – 'immediately!' – and puts in a third layer.

As he awaits their effect, he turns feverishly elsewhere. He
starts mopping up the blood that's been spilling over into the
abdominal cavity. Organs come into view, mesentery and bowel.
He uncovers something that looks like a kidney. But it can't
be. It's in the wrong place. It's the left ovary! Swollen beyond
belief! Lumpy, with taut pale cysts in it the size of golf balls,
each one looking about to burst, demanding to be deflated.
Dr Kostov siezes hold of needle and syringe and puctures the
cysts one by one. But only a few drops of fluid come from
each. And the ovary's no smaller at the end of it. Now blood's
succeeded fluid, and it's pouring from each puncture hole.

Dr Kostov throws down his needle and syringe. He's begun
talking to himself in Bulgarian. He's swearing, he's fighting
against despair. A high-pitched whimper tells he's not winning.
He knows it's too late now, but he should never have pierced
that ovary. Cysts are to be expected in moles, they come with
the condition. You leave them well alone. Once the mole's
been cleared from the womb, they deflate by themselves.

A pint of blood arrives from the laboratory, a mere token
of what's needed. It's run into her vein as fast as possible. But
a moment later, Dr Kostov's mopping it up from the ovary and
wringing it out over the basin on the floor. He swabs, but the
bleeding won't stop. He swabs more fiercely – each wipe a
blow. The blood still won't stop.

He finds one of the arteries feeding the ovary. 'I must tie it off,' he cries, 'I must!' – and then he hesitates, as if in expectation of an assent that never comes. Fine needle, fine silk thread. But the tissue's too fragile. It's not even paper-thin. The thread tears through it like wire through butter. He ends up tying fluid or air. There's no alternative. The ovary must be sacrificed. If not: 'She'll bleed to death!' He cocks his head, for the approving echo. 'I have no choice!' he cries.

Curved clamp across the ovary's origin, scalpel drawn swiftly along its edge, no pressure's needed. Here it is, lifted out onto the instrument tray over the girl's knees, an unfortunate, pathetic piece of meat, pale and lifeless, swollen and split, torn by so much catgut and black silk, all to no purpose, dribbling fluid through its puncture holes. Dr Kostov growls at it, and spits from behind his mask. His hand jerks forward and for a moment I think he's going to send it SPLASH against the Theatre wall. He relents, tosses it down to join the mole in the basin and ties off the stump.

Back to the womb, for yet another layer of stitches. If it doesn't stop bleeding, the womb will have to come out too. Dr Kostov will have no choice! He swabs, and waits awhile. At last. As dry as it'll ever be. The orderly runs in a bottle of fluid. Dr Kostov calls for more – 'and more!' – like a thirsty diner.

A final swab around, and we stitch her up. It's the only part of the operation that goes according to the book. But when we remove the covers, I'm appalled by the amount of blood the girl's lost through the vagina. It's been dripping off the table on to the floor and that's why my shoes have been sticking. She gets the right to some cotton wool between her legs. I feel ill. I can't believe she'll survive. What a picture, what a mutilation.

It's after ten when I get back. For more than two hours, and in this empty room, Calie's been listening to the screams from Maternity across the garden, and to the shrieks of the children in the surgery ward upstairs. She's in tears. We climb into bed. Our reunion's a fiasco.

12

We sit up in bed and watch the dawn together, a Kabyl summer dawn, day after day the same, and today her first. For once, there's no sound but the beating of the swallows' wings. We watch the boy on the hill opposite, driving out his four cows, and we hear his cries. It's beautiful and it's restful, to sit here like this, to cross the floor to the window, and feel the cool air on us. Then a child starts crying, setting off others in a chain reaction. Dawn has broken in the ward upstairs. I go down to Maternity for the round with Dr Vasilev.

Sandal on the edge of the bed, resting the charts on his knee, he writes in the same old drugs – iron, vitamins and antibiotics. The enthusiasm generated by the motorcycle has disappeared. We haven't a word to say to each other.

Upstairs: first bed, first room. The bed's empty, the sheets are off. Next to it, there's a rusty drip-stand, called a 'gallows' in French, with a half-finished bottle of saline hanging from the hook. The girl from last night is dead.

It's an awful shock, despite everything. Baya says that the husband is only nineteen. He came in last night with friends. They'd heard she was going to have an operation and they wanted to give some blood. But the operation was already over. He came back in the morning to find she was dead. He fainted, he lost his reason – Baya's not sure. At any event, he's admitted to the general medical ward under Dr Ivanova. His friends told Baya how he's spent all his savings having the girl watched by one of the Kabyl doctors in town, the one who specializes in women.

There's no comment from Dr Vasilev, head of Maternity, no comment from him on an act of criminal negligence by his colleague in town, crowned by an omission even more criminal by his own subordinate, Dr Kostov, who'd opened up a girl he'd never examined. All he will say is: 'Who was the midwife?' When Baya says it was Djamila, he goes: 'Eh!' But it's not even a 'what-do-you-expect' sort of 'eh!' He won't put the blame anywhere, not even on the obvious target, the Algerian midwife. There's to be no inquest, and already we're at the next bed where there's a woman in her twenties who's beautiful, who I've not seen before, sitting upright in bed, robed in a for-once clean sheet, head on one side, pensive and sad. The baby in the cot at the end of her bed is surely going to die. Premature and tiny, dry and wrinkled. Eyes encrusted by something. Dr Vasilev pinches its cheek. The baby doesn't react. The pinch stays in its skin. Tears start rolling down the flat cheeks of the woman, and I'm the first out of the room.

Two things keep coming back to me: Dr Kostov sitting on the stool in his incongruously pixie Theatre cap, before it all began, crying out: 'Lebess?' and the girl twisting her head and saying: 'Lebess' softly back. And then the nightmare sight at the end of the operation, taking off the covers and seeing the pool underneath. We'd been pouring blood down a hole.

Dr Kostov's in Dr Vasilev's chair in the office downstairs, writing out prescriptions. I say the girl's dead. He already knows. He's uncomfortable, there's no doubt about it. He's even unhappy. He says that Fatma called him last night at eleven, only an hour after the operation ended. There was nothing he could do. The girl was already cold. 'She must have died from a blood clot in her lungs,' he says.

Dr Kostov's no pathologist.

I make out new charts for all the observations that should be carried out in the delivery room. There's a form for the drugs that each woman's receiving, another for her progress during labour, one for the examination of each baby at birth, and one for the mother after delivery. Four in all. They're more or less a reproduction of the charts in the textbook. Then I get permission from the Econome to use one of the typewriters in the Director's office. I make a fair copy of each chart. It's a long job, with all the columns and dotted lines involved, and it takes until midday. The Econome comes to find me. He's admirative and enthusiastic, sure that we're on our way to becoming a real hospital. He's as tireless as a scout-master. When the forms have been checked over by Dr Vasilev, he says, he'll get one of his secretaries to make stencils. They'll run off 500 copies of each as a start.

I come to the doctors' office at the beginning of the afternoon with the forms all typed out. Dr Vasilev takes one of them and says: 'In Bulgaria, that's how we do things. But here . . .' When I ask him, he can't say why it isn't possible here. The question's too big. But he's happy for me to go ahead. He'll sign anything I want for the Econome.

Dr Kostov doesn't look at any of the forms. He has an odd sort of smile, a touch of hostility, as if to say: 'Are you trying to teach me my job?' Whereas Dr Vasilev seemed not to take the forms as an implicit criticism of himself, Dr Kostov is more professionally alert. Before doing anything about stencilling the forms, he says, I should go up to the delivery room. What I need to get while I'm here is some practical experience.

He's put me down. As far as Dr Kostov's concerned, I've overstepped the mark. I go up to the delivery room, even though it is Tamara. We do a normal birth together. I'd seen her as a two-fisted midwife, as a huge blond commandant in frightening rimless glasses, an Ilse Koch for the mothers under her care, a mate to surgeon Ivanov. But I've done her an injustice. She's a babushka. She's a grandmother, and she's knitting a white jacket for her grandson in Moscow.

The baby swings head down from her massive hand, and gets its slap on the bottom. She smiles at me as she wraps it up, and I think she's happy after all this time that I've come to join her on duty. We have a difficult, ponderous conversation. We have so few words in common. I show her the forms I've made out. She can't understand much of what's at the top of the columns – I tell her that Dr Vasilev will come to translate the headings for her – but she recognizes the multitude of little squares, knows they're meant for ticks and crosses and numbers, and she's glowing. They have the same in Moscow, she says. She'd like to have them here, but she's not sure about Dr Vasilev. He's tired, she says, and he's not a good doctor. He's not Savianov, her chief in Moscow, who's written a book on obstetrics and who's invented a method for delivering breech presentations that she'll demonstrate to me next time there is one.

She's almost radiant, and her size only helps. It helps too that there's a very pretty girl on the delivery table, in a yellow Kabyl robe, with all sorts of added colours. She's bright and strong, with perfect white teeth, she's everything a pregnant mother should be. It's her third baby, she's an old hand. She has scarcely any pain. She cries 'ai, ma,' she calls for her mother, but it's from habit rather than real need. It's not like the first time must have been. And Tamara cries 'sussem!' but she doesn't really want her to be quiet. When the contractions come, the girl gets on to her knees, puts her hands on her hips and presses downwards till her face is ready to burst. If the baby came now, you feel it would go straight through the bed to the floor. Between contractions, she swings off the bed on to the floor, kneeling there too. But it's not awkward and panic-stricken, like the women with their first babies. She's graceful and agile, she's happy as she is. Of course, she'd like to be having her baby on her knees, like the two she had before, but she doesn't mind when Tamara gets her up on the bed, lying on her back. The cervix is wide open, the baby's on its way down, she's content not to move any more. She purses her lips, makes huge sucking sounds, runs her tongue from lips to palate, and claps her hands at the height of each contraction.

Fatma watches too, calling out in Kabyl. She tells us how they deliver in the mountains. The men all go away, and an old woman acts as the midwife. She's usually a member of the family, or she's from the village. The mother kneels, legs apart, with her body bent backwards. Other women support her. There are all sorts of herbs that can be applied to her stomach if anything goes wrong. They tie the cord with string or wire and cut it with a knife. 'When I'm the midwife,' says Fatma, 'I always wipe the knife first.' Then they take some hairs from the mother and the other women present, burn them and apply the ash to the cord as a dressing. The mother mustn't get up for forty days, and she mustn't work or wash. She uses a pot in bed. If the baby's a boy, the midwife gets a new robe, some fine cous-cous or some meat. If it's a girl, she still gets something, only rather less. If it's a boy, there are cries of joy, 'you-yous'. If it's a girl, says Fatma, there aren't.

We wait for the baby's head to come down all on its own. Dr Vasilev arrives, to translate the headings on the forms. His Russian is fluent, and Tamara follows everything. When he's gone, she goes next door to the midwife's room and fetches me an enormous pear, as well as a Russian picturebook I've noticed her with before, that shows fauna and folklore from all over the world, in diluted colours on grey paper. She points out the peasant costumes for me as she turns the pages – Eskimo African, Indonesian, and regional clothes from the republics of the Soviet Union. She runs through the towns of her country for me, on her fingers, nursery-style. Moskva – beautiful and ugly. Leningrad – beautiful, Stalingrad – beautiful, beautiful. Kiev – and so on. Her 'ugly' may still be 'not beautiful', but 'beautiful' itself is an improvement. She's showing a new interest in French, a new ability.

A warning 'ai, ma' from the delivery bed, and Tamara fetches a box with clamps and scissors. I hadn't realized how well she keeps the delivery room. She's the reason why everything's ready when Zora and Djamila begin their shifts. When she's not delivering babies, she's filling the bottles of alcohol and antiseptic soap, she's twisting bits of gauze into umbilical ties, she's washing gloves and dipping them in talc. My admiration must show, because Tamara puts everything down and summons me in Russian to watch her, as she does a little routine on the delivery room floor. 'Mademoiselle Zora!' she announces, her cheeks puffed with outrage. She raises herself gracelessly by her thick ankles on to imaginary high heels, fingers above her head, rearranging the curls in Zora's freshly set hair, to mince to and fro in a grotesque parody of femininity.

The baby comes easily, pink and wet, streaked with white fat like cream cheese. It's a job to tie its cord, it grips the clamp so tight. It's come in its membranes. Tamara gathers them up, puts her hand inside and spreads them out, up to the light. In Russia, she says, it's a sign of good luck and long life to the baby. Sholokhov has written a story about it. Tolstoy was born in membranes too. It's confirmed her mood, and my experiment with the new forms couldn't start under better auspices.

Djamila wants me to go ahead and get the forms stencilled. Of course, she'll fill them in, she says, it's what she was trained to do. I mustn't get her wrong. If things are the way they are in Maternity, it's because of the doctors: 'It's for them to give the lead.'

It's the first time I've seen her since the night of the mole. She admits she never examined the girl: 'I hadn't time. All three beds full in the delivery room – how could I?' She must have invented something when Dr Kostov asked her. If he ever did ask her, of course. 'Besides,' says Djamila, 'who ever opened up a mole? It's unbelievable.' She's indignant. The mistakes made by others are so enormous that each can afford to ignore his own. Everyone's guilty, no one's guilty.

There's a tall, blue-eyed seventeen-year-old on the delivery table. She's been in labour nearly two days already with her first baby, and Djamila calls in Dr Vasilev. He arrives a long time later, drawn and slow, a cancer patient attending his last appointment. His fatigue and depression match anything shown by his patients. It's supper time, and he advises against a Caesarean. The operation will reduce the girl's child-bearing capacity, he says, and hence her status in the eyes of the community. The sociologist stands in for the tired obstetrician.

He sits on the chair in the corner, and I show him a specimen form we've been keeping, the girl's pulse and blood pressure, the rate of her baby's heart, the frequency of her contractions. He tells us (elbow on the ledge, hand against his head) how they organize things in Bulgaria. We've heard it all before, and it's exactly what the forms will try to introduce. 'Why can't we do it here?' asks Djamila in exasperation. 'Eh!' – an 'eh!' that goes quickly up, and comes quickly down, like those electrical signals that run across the screens on the cardiology ward in London. 'In Bulgaria . . .' is the flat trace, that means no heart activity. 'Eh!' is the little spike, the reluctant flutter that gets forced out of the heart by treatment. We're only nagging. Dr Vasilev gets up, pats the girl's belly and bids us a hoarse: 'Work well!'

It's ages since they've talked like that, says Djamila. It's been longer than she can remember since Dr Vasilev sat down in the delivery room and even talked to her about how they do things in Bulgaria. As for anything more . . . She lives in the same building as Dr Vasilev and Dr Kostov, she works with them, and yet they've never even asked her in for a drink. Only 'the Russian cow' has had that honour. 'Let's face it', says Djamila, 'we can't stand them, and they can't stand us.' I tell her of the welcome Dr Vasilev gave me. She agrees he can be nice, but he's finished, he's 'passé', he should retire. 'They don't give a damn,' she says, 'so we don't give a damn either.' She'd had her happy moments as a midwife, but now her work only disgusts her. She lets me in to a little secret. She's had enough of Kabylia and she's applied for a transfer.

She puts up a drip, of a drug to help the girl's womb contract. Her running commentary on the girl then goes like this: 'But she doesn't push, the great lump! She wants me to do all the work for her. I'm sorry, I'm not going to. She's got another think coming. But she won't PUSH! Just look at the great cow. Oh, how these women get on my nerves. But push, for God's sake! Push! She doesn't know what the word means.' The girl interrupts: 'Operation? Operation?' 'No, my little girl, no. N'ki, n'ki! Ernu, ernu! Push, push! More, more! That's better. Now take a little rest.' The girl pants, head tossing on the pillow, mouth open, tongue flitting from side to side.

Djamila and I rest opposite each other, on the girl's knees, and she shakes her head at me: 'Just you try this for a living.' She glances down the girl's thighs to the vagina, where there's still no sign of a head: 'It'll be born dead at this rate.' Fatma says to the girl: 'If you don't push harder next time, it'll be a little girl.' And to me, Djamila says: 'A dead baby, or a little girl – it's kif-kif, it's the same thing.'

I get back early in the morning, as the Kabyl day cleaners arrive for work, in shawls and veils. Underneath, they're gypsy queens. Henna hair, henna hands and feet, gold and gaudy jewellery, crazy-paving dresses. They laugh at my amazement. Then they put on their overalls and say: 'Now you recognize us.'

The baby from last night is on its way at last, and Djamila's there ready with her clamps. What a night it's been, she says, she hasn't had a single minute to herself. The Register shows nine births in all, seven of them live. The specimen form that we'd been keeping seems to have stopped at the time I went to bed.

The head's coming through, and Djamila wants it for herself. She's so anxious for there not to be a tear. As the head appears, she bends it under the pubic bone by pressing down with the heel of both hands, arms straight, harder even than you're taught to do for massaging a heart. The head jumps through, and there's just time, as the vagina closes round the neck, to see that there's been a tear. Djamila pulls the baby through – it's dead – and inspects the damage. The tear goes down to the anal spincter, perhaps even through it. It's the kind that needs to be sewn up under general anaesthetic, an operation in itself. But Djamila couldn't bear to do it, even if there wasn't only a quarter of an hour to go before the end of her shift. Instead, she puts metal clips in the lining of the vagina and the outside skin.

Then, as I leave too, for the morning ward round with Dr Vasilev, I hear Djamila ask this question of the seventeen year old girl – the days of labour, the consultation with Dr Vasilev, the drip, the panic ('Operation? Operation? – No, my little girl, no'), and now the still-birth and the tear whose consequences have yet to be discovered: 'Ismim? – Name?' She must need it for the Ledger of Deaths.

13

Exactly one week after the mole, I came into Maternity full of hope and enthusiasm. I'd had the promise of the Econome that the stencilled sheets would be delivered that morning – 500 copies of each, 2,000 in all. It was an impressive quantity, and more than enough for the month that lay ahead. From now on, there would be no excuse. The experiment was to begin on the first day of the week, in a new month, and with an extra person on the staff. We had limped through August without the help of one vital link, the *chef de service*. She was the departmental secretary and nursing sister combined. She was the link between doctors and staff. The others had always spoken of Malika with respect. 'When Malika gets back . . .,' Baya used to say. I shared in that feeling, and Malika became my last chance.

I met her in circumstances that were a perfect demonstration of how things had been during her absence. In a way, I could not have wished for anything else. The morning was an appalling advertisement for the new forms. Out of such bungling, and misery for all concerned, there could come nothing but good.

I was over in Maternity soon after seven, and there were two Biotic-Algérie boxes outside the delivery room door, Djamila's total for the night (though not as bad as it sounds, because the Register showed no fewer than eleven births for her period on duty). The telephone rang. It was an orderly from Theatre calling on behalf of Dr Vasilev who was all scrubbed up and ready to go. They were waiting to begin a Caesarean, and they wanted to know what had become of the patient. She was supposed to have been up there half an hour ago. I laid the receiver on the desk and went into the delivery room to check. There was only one woman inside, and she was screaming on the labour bed, pummelling the mattress and drumming her heels. It was difficult to hear anything over her belly. I turned the air-conditioner off and tried again, but I couldn't pick up the sound of a baby. I went back to the telephone and told the orderly.

A few minutes later, accompanied by Tamara, Dr Vasilev appeared on the landing, unshaven, very low, more haggard than ever. He checked with the stethoscope and he couldn't find any heart sounds either. There was no more need for a Caesarean, and Dr Vasilev sighed.

Djamila, who'd gone to bed at four, exhausted by all her births . . . Fatma left in charge who'd been frightened by the great scar of a woman who'd arrived at six . . . Dr Vasilev whom she'd dragged out of bed to decide on a Caesarean . . . the arrangements made and the change of shifts . . . messages truncated, messages lost, a different cleaner, the arrival of Tamara . . . The breakdown in communication was complete. All the information was secondhand, and I didn't press Dr Vasilev.

With flushed cheeks, and her steps even shorter and fatter than usual (she'd arrived on time after all, and was that a crime?), Tamara helped us move the woman on to the delivery table and tie her feet in the stirrups. I fetched the steps without needing to be told, and brought down the heaviest box from the highest shelf. Dr Vasilev donned his rubber-fronted apron, a pitiful figure. What a butcher! Embryotomies didn't suit him like they did Dr Kostov. 'This is the Maternity for tired midwives,' he complained wretchedly. His criticism was bogus, and he knew it. No one had deceived him. Everyone had been true to form.

What is there to say about a second embryotomy? I kept away, and just passed Dr Vasilev the instruments. He pressed the lever that opened the head of the perforator, and brought down a lump of brain. 'Eh!', he went, a little welcoming 'eh!', 'the head will be smaller now.' He fitted the cranioclast and, as he pulled the baby out, veins popping, a jagged piece of skull tore the woman's vulva. Tamara pulled the rest of the body through with her hands, and swung it down into a cardboard box. The head was a sight that a defence lawyer would have displayed to the jury with apologies, irrefutable evidence of the insanity of his client.

We left Tamara to stitch up the tear, and went out on to the landing. Dr Vasilev was so low. It wasn't even eight o'clock. What a way to begin the day. What a job to come back to after a weekend off. He sat at the desk, and wrote 'Embryotomy' on the woman's chart. 'Why wasn't I called just one hour earlier?' he asked. In other words, why was the department like it was? He was asking the question, and he was its Director. For a moment, I thought he was going to cry. But it was a depression too deep and too longstanding to be relieved by tears. He went back to his apartment to wash and shave.

I was still sitting at the desk when a girl in a clean white coat came up the stairs. Plump but pretty, in a homely sort of way, with dimples in her cheeks, she'd just had her hair done, European-style. She dumped a pile of papers on the desk, and put out a hand to say hello: 'Malika.' She was contented and relaxed, still on holiday. She could have had no idea about what had just happened. But I was full of it, and instead of saying hello back, I couldn't help telling her all I knew. Her face clouded over: 'What a scandal!' She said it with such feeling that I even began to wonder if it had really happened. But then, as if I had contrived the whole scene, the door of the delivery room opened and Tamara appeared like some ponderous stage-hand, to stack the cardboard box on top of the two others. Malika raised a flap and peered inside. She winced and said: 'The poor little thing!' Her face showed real concern. What a welcome back. She promised me she'd be feeling ill for the rest of the day.

One of the Econome's secretaries came up the stairs, his arms full of my answer to the situation, the new forms. He'd made the stencils and run them off, all on his own and without a mistake. There were four sheets for each woman, and I showed Malika how they worked. She hardly needed any help, because it was what she'd been brought up on. She'd worked for two years in a 'real' maternity, she told me, and they'd used the same sort of forms there. Each was headed by the names of the doctors and midwives, with dotted lines for their signatures in the appropriate places. There were ten observations to make every half-hour on every woman in labour, eight to make on every woman during a ward round, five to make on every newborn baby. There were columns and little squares for everything.

I stapled some of the forms together in sets of four, ready for the day, and with Malika's help I cleared out a filing cabinet by the desk where they'd be easy to get at. Then I filled in several sets with some realistic figures, one that demonstrated a normal course of events, and others that gave examples of the kind of things that could go wrong. I stuck them up on the wall of the delivery room. Tamara had Dr Vasilev's translations all ready, and she began filling them in. Malika looked happy, and said the place was beginning to look like a hospital at last.

She was right, there was no doubt it looked professional. There were extra sheets along the side to explain what all the terms meant, there were arrows and stars, and all the figures were in bright colours. It was the brain child you'd expect of the trim and stethoscoped 'Doctor on Duty', dangling on his pin further down the wall. I could sense my Dean's emotion, the halo of Hippocrates above my head. The flag of civilized medicine had been unfurled in Kabylia.

Tamara went to and fro between patient and wall, working things out aloud for herself in Russian. When I left for Dr Vasilev's ward round, she was bustling about the delivery room like a cook in her kitchen.

Dr Vasilev seemed happy with the forms, but he was so much slower than Malika, or even Tamara, in understanding how they were to be used. Every time he wanted to write down a woman's drugs, he'd put them first in the margin of the temperature chart, and then he'd duplicate them on the new drug sheet. I had to explain to him that one note in the right place was enough. Temperature charts were for temperatures, drug charts were for drugs. He seemed to follow, and we passed on to a woman who was sleeping like a corpse, entirely covered by a sheet to keep off the flies. Dr Vasilev decided to give her antibiotics, and again he began writing down the side of the temperature chart, until Malika pointed out what he was doing. 'Sorry!', he cried, and explained that for two years he'd been in the habit of putting everything down on the same sheet. He gulped, and promised hoarsely: 'Tomorrow, we'll begin!'

Dr Kostov was in a particularly foul mood that morning. He told me, with his face scarred by remembered disgust, that as he was walking into work along the path outside the ground floor windows, he was hit on the head by a discarded melon rind. The incident had helped to bring him to his peak earlier in the day than usual. This was how he examined the first woman on his lightning round: he picked her temperature chart off the bed, called out her name, and when she sat up, he put his fist against her forehead, with the words: 'Get down, prostate!' punched her back on to the pillow and, on the backward swing, in the same motion, ripped the sheet off her body. He jabbed her a couple of times in the belly, and then turned to the other bed, saying: 'She can go.' Baya translated. The woman lay there, moaning: 'Ai ma, ai ma.' There was suffering in her eyes but, as usual, no trace of criticism. As for the baby in the cot at the end of her bed, it didn't even get her kind of attention.

His scowl – that curled lip, that disfiguring grimace with which he would greet each Kabyl vagina – stayed on him throughout the round. Fading momentarily in the corridor, it would be revived with a vengeance as we came into each new room. The place appeared filthier than ever. On the tables by their beds, each woman had melons and grapes and biscuits. But they weren't only on the tables, they were in the sheets and on the floor and on the windowsill. Under their beds, meat juice seeped from bags in a brown and putrid trickle that was a banquet for the flies, Large and comatose flies, that used never to move when we came into the rooms, as if Maternity was theirs. Stale bread and rancid butter, curdled milk in lemonade bottles with paper stoppers, and outside the window, a balcony that was strewn with the debris of the surplus food of weeks, cooking in the sun, crisscrossed by trails of red ants.

Grunts and incoherencies from Dr Kostov who could take

no more and who dragged a woman off her bed to the window and pointed her nose down to the balcony to 'Look at your culture!' And he warned her, how he warned her, in his brutal French and with his hand over the nape of her neck that 'in 100 years' time', she and 'all her people' would be 'down, down, down' (a prophecy uttered with the head up, the jaw tight, the lips retracted over metal teeth, and a dictatorial finger pointing to the floor). He spun the woman back to her bed and followed her with an outstretched declamatory arm: 'I call her *"Madame"* – and all *Madame* can do is throw her food out the window!'

But where else could they throw their rubbish? There wasn't a bin or a basket in the whole of Maternity. At the end of the round, Malika found an order form in the desk and made it out for twenty-four bins, one for each room in Maternity. 'With Mademoiselle Malika back in command,' she promised Dr Kostov and me, 'there's going to be some order in the house. From now on, things will be as they should be.' But Dr Kostov wouldn't take her seriously. 'Ahhh, Mademoiselle Malika,' he said with his sex-face and his hand on hers, 'do you think the moon is made of cheese?' He winked at me and laughed. Malika broke away, to begin work on the drug cupboard.

That afternoon, I took Malika's order form to be counter-signed by the Econome. His secretaries, all four of them in grey overalls behind their typewriters, waved me into his office. His desk was covered with different papers and the place was full of people. They were walking in and out, it was impossible to register a single face. The Econome himself was constantly on his feet, conducting two or three conversations simultaneously, shaking two hands at a time. It was like Maternity after the doors had been opened in the morning, plus a telephone that never stopped ringing.

Between the call he was taking from Mustapha Hospital in Algiers and the Electrician's query about the type of ovens due to equip the new kitchens, the Econome examined the order form, muttered: 'Bins . . . yes, absolutely indispensable,' and signed his name with a flourish. The telephone operator pushed past me, crying: 'Mustapha's on the other line!' The Econome picked up his second phone and cried out above the hubbub for me to wait. Five minutes in that office would have reduced the average man to tears, but the Econome insisted on conducting a more or less coherent conversation about the new forms: how were they working, how were they being received, and so on. While grey arms groped past him for papers on his desk, while the ambulance driver hailed him from outside and shook his hand though the open window, the Econome told me to take courage, that the Director would be back from vacation in a day, and that Mademoiselle Malika was worth her weight in gold: 'She'll support you all the way.'

'How easy it's all been,' I thought in the calm of a deserted corridor. A form and a signature was all I had needed. I felt angry with myself for not having got things moving earlier. I knocked at the Stores. No one answered, and I went inside. A warehouse vast and sombre, with shelves of plastic pans and surgical instruments. Brushes and detergents, and tins of powdered milk. Three mopeds from Czechoslovakia, brand new, with the factory grease still on them. The storekeeper was in a corner by the window, reading a book of poetry. He started when he realized I was there. He took my form, and stood up. He was tall and thoughtful. He told me it was months since he'd had any bins. Two years previously, they'd been provided throughout the hospital, and they'd all vanished in a few days. He kept the order form as a bookmarker.

It wasn't so much the lack of bins, it was the storekeeper's resignation that worried me, and that I kept from Malika when I went back to Maternity. I didn't want to disappoint her. She'd struck me as someone different from the others. Perhaps it's easy to let yourself be misled by first impressions, especially when they're welcome, but I could tell that Malika wasn't Baya. She wasn't tired, beaten and finished (even allowing for the benefit of a month's holiday). She had determination, and she seemed to know what there was to do. She took a pride in her job and she gave the impression that she actually enjoyed it. She wasn't Djamila, she wasn't harsh and indifferent. Most of all, she wasn't Zora. She seemed to like me, but as an equal. Her hair may have been European, but she didn't have the aspirations that went with it. She didn't want to join my world, she had one of her own. She was at home, on independent territory, and she had the proper self-assurance. If I was Europe, Malika was Algeria. I told her the bins were on order, it sounded more hopeful.

14

That evening, I left Tamara alone with the new forms in the delivery room and I went back to write a report on Maternity. I addressed it to the Director of the hospital, and above him to the Minister of Health. It respected all the conventions. No mention was made of physical violence. No attack was made on personalities, either Algerian or Eastern European. Consideration was paid to local conditions, and a cap was doffed to Islam. The report was couched in language that was official and precise. The tone was neutral, and the sentiment humanitarian. It was a doctor speaking.

I handed it to Dr Vasilev in the morning. I had no choice. I didn't want to do anything behind his back. I gave it to him in its plastic folder, and he asked me what it was. 'A report on the department', I told him, and I showed him the subtitle: 'Measures to be taken, equipment to be provided.' He was absolutely silent. There wasn't even an 'eh' out of him. He sank on to the seat that happened to be there, and started to read. It didn't criticize him directly, but it was implicit in every line. He sat huddled, his face hidden behind his glasses, over the first pure print I'd ever seen him read. He made me think of a man shown his own death sentence, and doubly pathetic, because it was a verdict he couldn't possibly contest. The report was an appeal to the professional ethic, to all Dr Vasilev's training. I wondered if I should have done it after all. I went away, into the delivery room, and watched from behind the door. Someone asked him a question, he didn't hear. They asked again. 'Qu'est-ce que?' he cried with a jump.

When he'd finished, he pushed the report away from him and lit a cigarette. 'It's good,' he said, in so low a voice that I could hardly hear him. He blinked and cleared his throat: 'We'll take it along to the Director together.'

He got to his feet and looked about him, a scholar emerging into the street after hours of study. 'Mademoiselle Malika!' 'Yes, Doctor,' she said, all bright and breezy. 'Tomorrow . . .,' he announced, 'in the afternoon . . . at 4.30 . . .' He paused for breath. This was no recitation of joy, no trip to the Sahara, no excursion to the sea. No climax shone though his opening words, carrying him along. '. . . At 4.30', he repeated, 'you, all the staff, Dr Kostov, and of course myself, we'll hold . . .' – the end came flat, without punctuation, eyes dull, and arms by his side – 'we'll hold . . . a meeting'.

Malika looked at me with eyebrows raised, as if to say: 'Well, well, things are changing.' Dr Vasilev passed on to the delivery room and announced his meeting to 'Mademoiselle Djamila!' She didn't respond, just carried on her work, and he asked her a little sharply: 'Did you hear me, Mademoiselle?' When he'd gone, Djamila shrugged to me: 'He must be joking. As if a little meeting's going to change anything.'

I came across Dr Vasilev sitting outside in the shade, stroking the one-eyed cat. 'I'm going to write a report too,' he told me, 'and I want you to help me.'

As usual, Tamara had left everything ready for the day. She'd topped up the bottles of alcohol, she'd prepared all the swabs, ties and delivery boxes that Djamila would need. She'd also made a beautiful job of the new forms, filling in every little square. But on the landing outside the door, there were two cardboard boxes, out of a total of only seven births for the night. Both babies were full term and fully formed, a girl and a boy. It was this that the forms were designed to prevent. But Tamara didn't seem to see. For her, they'd become ends in themselves.

During his round, Dr Vasilev was filling in the forms on roughly every other patient. In between, he'd return to the old temperature chart. There were times when he'd write in what the midwife had left out, other times when he wouldn't bother. I'd make suggestions, and he'd follow each one individually, but I couldn't convey their general principle. I couldn't make him see that either he used the new forms properly, or like Dr Kostov he didn't use them at all. I ended up feeling embarrassed for him.

When the round was over, Baya came to ask if I'd mind helping her with the babies. She said she'd never get them done otherwise. Maternity was at maximum capacity, two women or more to every bed, and there were at least thirty babies to be washed and changed. Baya was all on her own, and she looked more tired than ever.

We collected two babies from the cots at the end of the first beds and carried them to the changing room, where there was a large table covered by a dirty cloth. We laid them on their backs and began unwinding their wrappings, old pieces of material that had once been parts of a robe. Mine was tight like sticking plaster, and the baby kicked and waved as soon as its limbs were free. I had to pull the last part away very carefully, it was caked with faeces that had dried and stuck to the skin. They were hard and black. I softened them with water, then brushed them gently with a sponge. It was ten minutes before I'd got everything off. The sponge was rough and old, the kind you'd wash dishes with, and the water was cold. There'd been no warm water for two months, Baya told me.

On my second baby, I brushed till the skin turned red, but the stuff wouldn't come away. When we'd got off as much as we could, we wrapped the babies in a hospital cloth and put them back in their cots. We didn't bath them, and no baby had been bathed for two months, said Baya, because of the cold water: 'Better leave them dirty than give them pneumonia.'

Handling the babies didn't bring Baya back to life. She didn't stop to play with them, she didn't talk to them. She unwrapped, she washed and she wrapped, in the same heavy, joyless way. A too generous squeeze of nitrate had burned a baby's eyelids black, and 'that's a shame', said Baya mechanically, as she went to fetch the next. The tablecloth became stained and wet. There were no clean patches left to lay each new head. At the tenth baby, we stopped. We'd run out of cloths. 'We're short of everything,' observed Baya simply. Cloths hadn't been needed before, she said, and this morning she'd wanted to make her own contribution to improving things in the department. With that 'what-do-you-expect' voice that had struck me in the storekeeper, Baya told me ('confessed' would be the wrong word) that not a single baby had even been changed since the day I arrived.

Till then, I'd always assumed that Maternity did *something*. I couldn't have said what, exactly, but I'd taken it for granted that a background activity did exist, the kind that gets done in institutions without you ever being aware of it. But if babies weren't changed, if rooms weren't cleaned, if temperatures weren't taken and injections weren't given, what did Maternity do? It provided targets for Dr Kostov's sadism, it fed the flies and ants of Kabylia, it caused intolerable depression and fatigue in all those associated with it, but what did it actually do? Apart from the occasional reluctant Caesarean, it didn't even deliver babies. It was just a building with an abnormally high birthrate.

I went to find Malika, nominally to ask for more cloths, but in fact to make her feel the way I did. It was no longer a matter of cloths and bins, it was everything. There wasn't a single reason for Maternity to exist a moment longer, and I wanted everyone to know. Malika crawled backwards out of the drug cupboard and listened. After several moments' thought, she locked the cupboard, pocketed the key and said: 'Follow me.'

She took me down the stairs, past the office where Dr Vasilev was turning the pages of a new brochure from Roche, past the bench in the hall, and out into the courtyard beyond. She led me across the blinding gravel towards a great building four floors high that I'd never visited before, opposite the Morgue. The Econome was out, Malika was telling me, and besides, he wasn't really the person for me to see. Those four secretaries of his were 'useless'. If she'd rung them about the cloths, they'd only have whined about themselves, sitting there over 'their little typewriters', unable to take any initiative. Even the Econome himself wasn't what you'd call 'a real man'. He may have been second in command of the hospital, and the Director's deputy, but he couldn't force respect. There was only one person for me to see, said Malika, and that was the hospital No. 4, the Supervisor: 'Fortunately, we have one man here who's a revolutionary.'

We'd reached the building. Malika walked in front with a sure foot, through a ground floor that was eerie, empty and dark, a labyrinth. Printed notices, wards of bed-frames and mattresses: the ghosts of the doctors who'd returned to France, of the patients who'd been transferred to the new sanatorium on the hill above Tizi-Ouzou. It was the old TB block, and the Supervisor occupied its four abandoned floors.

Malika found him at the sink in the treatment room, shaving. I'm not tall, but he was the first Algerian I'd met who was taller than me. When he heard us, he stopped his razor short, holding it poised for its descent down a neck thicker than my thigh, and told us to wait for him in the doctors' office. We left him as he went chasing facial hair even beneath his collar. I said nothing to Malika, but I felt I'd just seen Ivanov, an Ivanov with more brio to his razor.

We sat down in the office, and didn't speak to each other. Malika had said the Supervisor was someone I should see. But I didn't know who he was, and I wasn't sure why we'd come. The day's *El Moudjahid* was on the desk. It wasn't open on the game of the seven mistakes, but on a long speech to the Seminar on Islamic Thought in Constantine, by a Minister called Mouloud Kassim. Then I looked through the cupboard, at the old books and reviews on chest disease and tuberculosis, until the Supervisor strode in, fresh from his shave, 'all ours'. He switched on the fan and brought his chair round to the front of the desk, a gesture that would normally have won my confidence. He sat down, and the tails of his white belt swung between his open legs. Sire to that Turkish delight daughter, his genitals were like a bull's, bursting through his trousers.

Malika looked at me, expecting me to begin. But I'd lost the fluency I'd had with her. Only a moment before, I'd wanted to denounce Maternity to the whole world. Seeing the Supervisor had made me selective, it had dried me up. I'd hoped for an ally, and instead, I was feeling a surge of loyalty to Dr Vasilev. So Malika took over, and she told the Supervisor how Maternity had gone to pieces in the past month, how the place had become 'a dustbin', how the doctors were 'butchers' and couldn't care, how they treated their patients like 'animals', the very words I'd used. The Supervisor punctuated her account with responsible, decisive 'yeses', and Malika put me in an awkward position at the end by saying that I could vouch for it all if need be.

I tried to make my position clear, in the tone of my report, unimpeachable. I was at the hospital to work under Dr Vasilev, I said, and my first allegiance was to him. All that Malika had just described was indeed true, but I hadn't come to inform. I'd expressed my criticisms in the proper manner, in a report that would be shown to the Director when he got back the next day. Besides, things were improving. Dr Vasilev had called a staff meeting for the following afternoon. All I wanted at this minute, I told the Supervisor, was some extra cloths so that we could finish changing the babies.

He scratched at the bulbous mass between his legs and, to my priggish speech, gave an echo of preposterous solemnity. He respected my 'scruples', and declared them to be 'the true mark' of the medical man. The profession was bound by 'a code of loyalty', and in my position he would have acted no differently. Nevertheless, he said, bringing his great fist down on *El Moudjahid*, it had needed courage – 'yes, courage' – to tell Mademoiselle Malika what was going on, and 'the Algerian people' were deeply grateful.

Even so, he wanted me to realize that he'd known all this for a long time. 'We Algerians aren't fools', he said. After all, they'd fought the French for eight years, eight years against one of the strongest armies in the world, and the sacrifice, he reminded me, had been enormous, a million and a half dead. The Supervisor searched for an example, and came across himself. He'd fought – fist on newspaper – he'd struggled – fist on newspaper – he'd fought again – fist on newspaper – while comrades and family fell around him. No price had been too high to pay, 'my friend', for an Algeria both 'Muslim' and 'Socialist', words which he allowed himself to pronounce with luxuriously saliva'd 'S's.

I said yes. It wasn't what concerned me. Nor could it have been what really concerned the Supervisor. We hadn't touched on the hospital yet. His parade was an introduction, but to what, I couldn't tell. Malika was no help, she was looking straight ahead. The Supervisor was glaring. Then, from Algeria, he focused down on Maternity. And his voice changed, till it was almost conversational. When you knew your medicine as he did, he told me, when you were as familiar as he was with obstetrics and gynaecology, you couldn't fail to notice things. He'd always had his eye on Dr Vasilev, who'd worked well to begin with. The rot had started when Vasileva came out to join her husband. 'I know my nursing,' said the Supervisor, 'and don't tell me she's a nurse.' Even if she was, it was still illegal for her to be working in the same department as her husband, and he'd sent off an urgent report on the matter to the Ministry.

But the Supervisor had done his psychology too. He leaned forward, and with finger raised he announced 'the truth of the matter'. If things had become bad in Maternity, it was because Vasileva didn't know her place. 'She's not a woman.' She had her husband round her little finger. The Supervisor recalled an incident, and he described it for us with the same outrage that he must have felt at the time. It had marked him so profoundly, he said, that he'd never set foot in Maternity since. One day, he was there talking medicine with Dr Vasilev. Suddenly, interrupting their discourse, Vasileva had appeared from the curettage room to give 'her opinion'. The Supervisor had turned to her ('as I'm turning to you now') and had said ('as I'm saying to you now'): 'Medicine comes before women, Madame. Show some respect for your husband.' And he'd brushed her back to her work, with this imperious flutter of the hand. 'Besides', he added, 'everyone knows she has lovers.'

Even as the speech was being made, I was thinking it was impossible. It was impossibly conceited, base and irrelevant. I was sure afterwards I'd remembered only fragments. We'd achieved nothing. I even felt guilty when I thought of Dr Vasilev. I came away with Malika, and I could say nothing to her. I glanced at her face. Was that the man she really admired? Was that her revolutionary? Was that the solution to Maternity's problems, the way ahead for Kabyl women? I couldn't tell what she was thinking, and to the one hesitant remark I made, she gave no response. But then, I thought, how could I expect her to share my way of seeing things? We came from a different background, we were of different sex, and we'd only met the day before. I couldn't have explained myself clearly enough. When we got back to Maternity, I gave her my report to read.

15

There was a storm over the Djurdjura after supper. Calie and I went walking in the grounds, backs turned against the clouds of dust thrown up by the wind. Lightning showed the hills as clear as day. The hospital buildings stood firm, several storeys high, on the sloping ground. They looked warm and secure.

There followed an extraordinary twenty-four hours, in which Dr Kostov took a business trip, Dr Vasilev suffered another disaster and, against a background of Bulgarian medicine, I came face to face with Algeria.

That afternoon, a woman had come in who was nine months pregnant and beginning to bleed. Dr Kostov examined her, which means that he shoved his fingers up, guessed that her placenta was in the wrong place, and didn't listen over her belly for the baby's heart. It was supper time, his bottle of water was getting warm at the end of the woman's bed, and he decided against a Caesarean.

He arranged for a blood transfusion before he left, 'to keep her going'. The laboratory technician came down to group the woman's blood, and a pint bottle arrived after supper. Tamara set it up. Minutes later, there were shrieks from the woman's room, of the indescribable kind that only come from a girl left all alone with her first contractions. Yet the woman was in her twenties and she'd already had several children. We ran down to her room with plastic pan and delivery box, and everyone who could walk was standing wide-eyed in the corridor: 'Ai, ma.' We found the woman in her bed, shivering uncontrollably, her sheet drenched in sweat, her teeth chattering, her whole body shaking madly. Her belly was hard as a board. The needle had been torn out of her vein, and blood of the wrong group dripped from the bottle on to her sheet.

Fatma arrived with the trolley and we wheeled the woman to the delivery room. She had no idea where she was. She'd stopped screaming, and she'd begun to mumble incoherently. Tamara put in a hand and broke the membranes with her fingers. The fluid was thick and green, it smelled off, the baby was surely dead. I put a thermometer under the woman's arm (she'd have cracked it with her teeth), and the temperature there was over 40°C. With the next contraction, she delivered the baby. Tamara lifted it out, separated it from her, it was a boy and dead. Not so long before, either. The placenta followed complete. But the woman was oblivious, in another world, her body drenched, and Fatma the cleaner was wiping her face with a cold sponge.

After her Methergin, which she didn't seem to feel, she became worse. Her heart raced 140 to the minute, and her blood pressure fell to 80/40. Dr Kostov came up from a curettage he'd just finished downstairs and said the woman would need something to calm her down. He snapped the heads off two ampoules of Largactil.

He was preparing the syringe, Tamara was putting the baby in a box, and not ten minutes had passed since the birth, when the woman began struggling to get off the bed. 'Strap her down!' cried Dr Kostov, beside himself, and Tamara tied her hands and feet to the bed-frame with bandages. I didn't help, I watched, the warped professor and his assistant whose experiment had suddenly turned against them, I saw their feeble antidotes and imagined the woman rising from the table to strangle them both. Then Fatma pulled on my arm, and I escaped downstairs to clear my head, with a straightforward curettage on a Kabyl woman in Kabyl clothes, routinely bleeding, a face I knew I wouldn't remember and didn't, who I walked to a room afterwards, to the last empty bed.

And then back upstairs, to find that, sure enough, the woman had torn her bandages free and was pulling herself up off the table, like a dead person from a coffin. But Dr Kostov's feet were firmly on the ground. He wasn't afraid of her. He knew she wouldn't make it, not with that heart rate and blood pressure, and she didn't, because halfway up her forehead met his right hand with a wham, her head fell back against the frame, she let out a piercing scream, Dr Kostov cried: 'Prostate! Animal! Idiot!' over and over again, and buried a syringeful of Largactil in the muscle of her thigh.

He was Tamara's inspiration. She rose to new heights, she became the Tamara of old, of those first unrecordable days when I used to put my head round the delivery room door. She had the weight advantage, she had the advantage in temperature, blood pressure and pulse, and it had been many years, not a few minutes, since she'd last had a baby. She beat the woman's face, she grabbed hold of her legs, punched them, pinched them, scratched them and twisted them, lifting them up and banging them down, spluttering their orders in Russian. Her riot was grotesque, yet Fatma – Fatma! – followed suit, adding Kabyl words of her own, slapping the woman's hands. There was a lull, during which Dr Kostov and Tamara left the room. I told Fatma not to copy them, they were mad dogs, they deserved to be shot. But she couldn't understand. She did what the doctors did. Her world had made sense a few moments before. Why should she begin to copy me. All I'd done was to confuse her. Tamara came back with a sheet, this was how they did it in Moscow. They made a wide rope out of the sheet, over the woman's chest, and knotted it under the bed, where she couldn't get at it. I let Fatma help, I wasn't tying anyone down.

I took a blood pressure meter and went downstairs to check the two women who'd been scraped out during the evening. Calie was sitting on the bed of a girl who spoke French, and there were ten or more women around them on the floor, asking questions, laughing, talking among themselves. One was the woman I'd brought to her bed only an hour before. She saw the meter, and thought I'd come to take her photograph.

In the delivery room, Dr Kostov was trying to get some aspirins into the woman's mouth with a carton of water. But she vomited over the edge of the bed. He jumped away, but he couldn't avoid the splash. And he vomited back at her, all those words again. As he left, disgusted, he told me he might be taking a free ride in the hospital ambulance to Algiers in the morning. He had 'business' to attend to.

The woman looked pitiful. Alone and terrified, staring at the torn ends of the bandages on her wrists, not knowing what they were, murmuring the 'M's of the Kabyl words for mother and death, crushed beneath the sheet. Her vomit on the floor, her baby in the box, and Largactil coursing in her veins. On the sleeve of her yellow robe there was pinned a piece of bark. It was for luck, Fatma said.

A car on the gravel at dawn, while the swallows were flying madly. A curettage? I'd forgotten, it was the ambulance. Dr Kostov was ready. Light pants and a close shave, a short-sleeved, open-necked shirt, and a briefcase for that deal in Algiers. He got in beside the driver, and they sped away.

Relatives were already waiting outside Maternity. We could hear their voices in our room. They must have been up in the mountains before it was light. Women whose robes hung low over their belts, holding food, followed me with their eyes as I passed by to the kitchen, and men with cloth-covered panniers saluted and said 'Monsieur' when I came down later to knock at the Maternity door.

Fatma opened up and bolted the door behind me. She'd never seen so many people. If we didn't keep them out, she said, the work would never get done. I found Djamila in the delivery room, with a woman on the point of giving birth. The head was almost out and Djamila was there ready to take it. On the side, there was a set of the new forms, utterly empty, without even the woman's name. I asked Djamila if she'd decided to stop using them already. 'No,' she said, but from her face, and those blank forms in front of me, it was a lie, the honest kind: 'No, and that's a lie, the day's just beginning and I can't be bothered to invent something, so let's leave it, shall we?' I left it.

Dr Vasilev appeared in poor shape for what promised to be a momentous day – the staff meeting in the afternoon and, maybe, a visit to the Director with me and the report. He hadn't slept a wink, he said, and I believed him. It was the mosquitoes, apparently. Yet there was no trace of bites on his arms or face, and he didn't scratch. Perhaps it was their persistent buzzing or perhaps, I couldn't help feeling, it was just their weight.

He had something extra that morning, a spurned look about him, as if Vasileva had sent him packing to the sofa.

He began his round at a melancholy pace, strangely unsuited to the amount of work that lay ahead. With Dr Kostov away, he had an extra round to do, and then Out-Patients, plus any emergencies in between. It was as if he refused to recognize the fact. Again, he'd waste time duplicating information on the forms, and again I'd point that out to him. Many of the women were fully dressed and ready to go. They were sitting on their beds with their things wrapped in a cloth beside them, only waiting for a prescription. But twenty women going home from upstairs alone meant twenty prescriptions to write. That in itself was nearly an hour's work, and Dr Vasilev said he'd never manage. But he said it his usual way, trite and uncomplaining. It was clear, he didn't believe it. He didn't understand that this time, he really wasn't going to manage. He couldn't know that Dr Kostov was riding out of Kabylia to Algiers. Baya broke the news. 'Ahhh!' went Dr Vasilev in a drawn-out donkey bleat. He looked heartbroken and betrayed. 'Why didn't he tell me? Ahhh!'

Djamila came down the corridor to find us, about a woman in the delivery room whose baby didn't sound too good. She suggested a forceps. 'Mademoiselle Djamila!' cried Dr Vasilev, swivelling round to spell out his martyrdom on his fingers, 'I've both rounds to do, all the prescriptions, Out-Patients – and now you want a forceps!' 'Just letting you know,' said Djamila brightly, with a wink to me. Dr Kostov's trip to Algiers was going to mean another cardboard box. Even absent, he was making his presence felt.

Dr Vasilev tried to hurry. Scarcely anyone was 'examined'. Even on that desperately crowded morning, he insisted on rounding off Tamara's handwriting, on spending precious minutes sighing over her petty inaccuracies, on carrying out with Baya the little ritual of accusation and denial. There was only one bright moment for him when a Bulgarian woman doctor came along to see us. Introductions made him so happy. He presented 'a very sympathetic Bulgarian friend' to 'a very sympathetic English visitor'. They talked for a few minutes in Bulgarian, and afterwards Dr Vasilev put his hand on my arm to apologize, and tell me what they'd been saying.

But for the rest, how he wallowed where Dr Kostov had dropped him! How it suited him, the mantle of the betrayed! Djamila came back when we were halfway round the ground floor, in a room that smelled of excrement and sugary milk. Dr Vasilev was shunning the external world, enclosed in his own, and he didn't want to hear what she had to say. She didn't insist. To me, she said she didn't think she could hear the baby's heart any more.

Dr Vasilev went upstairs to listen when the round was over. He found the baby's heart, very faint, low on the right side. But he thought the head was still too high for a forceps. And in the margin of the woman's temperature chart, he wrote out a prescription – 'Nikolaieff's Triad', a mixture of concentrated glucose, coramine and Vitamin C.

He took all the prescriptions with him to Out-Patients, to get them done in between seeing the women. We had to push our way through the crowd of relatives being held at bay outside the Maternity door. They clamoured for their women, and Dr Vasilev waved his sheaf of prescription papers aloft and cried glumly: 'I am all alone!'

For once, the floor of the waiting room was clear. No woman lay out on a sheepskin that morning, whitelipped and barely conscious. Baya called for those who were bleeding to come first, and there were only two, both mild, whose curettages could wait till the afternoon. The next was a problem that delighted Dr Vasilev. He examined the woman first, at length, and then after I'd had my turn, he asked me to say how many months I thought she was pregnant. I said three, and that made him happy, because he was able to put his hand on what I'd taken for the womb and send it shooting up towards the spleen. It was a cyst, he explained, and he got me to put my fingers back inside so that I could feel the womb stay still while he moved the cyst all over the belly. It was a moment of bliss between teacher and pupil, our first, and Dr Vasilev had forgotten everything else.

We came back to Maternity to find the doors had been opened and the department flooded with men and women, papers being held up before us, pleas from anxious faces, buses to catch, circumcisions to attend, marriages to prepare for. Malika and Baya drove them all away, and we climbed the stairs to the delivery room.

The baby's heart was even fainter. The woman was on half a table, her legs in the air, ready for forceps. Djamila wiped her down with alcohol and Dr Vasilev tied on his rubber apron. He would have to be quick, he said. And he said it as if there were still a chance. In went the spoons of the forceps, and the woman shrieked. Dr Vasilev found it difficult to screw them together, the head was still too high. 'Too bad,' he said. We'd just have to try. Djamila climbed on to the table to kneel beside the woman and push down with both fists on her womb, in a diminutive 'Chris-Taylor', Dr Vasilev pulled back on the forceps with all his strength, and I leaned across to hold the thighs against him. The effort completely involved us. We must have been pulling for ten minutes, with the air-conditioner full on, but we were running with sweat. I thought of the baby, and my head ached in sympathy. I couldn't believe it wouldn't die.

Dr Vasilev stopped, examined with his hand, and found the head was no further down. He listened, and for me it was a miracle, but the heart sounds were still there. So we pulled again, harder still. Blood began running from the woman, she shrieked, her fingers clawed at my back, and above her Djamila shouted 'Ernu, ernu!' When we stopped, after a further ten minutes, there was a line across her womb that Djamila said was a sign it was about to burst. It couldn't take the strain any longer. Dr Vasilev listened again, and this time there were no more heart sounds. Forceps out.

I got the steps and pushed them up to the cupboard. Heaviest box from highest shelf, cardboard Biotic-Algérie from the cleaners' changing room, all things come to embryotomy. I left them to it. I saw Dr Vasilev picking up the parts of the perforator of Blot. In his place, at that point, I'd have turned it against myself.

And after lunch, Dr Kostov arrived back in the office, grinning, even splendid, all the better for his morning off. No one dared call him to account. 'Eh,' said Dr Vasilev weakly, oh so weakly (what's left in anyone after an embryotomy, what was left in Dr Vasilev), 'everything went all right, thank you.'

It was some time in that crowded morning, between coming back from Out-Patients and beginning the doomed forceps, that I remembered the report I'd left with Malika. But she didn't have it any more. At first, I didn't follow. I thought she meant that she wasn't carrying it with her, that it was in her desk. No, no, she said, quite calmly and definitely, she didn't have it on her, it wasn't in her possession, it wasn't even 'here' any more. But if it wasn't in Maternity, where else could it have been? The report was for us, to help us in our meeting that afternoon, and to show to the Director. Yes, Malika said, but she still didn't know where it was. The Supervisor had come and taken it away. I couldn't understand. The Supervisor didn't even visit Maternity as a rule. 'He came,' Malika repeated, 'and he took it away.'

She was keeping something from me, and she knew that I knew it. But she didn't care. There was Djamila in her, rising to the surface, breaking through. With a sickening feeling, I realized my mistake. Malika's face had changed, or rather, it was even more the same, and it was I who was different. Her dimples were still there, but now I saw them twinkling like warning lights. Anxiety crept over me. I picked up the telephone. But the Supervisor wasn't in his office, and the switchboard man didn't know where he was. I was afraid he'd be going home, it was so close to noon. I went down the stairs, pushed my way through the relatives out of Maternity, and walked quickly across the courtyard. His black Peugeot 204 was in its usual place outside the Morgue. I ran past the garbage truck, into the hollow TB block, down the corridor to his lair. The fan was on, but the office was empty. I ran out, to the main building, and I wasn't running just to get back to the forceps on time. Something was going wrong. Up the stairs, and I was beating the banisters with my fist. I'd been so stupid. Malika must have carried the report to the Supervisor. She wasn't just Djamila, she was more – a Djamila with connexions, a Djamila with a sense of duty.

I met the Electrician. He hadn't seen the Supervisor. 'Try the Econome's office.' The secretaries were taking off their overalls, and putting covers over their typewriters. They hadn't seen him. 'Try the Director's office.' Back across the main entrance, the gate-keeper hadn't seen him either. I stopped to get my breath, and to shake hands with the assistant director, a round, strange and self-effacing little man with whom I'd never been able to have more than one conversation, repeated even again, in the midday sun, for the gate-keeper's benefit: 'Do you want to become a gynaecologist?' – 'No.' – 'Not even if you'll be able to examine the Queen's vagina?' – 'No.' He hadn't seen him. But then I heard the voice, booming and unmistakable, coming from the Director's outer office.

I went in, and stopped at the door. It was the Supervisor all right, with a flock of the Director's secretaries. Huge and obese, in the centre of the circle, his white coat parted over the famous genitalia, he was worth the finding. It was the first time we'd all seen each other that day, but it wasn't an occasion for shaking hands. I asked him for the report he was holding. But he said he hadn't read it yet. 'Respectfully,' I pointed out that it wasn't addressed to him anyway, but to the Director, and, above him, to the Minister. 'Of course, of course,' he said, the dismissive way he must have spoken to Vasileva that day in Maternity. 'Don't be afraid, my friend,' he assured me in a tone from which friendliness was totally absent, 'I won't be giving your report to anyone else.'

The lie, uttered only a yard from the door into the Director's private office, was too flagrant to be worth denouncing. I came away, back to the doomed forceps, at a walk. I'd truly blundered, and I could say nothing about it to Dr Vasilev, who was himself only minutes away from the climax to a disastrous morning.

I got back to Maternity after lunch to find a message summoning me to the Director's office. When I arrived there, a secretary kept me outside until the Director had finished on the phone. He was the young secretary whose typewriter I'd borrowed to prepare the forms. At that time, he'd been all alone and glad of the company. He'd even confided to me that his dream was to emigrate to Marseille. But right now, official and unsmiling, he was very much in Kabylia.

The buzzer went on the desk, and the secretary showed me through the grey padded doors. It was an impressive office, air-conditioned and very large, with a conference room at the far end. The furniture was excellent – modern, executive-style chairs, and a proper company director's desk, with two telephones, a tape-recorder and an intercom. The day's *El Moudjahid* was folded at the football page. Among a heap of the usual papers, the Director had a French edition of the works of Lenin, and a photocopy of the report.

He insisted on the formalities. He was sorry not to have had a chance of meeting me earlier, but of course he'd been away on holiday. He'd heard that my wife was giving every satisfaction in the laundry and he hoped to be introduced to her shortly. Were we enjoying our stay? Did we like Algeria? Weren't we troubled by the heat, used as we were to 'London rain'? He was surprised to hear that we hadn't been to Algiers, and he offered to take us there for the day the following week.

Then he pushed the report in front of him. To business. There was something I had to understand. Independent Algeria was only eight years old. As a future doctor, I had surely done some pediatrics and psychology. He put out his hand some four feet above the floor of cool tiles, looked at it with understanding, tenderness and a certain pride, and invited me to think of a child of eight. He paused, for me to register the full effect of this argument. 'Need I say more?', he asked. 'The child of eight,' he continued, was full of faults – inevitable ones, lovable ones. Proceeding by question and answer, the Director sketched its portrait for me. Could the child of eight fend for itself? No, it depended on others. Did it know in which direction it was going? No, at eight it was still searching for its way in life, it was still experimenting. Could a child of eight be blamed for its mistakes, asked the Director. No, he answered, mistakes were how it learned. 'Algeria is no different.'

He sat back, plainly convinced by this miserable catechism. From the security of his inevitable process, and with a smile of thanks to the pediatric parable, the Director looked at me, hands open, and said winningly: 'How could things be any different from what they are?'

Naturally, he was grateful for any suggestions from someone who came from an advanced and adult country, where medicine was so much more professional. But in the wrong hands, my report could become a dangerous document. Why, for instance, had I addressed it to the Minister? There was an edge to his question, and he was obviously worried. I tried to set his mind at rest. The report was never part of some secret move against Dr Vasilev, or against the Director as the man ultimately responsible for what went on inside Maternity. But why, he asked, had I given it to the Supervisor, someone with whom I had no dealings in the hierarchy? I told him the Supervisor was a liar.

But the Director didn't believe me. I felt he didn't believe the Supervisor either. He made me promise I'd never in future deal with anyone else in the hospital except Dr Vasilev and himself. Did he think I was part of a plot by the Supervisor to discredit him? Did he suspect we'd actually sent off a copy of the report over his head to the Minister? He'd been away a month after all, and a lot of things could have happened. He looked uneasy and vulnerable. With the candour of a child of eight, he said to me: 'I'd never set foot inside a hospital before 1963.'

His next words were drowned in a flurry of car horns from the street, and he asked me if I'd seen a Kabyl marriage. I told him we'd been invited to Baya's village in the mountains. That suited us both. Nothing like a bit of Kabyl folklore to get off the point. Everything became amicable as he showed me out the door that, for good measure, was crowned by a portrait of the legendary Emir Abdelkader.

All was lost. I was into hospital politics, I'd found my place in the intrigues and hates that I remembered Vasileva once telling me about. My report had become like any other bit of paper in the hospital: where's he trying to get? Who's he with? Its actual contents would never be discussed. There wasn't a chance of its suggestions being implemented. The Director hadn't referred to them once. He probably didn't even know what they were. I'd simply denounced Dr Vasilev, and all to no purpose. Perhaps they'd dismiss him, all for the wrong reasons. Maybe there was the Supervisor's motive. Given his obscenities on Vasileva, he must have had a score to settle. He might well have passed on the report to the Minister, partly to increase his own standing as a trustworthy subordinate, but also to get the Vasilevs sent home. So happy to have seen me when I arrived, Dr Vasilev would have little to thank me for when I'd gone.

I had to settle things with the Supervisor. I couldn't go back to Maternity, I couldn't face either Dr Vasilev or Malika until I'd reached the end of the story. I hung about on some empty stairway, undecided, and two women came by. One I didn't know, the other was Madame Lambert, who ran the laundry. She was a Kabyl who'd married a Frenchman and had lived for many years in France. She was almost a fellow European. She'd been a mother to Calie, and she became a mother to me now. I unburdened myself to her, she was full of sympathy. Not only was the Supervisor not a doctor, she said, he wasn't even a nurse. He'd worked as an orderly in the Liberation Army, and his cousin had become the director of the biggest psychiatric hospital in the country. The administration was all the same, she said, and she advised me to trust no one in the hospital.

The girl with her was Kabyl too, a qualified nurse under Dr Ivanova. She told me how she used to be in charge of the ward, until one day the Vice-Prefect of Kabylia came in to see his sister, a patient, outside of normal visiting hours. The nurse had pointed that out to him, purely for his information, and then she'd taken him to his sister. The following day, she'd received a printed document from the Supervisor's office: 'Request for an explanation.' In it, he demanded a reply to the charge that she'd received the Vice-Prefect of Kabylia with her legs open. The actual words were: 'with your legs in an incorrect position'. She'd returned the document blank, with a note saying that she was too busy to reply to lies and obscenities. The document had come back, with the request repeated, and again she'd returned it blank. She'd since been downgraded to orderly status, and had taken a drop in salary.

We talked there on the stairs for half an hour, and when they left I knew that nothing had been achieved, that I'd only become enrolled in the Madame Lambert faction, but I felt much better all the same. We were in total agreement about one thing, the Supervisor, and that was enough. I was even glad that we didn't work together, that we wouldn't have the opportunity of talking some more. I distrusted everyone, them too. I didn't want to know what they felt on other matters, I didn't want to spoil them as allies, I wanted to keep them pure.

I went back to Maternity. Dr Vasilev was in the office and I think I might have spoken to him about what was happening had Dr Kostov not been there too. Instead, since it was past four o'clock, I asked him if the staff meeting was still being held that afternoon. He was far away, dissecting a matchbox. I had to ask the question a second time before he understood. He was still buried under the colossal effect of the morning. 'Naturally!' he said.

But it was all too painful. Sun and crickets, and the one-eyed cat walking in from the parapet to push her cheek against Dr Vasilev's leg. Djamila asleep in the midwife's room, Malika dozing on the labour bed, Zora's day off. Only Baya was around: 'We can't leave all these women alone,' trying to keep awake, reviving herself by trips into the delivery room to breathe the air in front of the Carrier. Four-thirty approached. Dr Kostov took a walk over to the paint shop. Dr Vasilev clung to the cat. I wasn't going to nag. Mercifully, at exactly four-thirty, a curettage arrived to fill the void. We got up a drip, but she pulled it out, fighting like a mad thing to keep her legs together, and her soaking dress between them, the last reflex to go before unconsciousness. For the first time, I saw Vasileva lose control, with some straight blows to the woman's thighs, like Tamara when she's warming up.

And then the black Peugeot drew up outside the Morgue, with a jolt as the handbrake was harshly applied. The Supervisor climbed out, slammed the door shut, and disappeared into the main hospital. I hurried after him.

We came face to face in the front courtyard, outside the Director's office, under the sun. Swathed in his white coat, the

Supervisor was an Algerian Kostov, only coarser still. But forget that, forget the genitalia. Forget the grotesque. The Supervisor had become sinister. In the background, behind him, at various points in the shade, I made out two of the Director's secretaries, and probably the Director himself. There was the switchboard operator, the round little assistant director, and the Econome. The Econome hurt. There was the gate-keeper, and others too. The details were blurred. I was so nervous. If I'd been holding a gun, I'd have pulled the trigger out of sheer fright. My voice was trembling so much that I was scarcely able to get out my first sentence, which was to ask the Supervisor why he'd lied to me that morning in front of witnesses.

'Lied, my friend?' The Supervisor stepped towards me, but I couldn't move. I just repeated my question: 'Yes, lied.' He reached for the lapels of my coat and pulled me close, inches from the enormous face. 'Little student on holiday,' he called me, 'who do you think you are? A novelist with copyright?'

He shook me, and I didn't resist. I registered the tanned skin, the black eyebrows, the strong nose, and I let myself be enveloped by the breath, the saliva and the thundering voice. In my passivity, he seemed to discover new reserves of anger, and wilder inspiration. He knew all pathology, more than any doctor in the hospital, he knew 'all the pathology in the world', all surgery and gynaecology too, and he gave me a shake with every subject. His knowledge was as limitless as his power. No hospital door was closed to him, no piece of paper was not his to do with as he wished. He walked the wards, the Theatres and the corridors. They were all his, and he had accounts to give to no one: 'I run this place.'

He dragged me in front of the assistant director, technically his superior, and grabbed his arm: 'Be my witness!' Never strong, the man was clay in the Supervisor's hands. Was it not true that 'in the black hours', he'd been a doctor to the guerrilla fighters? Was it not true that he was an officer in the Liberation Army? 'Precisely, precisely,' answered the assistant director, who at least had the decency not to look at me. I kept my eyes down too, I didn't dare seek support from anyone. The Supervisor released one lapel and struck his chest

with his free hand. He stood before us, confirmed and con-
secrated, as 'the representative of Algerian medicine, a free
Algerian citizen, an Islamic Socialist, a revolutionary!'

He turned to confront his entire audience, a limp Europe
in his hands. Cowed by the sacred words, the other men said
nothing. This had not been some wretched bureaucrat reciting
his catechism, it had been the performance of a prophet. The
Supervisor was strutting. He was puffing his chest. He was
bombastic beyond all caricature. It was pure Mussolini, a
Muslim Mussolini.

He came back to his 'friend'. His tone altered, to one of finer
feeling, and his grip relaxed. How it grieved him, he confessed,
to have foreign doctors on Algerian soil, waging 'germ warfare' against his people! How it pained him, that all the sacri-
fices of the black hours should be brought to nothing, by
'white-coated saboteurs passing their hands from vagina to
vagina, infecting my heroic people with syphilis!' He would
never tolerate it, never! His voice became hysterical. 'Get
out!' he shrieked, 'leave this hospital immediately! Leave this
country!'

He released me, and his huge arm pointed behind me, past
the fountain and the courtyard, back to Europe. I stumbled
away from them, and then ran down the corridor to our
room, to get the insane words on paper. Insane and official.

'A gigantic loudspeaker is what we need, never to be switched off!'

Mouloud Kassim,
Member of the Revolutionary Council

Dr Vasilev spots this sentence too. He even reads it out to me. But it's not in criticism. He reads it the same way he sometimes says: 'Islamic Socialism!' or 'Mouloud Kassim!' He reads it in his nursery rhyme voice and he gives it that exclamation of excitement at the end. 'Oh-ho!' he cries. Dr Vasilev is thrilled by the opinions of the strong.

16

I feel utterly isolated. Till Calie's back from the laundry, I've nowhere to go but Maternity, where the curettage room is home, the smell of old blood, the clatter of instruments, Dr Vasilev's cigarette. He looks up and smiles a warm hello as he's twisting the top off the tin of gloves. He must be wondering where I've been disappearing to all day. He's no idea what's been going on. I hold the gutter for him and while he does the curettage, I tell him everything. I'm glad to have told him at last, but he sighs. He's so sad. I wish to God I'd never handed the report round, and I know he wishes the whole business had never happened. Why on earth did I have to give the thing to Malika when I hardly knew her? How could I have been so blind? She must have taken it over to the Supervisor's office while we were in Out-Patients this morning. But Dr Vasilev won't criticize me. 'It's done,' he says, 'it's done.' I'm sure he wishes I'd never come here. Today he didn't need.

Later, when a woman arrives for a curettage, slightly shocked, I prepare her like the perfect intern, a sort of gift to Dr Vasilev, some way to make amends. I take her history, how many months since her last period, the number of her previous pregnancies and miscarriages, her general health. I take her blood pressure, temperature and pulse, clean her thoroughly with disinfectant soap, clear her vagina of clots, put up a drip of Rheomacrodex, hydrocortisone, coramine and Vitamin C. Then I call Dr Vasilev.

He takes a long time to arrive. I become anxious, and I go out on to the porch to wait. I see him coming down the steps of the doctors' building one by one, on the last seconds of a fifty-year marathon. He stops at the bottom to light a cigarette.

Then he comes down the Maternity path, stopping a second time to whistle to the one-eyed cat who's rubbing her head voluptuously against the fir-tree. He's easy to see under the hospital lights and a full moon, in his white coat, white trousers and vest.

After the curettage, we wheel her to her bed. He sees that she's comfortable, and then he takes my arm: 'Come!' He brings me into the doctors' office, and unlocks the cupboard where he keeps his drug samples. He brings out a white card, marked 'Invitation'. He handles it carefully, smoothing down the edges. He tells me he was going to present me with it tomorrow, but he'd rather I took it now, to make me feel better. He's inviting Calie and me to celebrate the Bulgarian national day in a week's time. I accept at once. I'm exceedingly grateful.

Baya has asked us into the mountains for her cousin's wedding, and in the morning I come to ask Dr Vasilev for his permission. He cries: 'Of course!' and waves us down the hospital avenue into the hills, past rushes ten feet high, through woods, on a road that winds beside a river bed. Nomads stare from their brown tents, wild-eyed, long-haired, stone age. Goats stand tethered to nearby trees, and nomad children run on the river bed in rags. Signposts point to the patients' villages. The slogan painted on a well in white says THE ONLY HERO IS THE PEOPLE.

It's early afternoon, and nature's on fire. Powdery brown earth, long dry thistles, twisted black branches that have died of thirst. Fields of figs and olives, inside stone walls and green hedges of prickly pears. Donkeys motionless under trees. When the asphalt stops, and the cars fly by, French registrations of Kabyl workers on holiday, occupants waving, we have to stop and wait for the dust to settle.

Bend after bend, we don't stop climbing. A village on every hill, sometimes so inconspicuous that it's only after a few moments of looking that we actually see them. We arrive in the Place des Martyrs, where the road divides round a memorial to the dead of the Algerian War into two dusty tracks that climb even more steeply upwards between the houses.

Baya comes down to meet us, hardly recognizable. She's just like one of the patients, only happier. She's barefoot, she's got the robe and belt, and the knotted sash with the vertical stripes, and henna on her hands and feet. 'It's the custom,' she says sheepishly. Behind her, there are women and girls, dressed the same way, unveiled, filling pitchers of water at a trough. They hump the pitchers on their backs, resting them on their belts.

A cousin of Baya's who's in medical school in Algiers comes to show us where we can park. He takes us along a road on the edge of the hillside to the mission school for girls run by the White Sisters. The courtyard's smooth earth, with a great oak tree in the middle. We leave the motorcycle under a wooden roof, next to the Sisters' Renault, and a row of lavatories whose doors are fastened by wire. The school's half-hidden by firs. It's clean, but not severe. We walk back, past a small cemetery on the hillside. It isn't enclosed – Kabyl cemeteries aren't, the cousin tells us. It's difficult to tell what is tombstone, and what is the rock of the hillside. Far below, there's the river bed, on the next hill there's another village, and then the Djurdjura mountains beyond. It's country you'd never tire of.

Baya takes us through a gate into a courtyard the size of a small room, overhung with vines. The grapes aren't ripe yet. There are great bunches of them that you have to avoid knocking with your head. The floor of the courtyard is uneven stone. There's an exit for water on the downhill side, there are some boxes, with baby rabbits in one, and wicker baskets of prickly pears. It's about all there's room for.

You can crouch, and squeeze into a stone outhouse the size of a large cupboard. Inside, three women are squatting round a wooden bowl that's a yard wide, squatting the same way they do in Maternity when they accompany their sisters or their mothers for a curettage, knees fully bent, and bottoms not quite touching the ground. We shake hands. One's a deaf-mute, she's irrepressible, the most cheerful of all. There's another outhouse, even smaller, where there's a pot of sauce on the boil for the cous-cous.

Baya introduces us to a host of people, parents, aunts and grandparents, with tattooed faces and no French, cousins, in-laws and countless children. The Kabyl I've learned is far too specialized to be of any help, it's strange to hear words like 'sob' and 'ernu' being used in such a different context. When Baya's not around, we have to stay with the cousin or his younger brother to find out what's going on.

They take us into the house. It has no door, no window and no furniture of any kind. There's a stone floor the size of an ordinary living room, and then on another level, about three feet higher, there's a platform half as big, supported on stone pillars. It carries a gigantic white jar, as tall as a man and three feet square, that must have been built where it stands. It's used for storing grain. The lid is sealed tight and down the side there are holes big enough for your arm, stopped up with cork from the forests of Azazga. To take the grain, you pull out the cork and help yourself. The jar is smooth to touch, and it's decorated all over with the same triangular patterns that the people of Beni Yenni use in their jewellery. The design is careful and meticulous, without fantasy. It gets whitewashed every year, with a powder that comes from the river bed.

There's a curtain of sacks, each 'a gift from the people of the United States of America', stretching across the platform from the jar. I can't go up there, nor can any man. But Calie climbs up with Baya to meet the bride-to-be.

Underneath the platform, between the stone pillars, there's a manger, with a goat and sheep and several rabbits. The main floor is bare, except for some sheepskins and woollen rugs in a corner, and a pitcher of olive oil with a wooden lid. There's a shelf along one wall that's made of clay reinforced with reeds. It's been whitewashed too, and laid with old newspaper, cut along the edge in a series of triangles. Clay and reeds make up the ceiling between the beams.

Calie comes out from behind the sacks, triumphant, Kabyl. She has a sash in red and yellow stripes, knotted in the front. The robe is new. It's yellow, and when we get out in the court-yard we find it's also transparent. Calie tells me how surprised Baya was to find she didn't have a bra, the first step to freedom for a Kabyl girl.

Two Swiss Sisters arrive from the Mission. They're pale, with bloodless lips and straight fronts, born blessed, without breasts, and absolutely charming. The Kabyl runs from their

lips, and they're no easier to understand than the Kabyls themselves, a sure sign of mastery. They're perfectly at home with
the family connexions, they have something individual to say
to everyone. They know who's in France, who's in Algiers,
they know who's ill and who's well. They're not in it for the
money, they're not in it for the conversions. When they leave,
the bride's eyes are full of tears.

Then from outside the courtyard gate, comes a sound like
the war-cries you used to make in the playground at school,
before your voice had broken. The courtyard's invaded by
colour, some twenty women in their finest robes and jewels,
the front ones bent double, carrying carved wooden boxes on
their backs, painted like Sicilian carts. One of the women
arrives with a baby entirely enclosed in a white cloth. Weddings attract strangers, says the cousin, and she's afraid of the
evil eye.

The women arrange the painted boxes on the platform beside the bride – they contain gifts from the groom's family –
and retreat to the courtyard, leaving a passage for the men
who've come behind them. How dull they are in comparison,
in their suits and ties, above all the groom, with a punched
and beaten expression more fitting to the Out-Patients' corridor than his own wedding. The curtain of sacks is replaced,
with the bride behind, and the men from the groom's family
sit on raffia mats on the main floor of the house, to eat cous-
cous and water-melon. Their meal is over in minutes, and it's
the turn of the women of the groom's family – at least, that's
how a sulking uncle would have it, until he's overruled by
Baya and her cousin, and we all eat together. We sit in three
circles round the wooden bowls of cous-cous.

Baya keeps away from her sulking uncle. Three years ago,
she tells us, she was in love with a foreign doctor in the hospital.
But he fell ill with malaria, and had to go home. She hasn't
heard from him since. She went out with him several times
into Tizi-Ouzou, the capital of Kabylia. They did nothing
more than have meals together. It's what she told everyone,
but they wouldn't believe her. Word spread back here to the
mountains and her uncle came down into town, in sombrero
and baggy pants, and under his hooded woollen coat he car-

ried his revolver, the one he'd used in the struggle against the French. He was going to take her out to the field between the hospital and the cork depôt and kill her. She had to run for safety into the Director's office.

'Ça y est,' she says, 'I can never hope to love anyone again.' Her life's finished, she just drifts from day to day. She went to nerve specialists and told them her story. They all said the same thing, that she must leave Kabylia, leave Algeria altogether, and try to find work in France. But she'd never get permission to leave the country, she says, and besides, who'd look after her mother. It's better not to hope. She's resigned, she says, and she's not unhappy. But she's made us feel very sad. Her anaemia's a broken heart.

The bowls of cous-cous are so big they're discouraging. We feel we're getting nowhere. Besides, it's not the cous-cous of our dreams. We heap it into our mouths like a heavenly food, only to discover that it's almost impossible to swallow. It tastes of rancid butter, it's mixed with hard-boiled egg, it's heavy and dry. A sugared bread follows, made of semolina dough, and deep-fried in oil.

We're sitting next to a woman in her thirties, with a few teeth still left, who slaps her belly and tells us she's pregnant for the ninth time. She's exactly like the deaf-and-dumb aunt, with the same cheerfulness and generosity, except that she's talking fast in Kabyl all the time, having a great joke with Baya who's in fits on the other side of the wooden bowl. She tells us about her five live children, about her village, Beni Yenni, about her house, the figs and so on. Then she pulls a silver ring off her finger. It's made in her village and she wants us to have it. We're embarassed. But she stuffs the ring in my pocket.

The bowls are taken away and we all stand, for the men to come back into the house. This is the marriage proper, a two-family affair, without any civil or religious authority to officiate. Two chairs are brought in, little schoolroom chairs, the groom sits on one, and the bride comes down from behind her curtain to sit on the other. The little house crowds round them.

It's a strange moment. They're side by side, and it must be the closest they've yet been. Everything's happened for them so quickly. It was only a week ago that the girl was asked for.

Her father's away, working in France, and the uncle tele-graphed him for his decision. Was he ill? Had he changed his address? – they didn't get an answer. The uncle wanted to send another telegram, but then the groom's family intervened. They'd take the girl this week, or not at all. They offered a good dowry and the uncle accepted. Baya tells us in confidence that her family is very poor.

The groom takes a matchbox out of the jacket pocket of his brown suit. The girl extends a softer finger. They're both very nervous, and they don't look at each other, only at her finger, as he pushes the ring home. And then the moment's gone, as flashlights pop and banknotes fall into their laps from every-one around.

The groom and his family go back to their house and it's the turn of the old woman who all this time has been mixing henna powder and water to smear it on the bride's hands and feet, with some for Calie too. The bride must stay inside, but Calie can come out into the courtyard to let the henna dry in the sun. The longer you leave it before washing it off, the deeper the stain that stays behind. Deeper still, says the old woman, if you press the henna into your skin by bandaging yourself with cloths.

The cousin's younger brother takes us to see the family field. Everything's either uphill or downhill. We go downhill first, steeply, along a stony path between hedges of prickly pears. I pick one, and I haven't seen the needles that cover it like fur. The young cousin says I should rub my hand hard in the dust. I hold my breath and try. The Kabyl remedy doesn't work.

We pass a house with an oak tree in front of it, and rocks and old gravestones. It's empty, there's wax on the floor from candles. Every year, says the cousin, there's a ceremony to commemorate the miracle that greeted the builders of the house one morning: they'd only finished the foundations when they came back to find the house completed. It belonged to a 'marabout', a word that the cousin translates by 'saint'.

We stumble downhill for two kilometres at least. The Djurdjura Mountains get no closer, they must be miles away still, the air's so clear. A man's coming up on a donkey laden with brushwood. He's old and he has everything you'd expect – the hooded coat, the sombrero, the stick. We stand aside to let him by and a few yards further up, he pulls the donkey round and asks the young cousin who we are. 'Good afternoon, ladies and gentlemen,' he says in an English that's almost without accent. He reels off a list of English towns that are all recognizable at once, and more phrases, like 'a cup of tea'. He's one of the original zouaves (it's a Kabyl word), and he tells us he spent a year in England during the First World War. The donkey goes off into one of its heart-rending cries in the middle of the recitation, and gets a whack from the stick that makes no difference. The zouave asks after members of the cousin's family, and goes on his way, crying out in English up the hill.

The family fig field is some fifteen fig trees in dry, stony earth, at an angle so sharp that you have to steady yourself with your hands. You can swing from trunk to trunk, they're so smooth. The fruit's ripe – twist the figs, and they fall into your hand. We make up for the disappointment of the couscous, we can't stop eating – it's not every day, in a field like this, off a path like this, with a view, with air, with a robe like this, and we eat on regardless.

Further downhill, there's a well where we wash our hands. Two sheep are drinking there. It's a little oasis. Women tend vegetables in a garden that's green and luxurious, fat beans, ripe tomatoes. They pick us sprays of mint and take Calie for Kabyl. On the ground beside them are pots where they keep their food, cous-cous under a cover of fig-leaves.

It's a long climb back. The women do the journey twice a day, down in the morning at dawn, back before noon, and down again after the siesta. Last year, before water was brought to the village, they used to come back from the well with the pitchers on their backs.

It's a difficult climb too, because the young cousin may only be sixteen, but he's tall and looks several years older. He's under unfair pressure, an afternoon with a European girl slipping about as she has been in transparent Kabyl clothes. He's not like his elder brother, who has medicine to keep him sensible. He plays tortured sex games all the way up, at the expense of a giant cricket that's captured and deprived of its hind legs, dropped in Calie's clothes and hair, hung on a hair pulled from her head, blinded in front of her with a cactus needle, and repeatedly stabbed.

Some women call out to us from beneath a tree. We stop and talk, one speaks French and she remembers me from Out-Patients. Here there's no problem, no veil. They're warm and affectionate, they talk to us freely, and invite us into their house. But it's getting dark and we have to be back. We're passed by a group of men and boys, talking among themselves, climbing fast, with woollen coats over their shoulders, and sombreros – we hear Mexican, not Kabyl.

We find crowds of women at the fountain, filling pitchers and metal cans. Others pass us, back from the fields or from the river where the old zouave had been, even further away, laden like his donkey was with brushwood, so low that you can't see their faces. Their pots of cous-cous are now filled with figs. A fine cow goes by, everyone stands back to admire it.

A man invites us through a heavy gate into a courtyard like Baya's, except bigger because it's common to four houses. It's night, the paraffin light is poor, but the design of the house appears exactly the same. A glass of mint tea is handed to us out of a dark corner where there are some women sitting. The man tells us about one of them, who had a baby in March. She's been unable to do any work since, she's depressed, she's convinced she's going to die. The woman stares through us from her corner. He's going to take her down to Tizi-Ouzou, says the man, when the psychiatrist comes back from holiday. I suddenly realize he's talking about his wife.

The cousin borrows a torch. We pass groups of women sitting inside open doors, watching the street from smooth stone benches. The beam catches two boys against the wall, the cousin's age, who don't move as we pass by, hands over each other's erections. Then the meeting-place, a circle of stone seats, reserved to males, where boys play on the wet earth round a tap, and men talk under sombreros in the dark.

The mosque is the highest point of the village. It's the only building that's whitewashed. Three very old men are inside on their knees, mumbling prayers in a carpeted room. One of the old men is the mufti himself, says the cousin, and even he isn't from the village, they had to import him from Constantine. We climb the spiral stairs of the minaret. There are lights on in Fort-National and Michelet, and to the north there's the sanatorium on the hill above Tizi-Ouzou, with the electric glow of the provincial capital itself. Scattered lights on the hills around, from all the villages without electricity. Voices beneath us in the dark, and the sound of pipes and drums. There are three marriages in the village this weekend besides ours.

The bride spends the last minutes in the house where she's lived all her life. She's still behind the curtain. She's had nothing to eat all day and she's come down only once, to have the ring put on her finger and the henna daubed on her hands and feet. There's a girl friend keeping her company, until the groom's family arrive in a few moments to take her away. Her things are packed and she's ready to go, with the climax to her wedding only a few hours off. In the manger underneath, the sheep waits to be slaughtered for the feast of the Aïd.

'You-yous' as the women of the groom's family arrive, with the mother-in-law in charge. They envelop the girl in a thick white woollen coat, like that baby in the cloth this afternoon. The mother-in-law then guides her across the courtyard and down the dusty path into the back seat of a Peugeot, for a drive of some fifty yards to the house of the groom's family.

The rest of us walk. We split up for dancing, men and women separately. Women may watch the men, but the reverse isn't done. The bride didn't dance, Calie will tell me, and Baya will explain: 'She was afraid, poor thing.' A group plays music on pipes and drums. It's monotonous, wordless, without peaks or emphasis, insistent to the point of trance. The men hold scarves as they dance, winding them round each other's waists. There's the inevitable village master, a long-haired motor mechanic who works in Algiers, winding his scarf sensuously above his head as he looks down his perfect hips at his perfectly hanging jeans, scarcely moving. Later, he'll dance wearing a robe.

Baya's floor has been spread with every blanket and sheepskin they have, just for us. The others simply wrap themselves in a coat, Baya, her sister, her mother, the uncle. Everyone sleeps in their clothes, and we hear the drums all night, faint like foetal hearts.

We get up at dawn, the two of us, before the others, and it's not the swallows this time, nor the sunrise, it's that fig-field catching up with us. There's no time to make it to the Sisters' lavatories, or to the fields, but just to the bucket in the courtyard that's already overflowing. It's an enormous inhibition, but the figs are more powerful still. We creep back to the bed, whisper what's happened to Baya, and lie there crippled with embarrassment as her sister and mother fetch water from the fountain and swill it away downhill through the hole in the wall.

The women bring out the wooden bowls to knead the semolina dough for the fried bread. The deaf-mute is the champion, starting with a lump I'm unable to move, and at the end of an hour she has it leaping into the air on its own, with strange cries of delight. The same job takes Baya two hours, and that's with cheating, the deaf-mute giving her a hand. She tells us she's going out to fetch an old woman who she'll pay to finish her share of the work. They'll criticize her, she says, but what can she do? 'Once you leave the mountains, you can't get back. Life's too hard here.'

The elder cousin arrives with the sulking uncle. Their job is the meat, mutton that's been in the outhouse for the last two days. They have to decide what bits are still good to eat. They sit on the porch with a sharp knife and an enamel bowl, and a whisk for the flies. Other men come and give their opinions. Judgments are made on the basis of touch. Each man feels, and feels again. The smell is sickening, yet most of the meat is saved. The cousin seems to find the division of labour natural. Kneading dough is woman's work, judging meat is men's. It couldn't be otherwise. It's like the weather, neither right nor wrong. It just is. He's quiet-spoken and gentle, the tone of voice that suits self-evident truths. He's not married yet, he tells us, and won't be for another six years, when he'll have graduated from medical school. His brother must wait until then, he says, because it isn't done for a younger brother to marry first. Things will be hard for the crickets.

He takes me up to the loft, via the platform that's now

vacated. We walk carefully, on the beams. An old donkey saddle, a small stone press for olive oil, a pile of black olive stones used for heating, a jar of acorns for food, a cradle made of reeds, a broken jar with water for the pigeons, an intact pot with a handle like the ones the women had with them down at the well, that I admire and am immediately given.

But there's no donkey for the saddle, no one in the family goes to the fields any more. There aren't enough olives for the press, no one looks after the trees. They produce what they produce. And the figs aren't laid out on reeds to dry in the sun any more. They're eaten fresh. What isn't eaten is left to rot, on the trees that once upon a time each used to be called by a name. The village lives on the money that's sent by the men in Algiers and France. Some things have been changing fast.

In a last walk through the village, we're invited inside, through a covered porch with cool stone benches opposite each other, by a group of women who live down in Tizi-Ouzou and only come back to the family home in the mountains for their summer holidays. Their clothes are fashion and their home, they tell us, is 'typically Kabyl', preserved exactly as it was, with a fireplace in the floor and the olive press in position – they live in the new brick building on the other side of the courtyard. They dance the hip dances of the women in front of us, and we have our photographs taken together. They're full of laughter. They're enjoying being Kabyls for a month.

17

On my first morning back, Malika's name catches my eye on the notice-board outside the Postmaster's office. Elections have been held to nominate shop stewards in the national labour union. Miss Malika B., *chef de service* in Maternity, has been chosen to represent the female staff of the hospital.

I assume that's the reason for her being so happy when she comes to the doctors' office. Partly it is. But there's something more. She's treating us all to sugared almonds from a cellophane packet: 'I'm announcing you my engagement!' We congratulate her. I ask her if she knows her fiancé. 'Oh là là,' she says, 'we're not like some families. We're liberals. We've known each other for two years.' 'Who's the lucky man?', asks Dr Kostov, with a wink to me. But Malika's too excited to tell us. 'I'm engaged to you all!' she protests. 'Ah!' cries Dr Kostov, 'I'm engaged to you then? Very well . . .', and he takes her by the arm. Malika breaks away, laughing. 'He's a captain in the gendarmerie,' she tells us.

Dr Vasilev waves good-morning from the end of the path. He hasn't changed over the weekend. He doesn't bear me a grudge. He's even strangely resolute, as if it's been a weekend of decision-making. 'Come!' he says again, and tugs me out of Maternity, across the bridge to the main hospital. 'You and I are going to the Director!' We'll tell him how the Supervisor behaved, and we'll make a formal complaint. We'll tell him about all the things that need changing, we'll take the matter over his head to the Director of Health for Kabylia, at the Prefecture in Tizi-Ouzou! The drums are rolling, and I have a job to keep level with Dr Vasilev down the corridor. When we get to the outer office, he wants to go straight through unannounced, but a secretary restrains him.

The Director invites us in, with apologies: 'What a shame, Dr Vasilev! I can't receive you this morning.' Behind him, the partition's fully drawn back, and a couple of hospital workmen are arranging chairs round the conference table: 'We're holding our monthly staff meeting at 10 o'clock.' 'Eh!' 'Haven't you been told about it? But we're expecting you! All doctors must attend.' Dr Vasilev lets himself be treated like a pupil. He almost apologizes for not being informed. 'But afterwards', he cries, 'we must speak to you!' 'Of course you must,' says the Director easily. He hasn't shaken my hand and while we've been talking, he's shut the drawer of his desk that had the photocopy lying on top of it.

The source of Dr Vasilev's energy has been extinguished. We walk back to Maternity, at our daily pace. The first patient on our round is the most recent embryotomy. In Kabyl, the woman asks Malika about her baby, and Malika tells her it's dead. Dr Vasilev pulls back her sheet. There's blood down the inside of her thighs, over her vulva and hair. Her bladder stretches up above her navel. The flies hum. Dr Vasilev stares at her, fixed in disappointment. 'These women aren't patients,' he says, 'they're animals.' He takes a breath and says: 'If you Algerians can't look after your own people, we will.' He goes away to the the delivery room and comes back with antiseptic soap, alcohol, cotton wool and some rubber tubes. He starts to clean the woman himself. 'Dr Vasilev!' cries Tamara, who's followed him down the corridor. 'Eh,' he says, 'if the orderlies won't do it, the doctors must.' 'It was all arranged,' says Malika, 'we were going to do it.' She slips the tube up herself. The urine begins to flow. The women's very grateful, waves from her bed, kisses her fingers.

'Why didn't you come to the meeting I called?' asks Dr Vasilev, 'didn't I tell you the day before: "Tomorrow, at 4.30, we'll have a meeting"? Nobody came. How many times have I tried to call a meeting?' Distractedly, Malika says: 'Of course we want a meeting.' Dr Vasilev becomes resolute again. He and I are going down to the Prefecture in Tizi-Ouzou, he says, we're going to tell the Health Director for

Kabylia about what we tried to do, and we'll tell him that nobody came: 'We'll tell him it was sabotage!'.

'If he wants a meeting,' says Malika professionally, 'then he's only got to call one in the proper manner.' 'It's nothing to do with me,' says Dr Kostov. 'Of course it isn't,' agrees Malika, 'it's the job of the department head.' 'Ah!' goes Dr Kostov ominously, 'if I was in charge, Mademoiselle Malika, how different things would be for you then . . .!' 'They'd be much better,' says Malika uncertainly. 'How wrong you are,' Dr Kostov tells her, 'I'd make you work harder than you've ever worked in your life. I'd call a meeting and if you didn't come, I'd take you to the Director, and if he did nothing, I'd drag you in front of the Health Director for Kabylia. . . I'd change everything.' 'It's only right you should,' says Malika securely, knowing that it will never come about, 'it's you, the doctors who should do something.' Dr Kostov says it's more complicated than she thinks.

I'm disenchanted. My enthusiasm's gone. I know nothing's going to change. Raffia bags on the floor with meat, eggs and grapes that stand in pools of gravy. There's more bread and melon than anyone could possibly eat. The women occupy their rooms like campers. Each patient's folder has my four stencilled sheets inside it, bare but for their share of blood, melon pips and juice. I don't want a part in it. It's better to withdraw.

While Dr Vasilev writes out prescriptions in the doctors' office, I collect up all the stencilled sheets that are left. Then I go into the delivery room – where there's Tamara, and Dr Kostov who's writing out prescriptions too – and take down the model sheets that I'd stuck to the wall. 'Oh!' cries Tamara, all aroused. I ask Dr Kostov to explain to her that it's not worth having two systems going simultaneously, the old temperature chart and the new sheets, without either being used properly. Tamara's breathing heavily. No more columns and squares for ticks and crosses and numbers. From her 'Dr Vasilev's!' and her 'Heads of Department!' and the tone of her lament to Dr Kostov, who listens without answering, I can guess who's the man responsible in her eyes.

I take the models and the spare sheets – there are still about

400 of each left – over to the Stores. Of course, I'm breathing a little heavily too, and my hands had been trembling, and I'd waited till Malika, my 'enemy', was out of sight before I took my work down. I didn't fancy her being there to witness my humiliation. I had to do it, though. I couldn't go on being surrounded by my failures, like Dr Vasilev. The store-keeper, the gaunt man I'd once come upon reading a book of poetry, listens sympathetically and arranges the sheets on one of his shelves, 'for when things will have changed'.

I answer the telephone and I'm asked abruptly: 'Who's speaking?' When I tell him, the man says: 'This is the Supervisor. Fetch Mademoiselle Malika.' What for, he doesn't say, but it's certainly not to remind her to reduce the death rate in the delivery room. Then he asks to speak to Dr Kostov, and I say he's already left with Dr Vasilev for the meeting in the Director's office. A thousand sarcastic remarks run through my head, the temptation to call him 'Doctor', to ask his advice on a medical problem, to enquire after the health of the Algerian people this morning. I feel so frustrated. He's far too strong. I end up by being perfectly civil.

Seconds later, the Supervisor enters Maternity with his court (his superior, the assistant director, and one of the Econome's secretaries), on an inspection round. He calls to Baya and she goes with him, to mark down the orders he gives. Unfortunately for Vasileva, he finds the one-eyed cat in the room where the meals are dished up. The higher cupboards he opens himself and 'inspects' (heavy brow, eyes narrowed, missing nothing). The lower cupboards are inspected by his shorter superior, without panache (shrugging his shoulders at Baya). They leave after inspecting the ground floor only, it's Vasileva's territory. The first floor comes under Malika.

The nurse who's friendly with Madame Lambert brings me some good news. The other day, she could hear everything the Supervisor shouted from her ward. She had to go down to the Director's office herself shortly afterwards, to answer the charge of having welcomed the Vice-President with open legs. She found the Econome in the outer office, waiting to go in.

As innocently as possible, she asked him what all the shouting had been about. With a firmness that surprised her, the Econome said it was precisely why he was coming to see the Director: 'The Supervisor behaved intolerably with the little English doctor.'

It's the first support I've had. I want to go along to the Econome and thank him. But maybe I'll only be falling into the same trap if I take him at his face value. Perhaps it wasn't from the goodness of his heart. Perhaps it's only a new move in hospital politics. Exactly what was intolerable for him? Was it the Supervisor's lies and obscenities? Was it his socialist imposture? Or was the hospital No. 2 outraged by the claim of the hospital No. 4 to 'run this establishment'?

I trust no one, and I stay in the office. A man asks me for news of his wife. She's eight months pregnant, he says, and she was admitted for observation because she hadn't felt the baby move for a fortnight. I put the paper away and go upstairs to the landing to find out who the woman is, and how she is. Malika tells me everything's normal. I relay the information down to the man, who goes away. I go back to the office, and then begin to feel uneasy. Perhaps the man came down from the mountains just to ask that question. Maybe, worse, the information I gave him was totally inaccurate. Who's examined the woman today? Who's listened for her baby's heart? Who's asked her if she's felt it move? No doctor surely, but Malika neither. I go back upstairs, fetch the stethoscope from the delivery room and go down the corridor to find the woman. I recognize her as soon as I see her. She gave birth in the night. I remember the size of her goitre, I remember her face, which seemed to lack anything human about it. It was flat, bestial, expressionless. Now she's sitting up in bed and between her knees is an old enamel bowl, identical to the one in the curettage room, with slices of meat in it. She's pulling them apart with her fingers, and pushing them into her mouth with hands like paws. She stares at me over her goitre. The sheets that surround her are brown, green and stiff. The baby's among them somewhere, wrapped in an old piece of robe. The room is high with excrement, infected with flies. She stops chewing, the meat hangs out of her mouth, and the brown gravy drips over her goitre. I return the stethoscope and take a walk in the sun.

Dr Vasilev and Dr Kostov come back. They have no news. For Dr Vasilev, the wave of reform is over. The meeting was even chaired by the Health Director for Kabylia, he'd come along specially from the Prefecture in Tizi-Ouzou. But Dr Vasilev raised none of those points that had so fired him earlier in the morning. He's not the man to bring controversy to an assembly. Absolutely nothing to do with Maternity was discussed. It was a routine meeting.

We sit the morning out in the doctor's office. Dr Vasilev picks up his paper. And Dr Kostov begins telling me of his first days in Algeria, when he insisted on working the same way as in Bulgaria. He used to disinfect the women who came in for a curettage, he had sterile cloths in the delivery room, sterile gloves, gowns and masks. But he had to do it all himself. He'd be called for a curettage by someone like Baya, who'd done a six-month nursing course, who'd had a training in the basics, and yet he'd find the women waiting for him just as they are now, covered in blood, filthy and unshaven. 'What's the point?' the orderlies used to say to him when he asked for the women to be cleaned. He used not to say anything. He'd been told before he left Sofia that he'd see big differences in Algeria, but he'd been ordered: 'You're going there to work, not to criticize.'

'Remember the pathology you've seen here,' says Dr Kostov, 'but not the way we work. Otherwise you'll fail all your exams.' He points over to the wood and paint shops, and says: 'That's how we work. We're painters, carpenters. We're not doctors. Proper work isn't possible here. In England, in Bulgaria, it is, of course. But Algeria isn't a civilized country.'

I ask him why he's adapted to what he found, and Dr Kostov tells a story. In the countryside round Sofia, he says, there are villages called 'shopps'. The people in them are poor, they have no culture, they've had no education. They're called 'shoppies'. They can't even speak proper Bulgarian, only a dialect called 'shoppy'. It was always said that it would be impossible to change them. They'd never be any different. But then an English professor arrived, full of the finest principles, and said: 'No! Shoppies are men like the rest of us. They're human beings, they can be educated and raised to our level.' So the government gave him a grant to take a shoppy back to London, to educate him in the highest achievements of the human race. For a year, the government had no news. They wrote off to the English professor: 'How's our shoppy doing?' No answer. The government became anxious. 'Is the experiment working?' they asked. There was still no answer. They wrote a third time: 'How's our shoppy coping with philosophy, medicine and nuclear physics?' At long last, the answer came back – in shoppy. 'We're the English professor,' says Dr Kostov with a great laugh.

I find Vasileva in the curettage room after the siesta, her hair under a plastic bonnet. She's boiling instruments in the sterilizer. Simultaneously, we say: 'Nothing.' Nothing's happening. She's the only one working, she says. The other staff are all asleep.

She's a big, strong woman, many kilos heavier than her husband. In public, she defers to him, as one of his staff. But in private now, she speaks for him, expressing something that for Dr Vasilev is totally foreign, the need to justify and explain. It's a need born of self-respect. Her French is very weak, she's difficult to understand, but she tells me that the first days she came, she used to work like a nurse should, the way they work all over the world, in England and Bulgaria. No one appreciated it, so she began working like she does now. What was the point of her doing everything, when the Algerians themselves did nothing? Is it her country, or theirs? I ask her why she came. The question delights her. She puts down her curettage box and takes two steps forward, as if about to recite. With a giggle and a great sweep of her arm, she declaims: 'To construct Algerian socialism!'

At three o'clock, before either of the doctors is back from his siesta, the Director comes by, 'inspecting'. It's pitiful. The Supervisor had entered Maternity like a king, opening cupboards and drawers, testing surfaces for dust, already a champion inspector in his own eyes and only concerned that he should become one for others. But the Director arrives alone, unhappy and surreptitious, to fulfil an obligation. He has no confidence, and he looks at nothing but himself. It's an extraordinarily self-conscious performance, conducted at high speed on his short legs, in which what he inspects isn't the department, but himself inspecting. He'll be back in his office in a moment, looking in the mirror and wondering: 'Did I inspect well just now?'

But before, there's a halt by Malika, who gets the consideration of one clan member for another – or is it the interest of a middle-aged director of an Algerian hospital for a girl with just the right amount of fat? He shakes my hand too, and without stopping asks me if all is well. I say that things remain as they were described in the report he has. Then I ask Malika what he said to her. 'He was very pleased,' she tells me, 'everything was as it should be.'

There are three curettages later in the evening. I do the first two (Djamila tells me I've become a *chevalier de la curette*). But the third is a problem. She's a woman of thirty-five in European clothes, speaking excellent French, who walks in on her own. She's bleeding badly, and she's already weak. She lies back on the curettage table with a sigh. She's a virgin, she tells me, and this is the heaviest period she's ever had.

I put up a drip and call Dr Vasilev. Because she's a virgin, he goes in via the rectum. He finds a lump in her pelvis. He doesn't know what it is. It could be a distended bladder, and he puts up a tube. But there's only a thin trickle of urine. Then, on some inspiration, he changes gloves and goes in via the vagina. The lump is a pregnant womb, and there's no trace of a hymen. 'You're no virgin after all, Madame,' he says, 'you've even had children.' 'No,' says the woman, 'I've never had children, and my last period was a month ago.' She's sweating badly now, and her blood pressure's dropping still further. The laboratory technician comes to group her blood.

Dr Vasilev puts on his rubber apron and gets down the box of instruments. The night porter is fascinated. Dr Vasilev says:

'We don't need you for a curettage,' but there's no shifting the man. He stays in the room throughout, something he'd never dare do with a married woman. 'We're not the police, Madame,' says Dr Vasilev as he brings out the embryo in a single piece, white, some two or three inches long, 'so why do you lie to us?' 'I'm not lying,' insists the woman, 'my last period was a month ago.' 'But I have your baby here, Madame, it's about ten weeks old!' 'My last period was a month ago.' 'Eh!'

When Malika arrives on duty in the morning, she says: 'The gendarmes must be informed immediately!' She collects a sheet of paper and refuses to let me accompany her. For this, she says, she must see the woman alone. She comes back puzzled. She knows the woman well – she's married, with a daughter of fifteen. The only explanation is that the baby can't have been her husband's. 'He's the person we must tell first,' says Malika, the women's representative, 'it'll be up to him to decide what to do afterwards.' She picks up the telephone. I ask Dr Vasilev if we can't stop her. But he says there's nothing we can do. We mustn't interfere, this isn't our country. Then the husband arrives to visit. He knows all about the curettage, and doesn't seem to mind. The fifteen-year-old daughter is with him. 'It's beyond me,' says Malika, screwing up her report, 'the woman must be mental.'

Newspaper in hand, Dr Vasilev leads the way to Out-Patients, with Malika in attendance:

lumps	defeat
disfigurements	depression
cripples	rags

– the appalling guard of honour the length of the Out-Patients corridor, and the overpowering smell of excrement from the lavatories at the end. Of the twenty-five women we'll see, eight will have goitres. One has a veil with golden tassels, a fashion in veils. Another is a woman in her forties, unsure of her age, unsure of her name, tattooed and toothless. She fetches in a 'Livret de Famille', a sort of family identity book, issued by the French in 1950. It has space for four wives and sixteen children. She's the third wife and there are eleven live children.

A woman tells us that her husband came back on holiday from France a year ago, and she became pregnant. When he went back, the baby 'slept'. It 'woke up' when he came back again this year. But yesterday, when a mother-in-law and daughter-in-law began fighting in her house, she became so frightened that she started to bleed. She's afraid she's losing the baby. Dr Vasilev's fingers come out, he holds them up to the light, splayed, and says the strands of blood are from an ordinary period, and not from a miscarriage. She leaves with iron and vitamins, the answer to all her problems.

It's routine stuff, and Malika's so bored. With Dr Kostov, at least there'd be some spice. The women come and go. In between asking them questions and telling Dr Vasilev the answers, Malika stares out the window, bubblegum ballooning between her pretty teeth. No one leaves without a prescription, and to every pregnant woman Dr Vasilev recites the same litany: 'Don't ride in cars, don't eat beans or cabbage or anything that makes gas.' Sometimes, to sound more medical, he'll add: 'None of those hot foods that cause peristalsis!' Malika's translation stays the same.

The soft popping of bubblegum and the rustle of *El Moudjahid*. The women dress and undress. Some turn away to untie the veil. The knot's at the back of their head. Often they'll slip the veil down over their nose and pull the knot round to the front, where it's easier to undo. But for some, this is difficult. They've tied their veil so tightly that it won't come down over their nose. These women have deeply ingrained marks across their cheeks.

One woman keeps on her veil all the time we examine her. She has a lot of pain with her periods. She's more listless and depressed than any of the others. Seven years ago she was married to a man who already had a wife. It made the first wife so jealous that she had to do all the work in the house. Life became impossible, and she went back to her parents after a month. She's been keeping home for them ever since. She doesn't think she'll be able to get married again, she says, as she's not a virgin any more. Dr Vasilev adds a pain-killer to her prescription of iron and vitamins.

When the women have taken off their veil and shawl, they unknot the striped sash round their waists. Then they unwind their belt, after taking out any papers or objects, like an apple or pear, that they might be carrying in the vast pouch above. The pants come off next. They're always a battle. When it's Dr Kostov, they end up anywhere that suits the fancy of his right foot. They're shaped like a sack, with two holes at the bottom for the legs. Their crotch is at knee height. And then, under the robe, the women are naked.

An unmarried girl is ten days late with her period. When Dr Vasilev asks her to take down her pants, she has a kind of hysterical fit – hands over her face, but without tears, mouth as if she's crying, but without sound. She reaches the table, and sits down on the edge. She tries to raise one leg on to a stirrup, but it just isn't possible. She gets the fit again, more strongly this time. Dr Vasilev whistles patiently, fingerstall poised. He's giving her the benefit of the doubt. He's treating her as a virgin, going in via the rectum if she'll let him. But it's all too much for the girl. She gets down, saying in French, 'I can't, I can't,' and hurries from the room.

The last woman has waited patiently all morning. She's a veteran from the war against the French. She was imprisoned and tortured, and she wants to know if she's entitled to any disability pension. She's already passed through Medicine and Surgery Out-Patients. 'And what did they find?' asks Dr Vasilev. 'Nothing,' says Malika, in that same bored voice she's had since we began, 'they say she's perfectly well.'

But the woman sighs, and limps towards the table. 'Allez, Madame,' says Dr Vasilev impatiently, 'stop groaning for your pension.' She's thin, she's in her fifties, and she has a fine, delicate face. Dr Vasilev whistles as he examines her. The pain she feels changes place twice during the examination. 'She'll hurt everywhere I touch her,' says Dr Vasilev.

He too declares everything normal. The woman begins complaining to Malika. I don't know who to believe. Is she lying, or has Dr Vasilev's magic hand missed something? I ask Malika to find out what the woman did during the war to get herself imprisoned and tortured. But Malika's looking out of the window. She won't ask the woman anything. Instead, she says sulkily, still looking away: 'So what? There are too many women who say they did things.'

Dr Vasilev wants to give the woman iron and vitamins. But he's run out of prescription paper. He calls for the orderly, who comes in with some more. Strictly speaking, says the orderly, this paper belongs to Out-Patients. 'But seeing as it's you, Dr Vasilev . . .' 'Yes, what's the difference,' Dr Vasilev chimes in, in the same spirit, 'Out-Patients or Maternity, it's still the same hospital, it's still the same family.' Plump Malika smiles approvingly and says: 'We're all socialists here.'

18

A taxi comes down from the mountains, a dusty Peugeot
station wagon with worn tyres. The driver opens up the back
and, in the hospital lights, from her bare, bloodstained feet,
along her soaking robe and clammy skin, to her upper lip
that curls over two long silver teeth, the woman looks already
dead. I catch Zora on her way over to Djamila's room. We lift
the woman out, and hurry her down the path. The stretcher
leaves a trail of blood and vomit.

The relatives crowd the threshold of the curettage room. A
shrunken old woman whose head barely reaches above the
door handle watches us lay her daughter-in-law on the curettage table. 'Eh oui,' she must be saying with those twitching
lips, 'eh oui.' A younger woman, looking fifty, probably
thirty-five, watches Zora hunt for veins in her sister-in-law's
elbow. A young man in white shirt and jeans sees his mother
receive repeated stabs from the needle. And an older man
stares at me, as I inject Vitamin C into a bottle of Rheomacrodex and hang it upside down from the gallows above his wife's
head.

There's no pulse at the woman's wrist, and there's none I
can feel in her sunken groin. Dr Vasilev gets into a vein at last,
with a little 'eh'. Zora holds the needle in place, and the fluid
drips into the woman's arm. Dr Vasilev lights a cigarette and
turns towards the door. 'This woman', he announces to the
audience of relatives, 'needs . . . blood!' He raises the woman's
wrist in the air, and lets it go. It flops back, off the table. With
his Italian accent brought on by the excitement, he's pro-
nounced the French word for 'blood' like the English word
'sang'.

There's no response from the audience. The fluid drips

through the needle. 'Sang!' repeats Dr Vasilev. Still no response. 'Dim!' cries Zora in Kabyl, 'du sang, nom de Dieu!' But it seems they've only come to watch. The woman's wrist hangs limp over the table.

Dr Vasilev goes to the door and pulls on the husband's arm: 'Sang!' The husband doesn't push Dr Vasilev away. He doesn't retreat either. He lets the hand rest on his arm, but he shakes his head. He's not giving any blood.

Dr Vasilev catches the son's forearm, bare below the rolled-up sleeves, where full veins ride over the muscles. 'Kharty! – No!' cries the sister-in-law, pulling the arm out of Dr Vasilev's grasp. Her nephew's had an accident, he broke a bone in his hand last year. He's not giving any blood. The woman wags her finger in Dr Vasilev's face: her nephew's giving nothing.

'Then take her home!' shouts Dr Vasilev, throwing the woman's wrist in their direction. We don't want her, he tells them. We don't want your women cluttering up the department, wasting our time. 'Maternity isn't a morgue!' The woman on the table brings a little vomit into her mouth, and it spills down her cheek. But the sister-in-law only wags her finger back.

The relatives leave, and Zora cries out in Kabyl after them. She turns to Dr Vasilev and me, licking her lips the same strange way she does in the delivery room. 'See how we're loved!' she cries, 'us Kabyl women!' Dr Vasilev says nothing. Depression's arrived, extinguishing his anger. 'Eh,' he goes at last, with bleary eyes and muffled voice, as if he were speaking with his head in the sand, 'every country has its customs.'

Just before lunch, a Peugeot 404 draws up. A man of about forty-five gets out and comes down the path to the office, with never a backward glance. He's in a summer suit and dark glasses. He's followed at a distance by a veil and shawl. The woman reaches her appointed place, the bench in the hall, and sits down. The man comes on into the office: 'Bonjour messieurs les médecins!' He shakes each of us by the hand starting with Dr Vasilev, and saying 'Doctor' each time. He's as familiar with us as if he were a doctor himself. It's Zora's father.

He presents the symptoms – bleeding since yesterday. And the history – nine pregnancies, including this one, with five children still alive. Zora's the eldest. Dr Vasilev asks for the date of her last period. The veiled woman gets up from the bench in the hall, and Dr Vasilev repeats his question. But she doesn't understand French, and the husband asks the question for her in Kabyl. She doesn't know the answer. 'That's the Kabyl woman for you, Doctor,' says Zora's smiling father, 'she doesn't know anything.' As far as he can remember, her last period was in June.

Dr Vasilev and I go into the curettage room. The man indicates to his wife to follow us. Vasileva closes the door, and Zora's mother disrobes in silence. Shawl on the back of the chair, with the veil folded on top. Pants in a bloody heap on the floor. White, low-heeled shoes next to them. A cigarette for Dr Vasilev as he waits. Laboriously, she climbs the two steps on to the table. Folds her knees over the cold, uncushioned stirrups. Inches down, till her vagina's over the edge. Without needing to be told.

Dr Vasilev uncrosses his legs, gets up. Extinguishes cigarette under tap, flicks stub into enamel basin on top step. Selects glove from tin marked 'Gants stériles'. Puts right foot on top step, right elbow on right knee, and parts lips with index and middle fingers of right hand. In, and out. Black strands of blood between fingers of glove. Carries them aloft to sink. Removes glove. Opens cupboard, brings down curettage box. Sits on chairs between thighs. In with the cold gutter, searching for the cervix with pincers. 'Pa . . . pa . . . pa', woman retreats up table. 'Ai, Madame Zora! Comme ça, je ne peux pas! Ai! Sob! Sob!' Woman comes back down, 'ai, ma's' and heavy breathing. Hands hovering between legs, to hold curette back. 'Ai, Madame Zora!' Deep-throated rasps from the big curette. 'Ai, Madame! Ne bougez pas, Madame Zora! Vous voulez quelque perforation? Ai!' Clatter of the changeover to the small curette. Froth in the vagina. A dry swab, and it's over. Methergin from Vasileva, and Madame Zora dresses in silence.

She follows us back out, to the bench in the hall. Her husband doesn't want her to stay in hospital. He's taking her home. He signs the form accepting full responsibility and goes off to the hospital office to pay the 120 dinar fee. He returns to shake our hands: 'Merci, messieurs les médecins!' And the mother, to whom none of us has properly spoken a word, gets up after he's passed the bench and follows him to the car. It's been normal. It's been routine. It's been a visit to the vet.

Zora's stitching a girl she went to school with. They talk to each other in French. They live in the same town, but they haven't met for years, not since the girl left school early to marry a man chosen by her parents. She'd never seen him before, she tells Zora. The first three months were the worst. She used to cry all the time: 'He thought I was ill.' 'But it'll be better now,' says Zora brightly, 'you've got a little boy.'

'That changes nothing,' says the girl. Despite the birth, despite the pain, she's lucid. She can see right through the Kabyl delivery room ethic that Zora's preaching. A baby boy brings no freedom with him for his mother, he only confirms what she was for in the first place. The girl swears she'll never make a daughter of hers do what she's had to do. She tells Zora to stay single, or else marry the man she loves. She winces as Zora puts the needle through, with her usual disdain for local anaesthetic.

'Last one!' cries Zora blithely, and looks at me. 'I'll do the same as my friend,' she says, 'I'll marry the man my father tells me to. He couldn't make a bad choice.' But she's laughing, and I can't tell if she means it.

Three gendarmes arrive in a jeep, late in the afternoon. Dr Kostov's showering in his apartment and, as we wait, I chat with the chief gendarme on the porch. He's young, he has scattered hairs on his upper lip and there's saliva at one corner of his mouth, perhaps a nerve injury from birth. We stand there and talk, as colleague to colleague. 'Officer', 'Doctor'; khaki uniform, white coat; revolver, stethoscope. The nurses' textbook that Zora's lent me begins its chapter on cancer: 'Its chief characteristic is ANARCHY.' The gendarme and I fight together in the same struggle.

He wants two women examined for pregnancy. Dr Kostov

asks why. 'To know what they've got in their bellies,' says the gendarme. 'Three of you for two women,' says Dr Kostov, 'they must be dangerous!' He roars with laughter as he brings the first woman into the curettage room.

She's small, ugly and wretched, in a patched, off-white shawl. She's charged with having 'offended public decency'. Her husband left her a month ago. She gave birth here only recently, she says. She's slept with no one since, but they've accused her of living with another man. Baya goes to check the register, while Dr Kostov waits on the stool, glove at the ready. When Baya tells him the woman delivered a dead baby twenty days ago, Dr Kostov sends her back to the hall without examining her.

The second is taller and finer-looking. Her veil's wet under her eyes. A man stole her watch, she tells us. She went to the gendarmerie this morning, and they arrested her for having slept with the thief. Dr Kostov puts his glove back in the tin. 'Ai, ai.'

In the office afterwards he explains to the gendarme with the hanging lip that a woman can't be found pregnant a few hours after intercourse, or even twenty days after delivery. He tells the gendarme a story, about a big square in Sofia that has a statue of a Russian general on horseback. It's in the city centre and hundreds of thousands of people go by it every day. Every time a virgin passes, so the saying goes, the horse gives a neigh. 'It's never neighed yet!' laughs Dr Kostov. 'In our country,' says the pathetic gendarme, 'things are different.'

Zora joins us from a stroll in the garden. She's seen the jeep outside, and she's intensely curious. 'Where do you find these women?' she asks. 'Anywhere,' answers the gendarme, 'everywhere.' Zora asks him if it's against the law to live as man and wife and not be married. 'Eh oui,' says the gendarme with the hanging lip. 'Ah,' goes Zora in awe.

Malika puts a sour face round the delivery room door, to tell me I have visitors. They're just the kind she'd expect me to have – two French friends in jeans, with sleeping bags and stubble and hair down to their shoulders. Zora's excited when I tell her they've taken pictures for *Paris-Match*. She invites them into the midwife's room and offers cigarettes. She even

smokes one nonchalantly herself after closing the door. She's
sure she's seen their pictures, and she flips through her latest
issue of *Paris-Match* to point triumphantly at two shaggy film-
producers. No, we tell her, she hasn't understood: they don't
feature in pictures, they only take them. She's a little disappointed. And in the end her education gets the better of her.
She points to *El Moudjahid* instead, to THE YOUNG PEOPLE'S
PAGE ('FORBIDDEN TO PARENTS!'), where there's a cartoon of a glum-faced, long-haired man sitting idly on some

steps watching the traffic go by. The caption says: 'I'm listening
to my hair grow,' and Zora giggles. Before I leave with my
friends for a drink in town, she confides to me that 'long hair
is for louts'.

Fatma's having one of her rare nights off. She couldn't have
been replaced by anyone more different. The stand-in cleaner
is Kabyl too, and about fifty, but she looks and talks like a

working-class woman from Paris, with the same intonation and expressions. I find myself talking to her non-stop. She knows Zora well. They once worked together in Azazga, a small town that's a short bus ride away. In the 1950s, Azazga was at the heart of the revolt in Kabylia. It was there that the cleaner did liaison work against the French. Once she was carrying a message when some parachutists shouted for her to stop. But she ran on. They fired, hitting her in both legs. One bullet went through her thigh, the other lodged in her knee-joint. When the parachutists reached her, they broke her jaw with a rifle butt. Now she limps from osteoarthritis and has several false teeth.

She joined the women's section of the Party when the war ended. For a while she lived in Algiers. She went on demonstrations in the streets, campaigning against the veil and calling for improvements in the laws for women. For a year or so, she hoped for a change. Then Boumediène arrived and said: 'The veil is not a problem in Algeria.' He dismissed the militants and appointed more docile women in their place. The cleaner took her cue. She surrendered her Party card and withdrew from everything: 'The real war hasn't begun.' I'm glad she chooses the word 'war'. As for Zora, she listens but doesn't join in. This sort of conversation bores her. Prolonged, it would irritate her. Soon the cleaner and I seem to reach a dead end. That's the situation, and there's nothing that can be done about it. 'It's sad,' she says. Births and curettages come to sweep us off our feet.

Around eleven o'clock we take a break. She sits with Zora on the labour bed. They begin reminiscing over the time they worked together, the little events, the people they'd known, Azazga itself. In retrospect it seems to have been a happy time, happier perhaps than here. But I'm only listening with half an ear because I'm still on my feet – there are so many things the cleaner's left undone. Her knee gives her a lot of pain and she's been seizing every opportunity to rest it. Nothing's ready, and there's a girl who's close to delivery. After all the woman's been saying, everything I've ever wanted to hear, it's terrible to be noticing these petty things, terrible to be feeling nostalgic for Fatma and her efficiency, learned in the service of the French. Why clean after all, what's the point? If things *are* sad, then let them *look* sad. I stop doing her work and sit with them on the labour bed.

The girl's contractions come fast and hard, she calls for her mother. The cleaner considers her a while and then, with a sophistication quite foreign to Zora, she says in her Piaf accent: 'All that pain for a moment of pleasure . . . if there was any pleasure.' Here she is, she says, touching fifty and with three grown-up children, and she's still not ready for a man.

The sun has cooled and Zora goes hopping from parapet to grass and back again, her excellent figure. She's prettier than ever. Her hair in particular is a feminine masterpiece, fruit of those hours spent over in Djamila's room. It's jet-black and sculpted in waves and curls. But she's crying all the time. An engineer in Radio-Algiers has asked her parents for her. He saw her on the beach at the weekend. She was with her parents, he was with his. Her face is so tanned from those two days that she's turned almost black. It's the first time her father's ever accepted.

'I get asked for every week,' she says. But there's 'someone else', a surgeon, and she's 'in love' with him. He's on holiday in Rome. 'Oh please!' she cries, 'tell me what I should do!' She's alternately laughing and crying: 'It's stupid, but I can't stop.' She sits on Fatma's knee, on the chair at the desk on the landing. They talk in Kabyl, and Fatma rocks her. She advises Zora to marry the surgeon. She knows him, she's used to him and she must explain that to her parents. But Zora says that wouldn't be possible.

We do two births together. Like Djamila, she never seems to care. When she asks me again what I think, I say that it doesn't really matter who she marries, as really she's rather a cold person at heart. But she might as well marry someone who'll provide for her materially and, on that score, between an engineer and a surgeon, I find there's little to choose. 'Of course I'm cold and hard!' says Zora angrily, 'what else do you expect me to be in this system? Oh to hell with the lot of them! I'll just never marry.'

A small hospital on the coast sends in a woman by ambulance. A Kabyl girl's come with her, younger than Zora, and only an orderly. The girl helps her patient on to a bed in the delivery room and then stands back, to let us experts take over. She's overawed by the surroundings and fearful of getting in our way. She's particularly fascinated by Zora, and watches her every move. Zora sheathes half a Kocher's forceps with her fingers, the way you're supposed to (and the way she so rarely does) and slips it through the cervix with exaggerated nonchalance. The girl's mesmerized. She's quite forgotten the bedpan she's holding. Zora calls for it as the membranes break, with an imperious click of her fingers. The girl starts, and blushes as she realizes she's been standing there idle.

She goes to look after the baby born on the next bed while Zora and I wait for her patient to deliver. The girl has a way about her that's immediately different. She's careful and affectionate. Instead of using one cloth to wrap the baby in, she makes a proper nappy with the first cloth and then uses two more for the rest of the baby. I ask her if that's how she always wraps up her babies. She says it is. She thought it was how babies should be wrapped up. She's blushing again, afraid she's made some mistake. How often does she think babies should be changed? Twice a day, she says. Should they be washed entirely, or just their bottoms? Entirely. What about the water, should it be warm or cold? 'Warm!' She's laughing now.

But she's only an orderly, she says. She's not a nurse, she has no qualifications. She'd love to be a midwife, of course, but she doesn't think she's clever enough. It's music in Zora's ears. The girl obviously worships her. There's nothing she wouldn't do for her. Zora's been ordering her about, fetch me this, fetch me that. Her 'tus' have not been very endearing, but the girl's not minded. I break the spell horribly by saying that of all the things I've just asked her about, there isn't a single one that we do here in Maternity.

'How can you say that?' cries Zora, 'you know it's not true at all.' She even says she doesn't shave the women because they arrive shaved. It's true, sometimes they do, but at this moment she's pressing out the placenta through a great bush of pubic hair.

And then Zora leaves me to it, as she tends to these days.

She goes over to Djamila's and won't come unless called. She no longer pretends to be interested in her work, or in me. I had little hold over her in the first place, and since my marriage, I've had none at all. Zora's vocation is elsewhere. I imagine her in London, doing her shopping and attending hospital parties. It's where she could so easily be, and why not. There'd be many who'd want her, with that touch of the exotic. She even knows a little English already. She'd feel happy and free, without regrets for her surgeons and engineers. Fantasies on Zora in the West run through my mind as I deliver her babies.

I suddenly realize: this girl is beautiful. She's seventeen, and her hair's tied in a red scarf and when she kneels on the delivery table and Fatma draws her robe off her uplifted arms, her pregnancy only adds to the rest. She lies back and draws up her legs. Zora arrives, to slip her hand inside and break the membranes. She's too soon, because Fatma's not yet back from the lavatory with the pans from the other women. Zora jumps clear as the fluid gushes out, pint after pint of it. 'My sheet! My floor!' cries Fatma, a rinsed bedpan in either hand, 'why didn't you wait?' 'You get on my nerves,' Zora tells her.

I put on a glove too. What I want to feel is the back of a firm, rounded head, pushing its way down. But what I actually feel is something rough and hard, with no shape that I recognize, a piece of wood, a stone. My scalp begins to tingle, and no matter how much I press my hands down on my head to stop it, I can't – the tingling's inside. Zora grabs that shape, a little frantic, as she's been all evening, and begins to pull. The beautiful girl pushes hard. 'What is it?' I ask Zora. 'A monster,' she says. 'But what part of a monster?' She doesn't know. It felt like a sea-shell. Perhaps it was some scale or spine that I felt. But are there such things as monsters with spines? I don't know.

It comes through easily enough. Its limbs and trunk seem normal. There's a face that's normal too, perhaps. It's difficult to tell, because it's not part of a head, it's just a face. It's a baby without a brain. From above its eyes, and back past some rudimentary ears to the shoulders, there's just a knobbly ridge, more or less flat, hard and black. It makes you do the same, it makes you bend your own head back and draw it down between your shoulders. It really is a monster.

Zora's hand rests on its chest, her eyes alight: 'Its heart's still beating!' It beats on for two or three minutes. The monster doesn't move, it never breathes. Zora sings as she puts it into the first Biotic-Algérie box of the evening. She makes no effort to hide it from the beautiful girl, who stays quiet, staring at the wall. 'Aren't I cold and hard,' says Zora.

Things are going ahead with the engineer from Radio-Algiers. Her fight was shortlived. If I'm still here, she says, she'll invite me to the wedding. She's trying hard not to think about it all too much. The man she 'loves' will be shocked of course, and she does feel bad for him. But he'll get over it. I ask her what kind of a surgeon he is, and she tells me he's a dental surgeon. And his car, the sports car she told me about, is a Renault 16. She's already getting him into perspective.

Anyway, she says, the radio engineer – she doesn't refer to him by name – is 'très bien – very suitable'. He'll be someone for her to talk to, someone 'to share ideas with'. She laughs: 'At least, that's what I tell myself.' Angrily: 'What else can I do?' And so she talks on, in a monologue, as we deliver two more women, she on one bed, me on the other. We meet on the third bed, to tie the cords and wrap the babies up. 'You know,' she says, 'I'm two different people.' Here in the delivery room, she's happy, she's in charge, she talks and she sings all day long. She can do what she wants, she can be a tyrant with the women. But at home, she's nothing. She never opens her mouth, she never reads, and no one ever asks for her opinion. 'You only know half of me,' she tells me.

The women lie dribbling blood into their plastic pans. I go back to Calie, and the delivery room's all over me. There are clots of blood on my shoes, and the smell of rubber and talc on my hands is sickening. I have a headache from the monster, and above us there's a child wailing with every breath.

In the morning, I go out early into town to buy some paper. On my way back, I pass Zora, eyes down, walking briskly home. It's the street, her other half, and she won't acknowledge me.

19

I'm always seeing the gate-keeper with patients. He filters them off into the different departments of the hospital, Medicine, Surgery, Pediatrics. If the pathology's on the surface, he expects to be shown it. He tugs on old men's ears, inspects their eyes. Mothers unwrap their babies for him, and carry his diagnosis to the pediatrician. Women climb on to the delivery table telling us they're eight months pregnant, the doctor said so at the gate. Some patients he refuses – he sends them back into town. There are others, believes Dr Vasilev, whom he actually treats.

This morning I slipped into town without him seeing me. He was busy with an old man from the mountains and a pregnant woman in veil and shawl. They were still there when I came back. I ducked again under the red-and-white pole he uses for the traffic and began walking down to Maternity. But this time he saw me. He called out for me to wait, and came hopping angrily towards me on his wooden leg.

He's the hospital watchdog, never off duty. His stick's always hanging on the nail outside the sentry box. That wooden leg of his, extending into the red-and-white pole, itself relayed by the high concrete wall – he's part of the hospital's armour. His infirmity seems to have heightened his senses. He'll raise the pole on the baker's van without needing to turn round, he'll catch the peculiar note of the jeep before it's entered the hospital avenue – and he'll be standing ready with a salute for the gendarme with the hanging lip, prelude to a minute's conversation between responsible citizens, his hand resting on one of those deeply furrowed tyres.

'Those French boys I saw you with,' he splutters to me now, 'they should have been arrested and shaved!' Stored under pressure, his indignation bursts with a vehemence that sets off a fit of coughing. I help him to his red-and-white pole. And as he leans there catching his breath, he tells me, alas, of 'an even dirtier story'.

Do I see that pregnant woman standing by the sentry-box? He sizes her up through her robe. 'She's nine months,' he says. He – and no doubt I – can tell such things at a glance. But her father, the old man, hasn't the faintest idea. He thinks she has 'a swollen belly'! He lives up in the mountains, 'in the clouds'. The war created havoc in Kabylia, says the gate-keeper. Men died in the maquis and their widows were left to fend for themselves. They lived from hand to mouth. Some have remained intact and pure, resisting every temptation that has come their way, fighting off the wolves who've taken them for easy prey. But others, 'the black sheep' . . . The gate-keeper's nostrils wrinkle, at the moral pathology beneath the daughter's shawl.

He orders them to follow me, then hauls himself back along the pole to his sentry-box, muttering Kabyl. The old man walks beside me, sombrero and stick, tattered cloak impregnated with goat. Behind us, we see the belly that rounds out the silent daughter's shawl. The old man points at it with his stick. 'Her husband died during the events,' he cries, 'and now she has a swollen belly!' We meet Baya on her way in to work, at the main doors of MATERNITÉ. She takes care of the daughter and the old man leaves us, none the wiser, under those letters he cannot read.

Baya comes into the delivery room grinning: 'Look what I've done to myself!' She's put on lipstick and make-up. She looks ridiculous, with her chin all covered in grease. She borrowed it from Djamila's room: 'I've no idea how to put it on.' She wipes it off on the sheet under a woman on the delivery table. 'Ai, ma,' says the woman as she gets another contraction. 'Ai, maaaa!' echoes Baya. The woman smiles and flaps her hand wearily.

Baya's been looking everywhere for Djamila, who arrived

two hours late and has hardly been seen since. 'The swollen belly' has been screaming, she says. She must be having contractions, she may be about to deliver. We hurry down the corridor to her room. But the beds are empty. Baya opens the door of the lavatory. It's the seatless kind, except that the woman we're looking for is sitting in it, bottom in the bowl, back against the pipe, thighs out along the steps where you normally put your feet, straining. Baya lifts her up and she comes with us to the delivery room. I'd thought she was trying to hide, to have her baby and dispose of it in secret. But she follows us meekly. It's her first baby, and her first lavatory. It seems that's what she thought Maternity was, a place with 'lavatories' where you went and had your baby. She doesn't know there's a delivery room till Baya tells her.

Baya installs her on the table and sits beside her, half for a rest in the cool air, half to give the affection she really feels. She strokes her and tells me in French: 'She's a lost woman.' If she goes back to the mountains with her baby, her father will kill her. If she stays here, she will be reported to Malika's fiancé and she'll go to prison. Either way, says Baya, she's 'lost'.

News of the impending delivery seeps through Maternity. Fatma arrives with her mop, but stays at a distance, almost in awe. Malika brings the Register, more businesslike. 'Ah,' she says ominously, 'it's that woman. I must prepare my report' She stays a moment, then goes back outside. 'The swollen belly' is a police affair.

The woman's gripped by a contraction. She reaches out for Fatma's hand. Her face shows the pain and effort of labour. It relaxes as the wave recedes. At rest, her face shows nothing. No drama's there. It's all in her situation. Fatma comes to her side, pats the enormous belly, reassuring herself. It's a belly like the others, and the woman speaks, a few listless words. What's she saying? That she's not a bad woman, says Fatma. What happened to her? Fatma climbs on to the delivery table and sits against the swollen belly. But the woman can't tell her. She shrugs under Fatma's hands. It was a 'djinn', she says, a genie.

Fatma asks me if I believe in such things. I shake my head. 'In the mountains,' she says, 'they all believe.' I wonder if

161

she does too. She's half in the mountains herself. Perhaps she half-believes. She's forgotten her mop. She's turned back to the woman, asking more questions. This case is for her, not the doctors.

It was many years ago, relates Fatma, it was during 'the events', that the woman's husband died. She hardly knew him. Sometimes he'd come and stay overnight, arriving at dusk and departing at dawn. At other times the sky swarmed with helicopters, paratroopers combed the villages, and he'd be away in the maquis for months on end. News filtered through in brief messages that were weeks out of date. The woman helped in her husband's house. She prepared food and tended his fields. In the winter she began weaving him a woollen coat. Then one day she saw her father arrive in the courtyard with the donkey. Her husband was dead.

She gathered her things and packed them into a wooden chest. To tell the truth, says Fatma, she had very little: her jewels and her mirror, a robe and a pair of shoes, and a bottle of perfumed oil for her hair. Her father loaded them on the donkey with the half-finished woollen coat, and they took dried figs for the journey. They crossed the stony bed of the Soummam river and climbed between the prickly pears on the other side. They reached her old home before dark. She found the pitcher of water empty, and she went to the well. There was her father's meal to prepare, and she lit a fire. His loom stood idle, and she brought over the half-finished woollen coat. In the morning she rose early and went to his fields. 'A house without a woman,' says Fatma, 'is like a sea without fish.'

She's conducting no ordinary interrogation, of the kind Malika will undertake when the baby's born. Fatma doesn't ask a question and receive an answer. The woman's uttering single words, monosyllables, stones cast in a stream and Fatma's leaping from one to another, creating a folk-tale out of unhappy chance.

At long last the fighting stopped. The new government declared the woman a war widow. She became entitled to a pension. Her father went down to the Prefecture in Tizi-Ouzou. The building was new, all glass and steel, but the administration was just getting to its feet. Payments hadn't even begun in Algiers, he was told after a day of waiting. The years passed, her father paid his regular visits to the Prefecture, but the money never came. He was too poor to force their attention.

They turned to pottery to keep themselves alive. Every so often, her father would fit wicker baskets on the donkey and fill them with clay from the river bed. At dawn the woman would leave with the donkey and the clay, and go down to the fields. There she'd make her pots, the way her mother used to, and she'd bake them in the hollow her father had dug in the earth. She'd work all day, says Fatma, barefoot on the stony ground, and she'd only stop to talk to the women drawing water from the well.

And then, one day . . . Fatma seizes her cue. The woman has spoken one word only, but Fatma 'knows': 'It was a day when she was feeling heavy and sad . . .'. The woman was surprised by night. She loaded her pots on to the patient donkey and they hurried up the path to the well. Fatma hears jackals in the field beside them and she sees the woman laying a hand on the donkey's harness. Never before has she been to the well at night. All the other women have gone. It's empty and still. She's impressionable ('like all Kabyl women, say our men') and 'like all women' she knows her folk-tales. Good faces evil, at wells after sundown. What are her fears? That she'll meet a 'tseriel' drinking in the form of a solitary goat, or a serpent rearing from the trusted pitcher, or a 'djinn' lurking beneath the water in the guise of a gelatinous toad. She's at the mercy of every genie in Kabylia.

Fatma describes the water as it runs into the trough without a sound, 'like a black syrup'. She pictures the donkey drinking, and the woman washing her pots one by one, without ceasing to look around her, though she can scarcely see further than her hand. She rinses them clumsily, in mounting panic, careless of her father's anger should they break. She's finished, and no toad has spoken to her from the trough. She's replaced the pots on the donkey's back and she's filling the pitcher with fresh water for the night, believing herself safe, when . . . 'Ai, ma!' and the pitcher sinks from her grasp.

The genie. But in what guise did he appear to you? A light shining in my eyes. With what tongue did he speak to you, bleating of sheep or barking of jackal? Kabyl. Human or animal, goat or multi-headed serpent? Human. Man or woman, hooded cloak or coloured robe? A man, in shirt and trousers and heavy boots. What were his demands, to eat you alive, to have you move the Djurdjura Mountains with a shovel or drink the Soummam in full flood? None of these. To 'cover' me. By the well? By the well. His face? The woman shrugs, shielding her eyes against the blinding light.

It's my turn to question Fatma. Does she believe that story? And besides, how much of it is her own fabrication? She was speaking ten words to the woman's one. She was too inspired a translator. But Fatma won't say, she won't commit herself. She only laughs and makes me feel I've missed the point.

Malika goes off duty at 7.30, glancing into the delivery room as she leaves, to see if there's been any progress. There has been. 'The swollen belly' will soon be delivering. 'We'll do the paperwork in the morning', says Malika.

I draw back the robe over the enormous belly. The skin's taut, and the navel's inside out. A dark line runs down her middle. On one side of the line I can make out the back and head of a baby, and I can hear its heart beating extra fast. But down the other side, there's a lump that baffles me. I tell Fatma that something's wrong. She says: 'It's the best solution.' The baby will die, Malika will lose interest, and the woman will return to her father with a flat belly and empty arms, her swelling cured.

We call Dr Kostov, on duty for the night. He arrives a little sluggish from his supper. 'She's an unhappy woman,' Fatma tells him, 'a lost woman.' Dr Kostov waives the social history. He points to his stomach and asks us: 'What's she got *here*?' Then he feels the belly for himself. 'It's a fibroid', he declares. Sometimes they'll grow with the pregnancy, he tells me, just like the baby. He might even have to do a Caesarean, if the fibroid's lying over the cervix. But first he'll try and push the baby past it. He climbs on to the table, and the woman looks up at him in alarm. But he's really what she needs, an obstetric textbook turned upside down, with every 'Don't' a 'Do', and every 'Never' an 'Always'. He brushes her hands from her belly, rests both fists in their place and begins his 'Chris-Taylor' chant, low-key at first: 'N'ki! Ernu! – Push! Harder!' Fatma takes her hand and tells her in Kabyl: 'The harder you push, the quicker it will be over.' The woman loses her head and screams.

I listen again over the gigantic belly. The heart's faster – and fainter. Dr Kostov takes a well-earned rest against the oxygen cylinder, and wipes his forehead on his coat. I ask him if what he's doing couldn't burst the woman's womb. He admits that it could, but he'd know if it did. The womb would suddenly give under his hand, in a sudden loss of resistance that he mimics for me. Then he'd operate. Theatre's only upstairs, after all. 'It's not an emergency,' he says, 'as it would be in England or Bulgaria.' Half an hour with a burst womb is nothing for 'these women'. I ask him how the babies manage. Dr Kostov tells me what I suspected, that they always die.

He returns to work, bearing down with both fists. The woman shrieks, and Fatma holds her hands away. Wet black hair appears between her legs. 'N'ki,' says Fatma in her ear, 'n'ki.' A colossal surge of effort from Dr Kostov and the head's forced out, to turn sideways in my hands. I pull, and it comes through easily. But the baby's alive – it even grips a clamp tightly in its fingers. And I look up, to see the woman pointing frantically at her still-swollen belly, shrieking she's not finished yet. Dr Kostov's shouting too, he's tumbling off the bed and coming round the front. I lift the baby from his path. He jams the stethoscope between his ear and that lump on the other side of the woman's belly. 'PROSTATE!' He's heard another heart. The fibroid's a twin.

Six in the morning: the sun's been up an hour. I can see the women in their rooms through the open windows of Maternity. They sit on each other's beds, undone hair reaching to their waists, over their enormous bellies. They pour lemonade, or curdled milk from home. They tend their babies, tend each other, combing hair, resting on a shoulder. Some will lean on the windowsills for hours, heads on their arms, green ribbons round their hair, staring downwards. There's nothing for them to fetch, nothing for them to make. They've no experience of having nothing to do. Men might feel at home in a hospital ward. But for the women, it doesn't fit. Maternity's a camp for displaced persons.

I discover the woman-with-twins in her room, putting on her shawl with Fatma's help. She's still very weak and her babies cry feebly on the bed. Fatma wants her to leave before Malika comes on duty. But at the same time, she's afraid and she asks the woman: 'What will you do?' The woman-with-twins can't say. She knows two villages, her father's and her husband's, and she can keep a house. She has no money. She cannot read or write. She cannot count or tell the time. She doesn't know the date. She's never walked in a street alone, taken a bus alone, or been inside a shop. She's stepping into the wilderness.

She follows us to the door, a twin in either arm. Fatma draws back the bolt, and we find Baya the other side, arriving to work. 'Athamtot! – Madame!' she cries, and for a moment I'm afraid she'll stop the woman leaving. But she's spied something in her shawl. She opens its folds, to reveal hospital cloths round the twins inside. 'What would happen if everyone took our linen,' she says, 'we'd soon have nothing left.' Dully, the woman goes back to her room and unwraps the twins. She's a thief, and no one watches her leave. She walks up the path to the main gate, and out into the street. The world can never have received someone less likely to survive.

Malika takes the news philosophically when she arrives later in the morning. The gendarmerie is vigilant, she says. They have jeeps and radio, and practice in this sort of thing. The woman-with-twins won't escape. Sooner or later they'll catch her.

Later that day I stand behind Dr Kostov as he washes a bloody forceps from his fists, scowls at the damp patches on his coat and strides from the delivery room. I follow him. Even as I'm on the stairs I hear a fresh set of screams and after I've fought my way through the crowd outside the curettage room door I find him seated between a fresh set of legs. The girl's about sixteen and she's naked. She's running with sweat and sobbing 'ai, mas' into the elbow crooked about her face.

It's not a curettage. I become aware of the girl's pink breasts and flat belly. She's not even pregnant. I see the fresh henna on her hands and feet and then, as Dr Kostov readjusts the spotlight – she won't stop moving – I notice how carefully she's been shaven. She'd look just like a little girl, if it wasn't all so swollen and sore. Simply to be touched there with cotton wool makes her jump and squirm. It's a marriage injury – a torn hymen, a lacerated vagina – and blood's everywhere. The discarded wedding robe's steeped in it, it's dripping into the enamel bowl. As Dr Kostov draws up his stool, a huge clot catches him by surprise. It springs from between the girl's legs, to send up a shower of red spots on to his coat and glasses.

The first touch of the needle produces monstrous 'ai, mas'. Dr Kostov shakes his head. The girl lies panting, drawing in hoarse lungfuls of air, energy for further screams. Those men I had to push my way through to get in here, four or five of them, all in fine suits, their best clothes, must have been the marriage party. The husband, his brothers, his cousins, I can see their shapes through the opaque glass door. 'Ça y est? – Is it done?' comes the cry, that same 'ça y est?' that Baya told us about in the mountains, the 'ça y est?' they shout after the dancing stops, outside the marriage room door.

Dr Kostov accepts the needle Vasileva's offering him, though it's far too big. He accepts her catgut too, though it's thick and coarse. He puts in two stitches, and he does so like a robot. He ignores the girl's sobbing, her sudden movements. He accepts it all, much as Ivanov accepted the spurting urine and nightmare panic of the boy on the Theatre table. He can't even see what he's doing. He puts in those stitches with X-ray eyes. And as he's tightening the second one, index finger over the knot, it comes clean away. He flicks it into the enamel bowl and leaves the room.

Outside, his finger points, dripping water from the tap. One of the men comes forward. 'No love for twenty days,' grunts Dr Kostov. The husband smiles, with an air of complicity. 'Come now, Doctor.' He's about forty, trim and sophisticated in an English blazer with colours over the breast pocket. He's no peasant, he's telling us. But Dr Kostov won't have him for an equal, he turns his back on him. 'She's staying in till the bleeding stops,' he says, trusting Nature to do the work of that second stitch. The husband follows him into the office, incredulous: 'But there's nothing wrong with the girl!' Dr Kostov wheels on him viciously: 'Are you a doctor?'

The husband appeals to me instead. He offers a cigarette, to the European in me. He understands we're very busy – he's been very busy himself. The tourist in me will appreciate that Algerian weddings are a family affair. They can last for a week. The cars go from village to village, from relative to relative, eating cous-cous and meat in the different homes. If he'd known me before, he could have invited me along. Put yourself in my position, says the husband: what's left of a marriage when the bride has to stay in hospital? Besides, he says, he likes his young bride very much. And he winks, to the man in me.

At this point, the Bulgarian paper is lowered on a remarkable sight, a Dr Kostov twisted by circumstance into adopting an attitude of Christ-like concern, the doctor of the advertisements, whose patients' interests are always uppermost in his heart. 'Your wife needs gentle treatment,' he says in an unreal voice. The husband assures him she'll get it. But he's not seized Dr Kostov's meaning. He's not understood that Dr Kostov quite simply doesn't want to have to stitch up that hymen again. Dr Kostov shakes the Schweitzer mantle from his shoulders and makes his meaning clear, in his normal voice: 'If you bring her back again, I won't touch her.' 'Then I'll take her to Algiers,' says the husband. 'She'll be dead before she gets there!' shouts a triumphant Dr Kostov.

Fatma wheels the girl from the curettage room. As soon as he sees her, the husband runs forward and bends over the head of the trolley, talking furiously in Kabyl. Dr Kostov comes over at a more leisurely pace, newspaper in hand. The husband takes the handkerchief from his breast pocket to wipe the vomit from the girl's mouth. His mother comes forward, and together they lift the girl into a sitting position, swinging her legs over the side of the trolley, first stage of getting her to her feet. Dr Kostov stands by, Bulgarian paper in hand, sardonic witness to this lower form of life.

The twins are back. They were found by a nomad boy and the gendarme with the hanging lip brought them in by jeep, One has bruises on its head and ankles, the other has bloodstains round its cord. But on the whole they look none the worse for their night out.

Baya comes to look. She's joined by Fatma, who leans on her mop over the cot. They're immensely curious, and their Kabyl is respectful. In a way, their curiosity over the twins is homage to the mother. They're investing her with a free will, a spirit of defiance, an opposition to the system. But of course, it's what she never had. The woman-with-twins is no heroine, she's no militant in any cause. She didn't stand up and shout her name. Trapped in the system, with illegitimate twins, she's answered within the system, by abandoning them. She's a woman like the others, but a woman two times over.

She gave herself up to a small gendarmerie in the mountains, says Malika. They're charging her with 'abandonment in a solitary place'.

I thought we'd hear no more of her. But first, about one week later, the gendarme with the hanging lip drove in from prison, saying her breasts were swollen with unused milk. Dr Vasilev wrote out a prescription of hormone for 'mon ami, Monsieur Gendarme'. He stayed on a while, as his habit was. He'd enrolled on the gendarmerie nursing course, he told us. Dr Vasilev thought it a wise decision and wished him every success. I asked him how he'd come to be a gendarme in the first place. It was pure luck, he said. His father had died 'on the field of honour', in battle against the French, and as a war orphan he'd been given priority. Then we made small talk, of the usual kind about the hospital and the prison, and he left.

We were to see him some two weeks later, with the woman-with-twins. It had been one of those empty afternoons when everything was hot and still, when siesta was prolonged into supper. Dr Vasilev had slept until late, and when finally he arrived in the doctor's office, there was only one emergency for him to see, and even that was not truly his province. An anxious father came into the office and laid a pair of baggy pants upon the desk. They belonged to his daughter, a little girl of eleven being held by her mother on the bench in the hall. They had flecks of blood between the legs. A jealous woman neighbour had attempted to deflower the little girl with her finger, in revenge against the family. As Dr Vasilev examined the pants, Fatma held the father back. It was a field in which she came into her own. Her face was responsible, dramatic. She went next door with Dr Vasilev and the little girl. Together they certified the hymen intact, and Dr Vasilev was able to make out a certificate of virginity for the father.

Then we'd taken a little walk in the grounds. It was almost suppertime and the sun was setting. The one-eyed cat followed him at a distance, and her kittens sprang in the grass. We paid a visit to the paint shop, to see 'mon ami, Monsieur Peintre'. He was the only hospital workman who was strictly Muslim. He wouldn't touch tobacco or alcohol, and of course he never ate pork. He was often to be seen outside the workshop, a glass of lemonade in hand. Dr Vasilev examined his brushes and pots, sniffed his turps, and they'd agreed over the advantages of rollers. Then he'd gone hunting in the painter's cupboards, 'looking for the beer'. Surely you allow yourself a beer at the end of the day! It was an old joke between them. We'd come back to the courtyard with Dr Vasilev still chuckling.

He seemed happy, and Bulgaria loomed large on the horizon. He began looking forward to the time when he'd be back and we'd be able to pay him a visit. He'd show us his hospital of course, but we'd spend most of our time at the sea, with an excursion into the mountains to see Vasileva's childhood village. Then he gave a little wave as the jeep drew up.

He took me over, to welcome the gendarme with the hanging lip, sitting beside his driver in the front seat. The jeep had a springy aerial attached to the back and it was painted brown, with letters along the side in white, Arabic and French. It carried jerrycans slotted behind the front bumper, one for petrol, one for water. We peered through at the dashboard. The gendarme showed us the guns on their clips inside, and his heavy-duty torch, embedded in black rubber. 'Eh, Monsieur Gendarme,' asked Dr Vasilev, 'what have you for us today?'

Only Fatma recognised the woman-with-twins beneath the veil and shawl in the back seat. She came up the path behind us and took her place on the bench in the hall. Then she watched from over her veil the ensuing encounter between Medicine and the Law.

Dr Vasilev could have had no idea what the gendarme wanted. I suppose he thought she might still have been having trouble with her breasts, or that she'd caught some infection in her womb. But it was nothing of the kind. The gendarme laid an official form on the desk, signed by his commanding officer, requesting that an examination for pregnancy be performed on the woman-with-twins. 'Qu'est-ce que!' cried a startled Dr Vasilev. The miserable gendarme shuffled in his boots. 'It's been judged necessary for her trial,' he mumbled. Had the charge been changed, to witchcraft? What doctor in the world could have found the woman pregnant so soon after delivery? Dr Vasilev had everything on his side. But the protests faded on his lips.

Fatma brought the woman after us into the curettage room. She took off the veil and shawl. She was taller than I remembered her, and downcast. She lay back on the table and exposed fat thighs to the spotlight, and a belly striped and loose, to do with what we would. She submitted passively to the absurd examination that Dr Vasilev actually performed. But then what would she not have allowed, and what would Dr Vasilev not have accepted? Fingers without knowledge, numb fingers, felt a body-become-débris, uninhabited.

The woman drew on her pants. In that same dull voice, she told Fatma that she was going mad. Fatma rebuked her for having left out her babies to die. But I don't think she really meant it. What else could the woman have done? It was the traditional solution, and Fatma had pushed her to it when she'd hustled her out early that morning. I asked Fatma if the woman still believed that story about the 'genie'. It wasn't likely to convince them at her trial. But the woman had ceased to believe. It was never a genie after all, she told us, it was the gendarme.

171

Fatma jumped away: 'Ai, ma!' I'd never seen her so shaken. 'Ai, ma!' But then she fought back, casting doubt over the new accusation, calling the woman to order over a point of folk-tale orthodoxy. Genies were notorious for adopting different guises. They'd take on any shape, and why not that of a gendarme, especially one with a special sign like a hanging lip. But even Fatma didn't persist, the way she could have done. I felt she didn't really mean this either. The woman's baleful stare, her melancholy voice – her statement carried a lack of motive that stamped it as the truth.

When the gendarme passed her bench, signed form in hand, the woman-with-twins rose. She looked such a model wife. She followed him down the path, so dutifully. Never had a shawl seemed whiter or more flowing, never a veil more virginal. She glided across the courtyard and mounted the jeep, so daintily. Then she turned and looked down on her erstwhile genie, over her veil with its black lace border. The embroidery had become mockery.

Later that evening, I had to call Dr Vasilev for a forceps. A little tug, and it was over. We went down to the office, and Dr Vasilev had a smoke. For a while, we didn't talk at all. We sat with the office light off, in near-darkness, to avoid attracting the mosquitoes. Then I asked him about the woman-with-twins. What did he think? The story had seemed plausible to me, with the gendarme going to the well to fetch water for his radiator and using the torch to find his way. But did Dr Vasilev believe him capable of such a thing?

The cigarette went up, and down. Dr Vasilev wouldn't think. He wouldn't get involved. He had not struck the gendarme from his list of friends. He wasn't even disappointed. The gendarme or a genie, what was the difference. It wasn't for him to say. 'Eh,' was all he'd venture, 'every country has its customs.' Then he reached across the desk and found my arm. He gripped it with a return of his old brightness. When I came to visit him in Bulgaria, he promised, I wouldn't find such things! They no longer happened. I asked him why not. 'Chez nous – In our country,' he told me, 'we have no more gendarmes. We have a people's militia instead.'

20

EL MOUDJAHID

SHORT REPORTS

SUICIDE: A girl of about 18 years of age, as yet unidentified, threw herself off a building on Che Guevara Boulevard yesterday. The unfortunate victim was rushed to Mustapha Hospital. The police have not yet been able to discover why this young girl should have sought to put an end to her life. An inquiry is under way.

The Postmaster stamps across the courtyard from Pediatrics. His surgical boots seem to give him poor hold on the gravel. He hands over his monotonous mail. An 'important communication' from the laboratories of Roche to Drs Vasilev and Kostov, the bright and enterprising voice of Western capitalism; the Bulgarian daily paper and *El Moudjahid*, the grey mouthpieces of the governments in Sofia and Algiers.

The Postmaster's dour and colourless too. He wears shirts in dark blue wool. He has thick trousers that he holds up with an empty cartridge belt, and a beret pulled down over his ears. And, of course, there are his heavy boots. He's aggressively proletarian.

Noticing that I'm alone, he fishes out something extra from his grubby army bag. It's an envelope addressed to the Ivanovs, husband and wife, with a Geneva postmark and a Swiss stamp. It comes for them every month, he tells me. 'Algeria is their America, it's their gold-rush.' Such people, says the Postmaster, aren't the solution to Algeria's problems. The government knew this from the start, and none of us had any illusions. That's why we chose yellow for the number plates on their cars. Yellow is the colour of gold. The Co-opérants

Techniques were flattered, they couldn't see the sarcasm. Besides, says the Postmaster, everyone knows that the initials CT really stand for 'Chercheurs de Trésor', treasure seekers.

He has a very simple explanation for their behaviour. It's political, he tells me darkly, and he'll discuss it if I care to come along to his office one day. He swings the old army bag over his shoulders, hitches up the cartridge belt and stomps off on the surgical boots to deliver the Ivanovs' bank statement and their airmail edition of *Pravda*.

The Postmaster's office is up by the main entrance. His desk is not the smooth executive kind favoured by the Director. It's thick and wooden, like a teacher's desk in an old-fashioned school. The Postmaster might have hewn it out of one of the carpenter's sawing-blocks. It suits him admirably.

'They're revisionists,' he's explaining gravely. Countries like Bulgaria and Russia have lost the socialist ideal. It's only to be expected that their doctors are commercially minded. They've nothing to teach the newly independent nations. The Postmaster has a large portrait of Mao Tse Tung over the desk in his office.

He's the hospital's union representative, and a member of the national Party. In fact, he tells me, the two things really go together. All labour union representatives are also Party members. It's a sort of unwritten law. Thus Malika is enrolled in the women's section of the Party. As for himself, he says, his leanings towards the China of Mao have never been held against him. He's made no secret of his beliefs. The portrait is even there as an advertisement for them.

In return, I tell him of the cutting I've stuck on the wall of our room, showing a squad of barefoot doctors marching through Shanghai. The Postmaster's pleased. He looks at me with comradely warmth. He opens the doors of his cupboard, it's chock-full of *China Pictorials* and their North Korean equivalent. We both agree that Algeria must outlaw private medicine. And it mustn't waste time, like the developed countries, educating its doctors for six years. What the country needs is barefoot medicine.

He gives me an armful of magazines to take away. The cover

on the top one shows a rainbow in the sky over Marshal
Kim Il Sung's birthplace.

I notice an old man in the courtyard with a brown paper
parcel, the size of a swimming costume and towel. He finds a
spot by the Morgue in the shade. He unwraps the parcel carefully, religiously, and rolls out a coloured mat in front of him.
He takes off his shoes and kneels. He mutters, and prostrates
himself in the direction of Pediatrics. He has a wet nose. He's
the first person I've seen praying publicly in Kabylia.

'Supposing the Chinese system were applied in Algeria,
what would become of the Muslim religion?' The Postmaster
welcomes my question. He enjoys the paradox, and he's
obviously had to deal with it before. We've discussed Vietnam
and the Middle East. The Postmaster has been severely critical
of Nasser for failing to support the Palestinians as he should.
He's been even more critical of the Russians. He's certain
they're responsible for Nasser's hesitation. We've agreed once
again that Russia's policies have nothing to do with the
advancement of socialism, and all to do with the preservation
of their colonial interests.

The Postmaster is concerned that we should now extend our
agreement to the question of Islam and socialism. The con-
tradiction between the two, he says, is only apparent. When
we talk of Islam, we don't mean the religion we find around
us. What's left today is only a perversion of the original. After
all, the French colonized the country for 130 years. They introduced a foreign culture. They even made a number of conversions in Kabylia to the Catholic religion. Algerians no longer
knew who they were. They couldn't be really French, because
the French would never allow it. But, on the other hand, they
couldn't be really Algerian, because a foreign power occupied
their soil. They hung in mid-air between two worlds, and two
identities.

The Party's task, and the task of the government, says the
Postmaster, is to give back the people an Algerian identity.
What was it, throughout the 130 years of colonial rule, that
kept the Algerian people in touch with themselves, if not
Islam? Independence has given us our chance to return to the

175

original sources and develop the true Islam. Between that and socialism, there's no conflict at all: 'They're kif-kif,' says the Postmaster, 'they're the same thing.'

'For instance,' he offers, 'in the original Islam, men and women were equal.' I haven't referred to women myself. It's simply that whenever Islam is mentioned, either in private or in the newspaper, it's always about 'the problem of women' that everyone seems to be speaking. The Postmaster's no exception. 'Equal in Islam,' he says, 'and equal in socialism.' He leafs through one of the *China Pictorials* I've returned, till he comes to the picture of a textile mill in Kiangsi province. He reads me out the caption: 'Men and women weaving the same cloth together.'

The Postmaster considers his point made. Besides, he says, women are becoming essential for Algeria's economic development. With a rare laugh, he tells me of his own contribution to the nascent labour force: 'eight daughters – and each one of them as good as a son!'

I'm on my way down the corridor to join Dr Kostov in Out-Patients. I see a boy with a red swelling the size of an orange between his eyes. I see a woman from the mountains sprawled on the floor, with just her shoulders against the wall, her head cradled by a little girl, so old that wrinkles have deformed her tattoos, she must be dying right there. I see babies in rags and string, smelling of herbs. Young men with their legs in plaster hop aside to let me pass. The expression on the faces is terrible. Utter submission.

I open the door of our waiting room. Because it's women, it's kept shut. Twenty pairs of eyes look over their veils. They can see without being seen. It's still uncomfortable for me. I can't get used to it. How must the French have felt during the war, when there might have been grenades under the shawl? Eyes are supposed to open in fear, to narrow in suspicion. But the clichés are no help when the rest of the face isn't there to guide you. They give nothing away. What do you make of just a pair of eyes? You have to make *something* – after all, if the face is covered, there must be something to hide. They might be smiling, contemptuous smiles for what they see around them. They might – but that's so unlikely – be a sort of underground in our midst. More probably, they're just very curious. It's impossible to tell. The eyes are an ink-blot. They say more about you than about the women behind the veils.

There's a woman lying out on a sheepskin in front of the door into the consulting room. It's the position of the doormat. I shall have to step over her. Her eyes are closed, her robe and feet are stained with blood. Then the door to the consulting room opens, and Dr Kostov appears framed within it. Perhaps it's just the way I'm seeing him, with this collapsed Kabyl woman at his feet, but there's definitely something superb to him this morning. His face is a little tilted, he's looking down at us, his right hand is gloved and up, and there's a grin, even a faint swagger, as he beckons: 'Next!' – an abortionist in the prime of life.

Pushed into the room in tears, a girl of sixteen with her veil round her neck, who turns her head away, searching for somewhere to hide. Dr Kostov drums impatient fingers on the desk. Motherly, Baya goes into the corner and gets the girl's story, to a background of commotion from outside. She's been married four days, and there's still been no blood. Her husband's family want a certificate to prove that she was a virgin. I remember from *El Moudjahid* that in the Mahometan era we're in 1389.

The girl comes towards the table with her face hidden under her arm. Baya guides her up the steps. Male voices rise above the hubbub outside. Dr Kostov isn't rough, and he opens the girl with his fingers, revealing a pink annular hymen, the kind the penis can go through without tearing anything, without drawing blood, the kind that's possessed by one woman in three. Baya gives the girl a kiss to tell her that everything's all right. The girl stumbles to the corner of the room, where she stands still, turned away, her face shielded.

The door opens and the men we've been hearing over the partition burst in, and seem to surround us. Their hands are out, it's the custom between men, but I can't shake them. They're the husband's father and elder brother. They ignore the sixteen-year-old thing in its veil and shawl. They're Kabyl

speakers only, their French is too poor. They're small and thin
and wretched and, in a sense, their ordeal is as desperate as the
girl's. Her virginity is all they have. Baya explains to them that
not all girls bleed on first intercourse. Only some do, it
depends on the shape of their hymen. Dr Kostov makes out
the certificate, but Baya's sceptical as she watches them go.
She's sure the girl will be sent back to her parents, where
she'll spend the rest of her life. She says it's better to do like
some families and come for the certificate before the marriage,
'to make sure of the quality of the goods'. As for Dr Kostov,
he shakes his head. Islamic belief is ridiculous, certainly. But
so are all beliefs.

The Postmaster with the surgical boots raises a cautionary,
schoolmasterly finger when he hears of the virginity certificate.
Union representative and Party member, he's the hospital
theoretician. Not for him the Supervisor's lies and obscenities.
Foreign to him too is the Director's secondhand phraseology.
Instead: a simple worker on the ideological front.

He points out that in discussing such matters as virginity,
we're leaving the arena of our political discussions to enter
'the moral sphere'. The two are quite distinct. 'In the moral
field,' he tells me, 'I'm in favour of a strong line.' Just how
strong is indicated by a karaté chop with his right hand.

When we fought the French, explains the Postmaster, it was
for cultural independence too. It wasn't only political. What
we wanted to avoid was the situation that exists now in
Tunisia and Morocco. There, Western capitalism runs ram-
pant. Economic colonization has brought cultural enslavement
in its wake. Morocco and Tunisia have lost their identities.
They think and they live the way the West tells them to. The
same would have happened in Algeria, says the Postmaster,
had it not been for Islamic Socialism. In Tunis and Rabat,
girls are allowed to do as they please. They smoke tobacco,
they drink alcohol, and apparently they even go out with men
in the evening. The Postmaster admits that 'that' exists to a
small degree in Algiers, but if I look around I won't find any
of it in Kabylia.

Here lies the fundamental lesson of China. What was

Shanghai, the Postmaster asks me, during the heyday of Western imperialism? A city of depravity and vice. Take a walk in its streets today – as did the Algerian ambassador to China a few months ago. He lost his way and without thinking turned to a young girl for guidance. He was called to account by the Chinese police, for not having asked a young man instead. 'What has China done?' cries the Postmaster, 'she has built a wall outside, and Man inside!'

In Islamic Socialism, 'voyez-vous', woman is a mother. She's the keeper of the house, the educator of the children. She's the cornerstone of the family, its vertebral column. And families are the cells of which society is made. Naturally, provided these obligations are fulfilled, she may leave the house to work. She may, as the Postmaster puts it, 'participate in the national economic struggle'. But that is not the same as 'being allowed out'. A street, believes the Postmaster, is a straight line joining two places of work. It is not a place in its own right, for idling, dallying and striking up dubious relationships.

Once again, therefore, there is no discrimination. Men and women are equal, in their respective roles. Woman's role demands she be absolutely pure. If she is not, then she fails in her role and cannot possibly be man's equal. Thus the purity we demand of women is for their own sakes – and the best of them, 'the most politically conscious', Party members like Malika, will insist on it for themselves. Smiling at me, as sure of my approval as he is of theirs, the Postmaster promises that with his eight daughters, 'I'm like this' – the karaté chop.

Gunshots at dawn. It's the opening of the hunting season. The Postmaster will be putting his empty cartridge belt to use. He's going hunting wild boar next week in the forests beyond Azazga. He offers to take me with him. But by that time, I tell him, I shall have left.

I ask him how he manages to follow the game on those surgical boots. He's had them so long, he tells me, that he hardly notices them. The front half of both his feet were amputated when he caught frostbite in the Italian campaign during the second world war. The French pay him an 85 per cent disability pension. 'I fought in their army for six years,' he says doggedly, 'and, believe me, I know what socialism is.'

It's an empty, very hot, late September afternoon. The men have gone back to work in Algiers and France, the marriages are dwindling. It's very quiet. Dr Vasilev sits in the shade on the parapet, stroking the one-eyed cat and whispering affectionate words to it in Bulgarian. There's a simple curettage he asks me to do, on a woman from the mountains with more tattoos than anyone else so far. Crescents and crosses on her face, other designs on her elbows and hands. Vasileva's delighted. She hugs her and gives her a kiss. But the woman's unhappy. The curettage doesn't bother her. What she wants are the tattoos taken away.

I sit beside Tamara in the cool of the delivery room. She's spread her knees and she's concentrating hard on her enormous lap. She has a pile of gauze swabs there, and she's folding them into quarters. When she finishes each little pile, she gives it a blow with her fist, to press it into shape. She hums as she works, and mutters a Russian commentary to the various little incidents in her world – Baya passing through with the blood pressure cuff, a cleaner collapsed on the other chair, depressed because her little girl has a temperature of 40° C (Tamara tuts sympathetically), a whimpering premature baby parked on the scales, and commentary on events I can't recognize, the number and consistency of the swabs perhaps, or happenings in her internal life.

Fatma comes in, with her great-occasion face. She tells us to come and look. She's fetched her blue scarf and she's knotting it round her, to cover her face like a veil. We find the other cleaners and Baya standing at the window overlooking the courtyard. Under the sun outside – green garbage truck, mound of rubble with the retriever on top, an orthopaedic patient of Ivanov's staring from his crutches – there's an old 403 Peugeot station wagon with a tyre on its luggage rack. Its bonnet is propped up, and I recognise the Electrician in his overalls bending professionally over the engine. The car is backed against the Morgue, and there's a rough wooden coffin with an unsteady lid that two men are trying to slide inside. The Postmaster, in beret and surgical boots, seems to be supervising.

Scraps of the story from those around. In the coffin is the Postmaster's sixteen-year-old daughter. He'd arranged for her to marry a distant relative of theirs, a man of forty. So she took his hunting rifle this morning, and shot herself through the head. Says Baya: 'I'd never have the courage.' Says Fatma: 'She was beautiful.' I ask if she's seen her. 'We saw her little feet, Doctor,' says Fatma, 'she was beautiful, like your wife.' The girl's a legend already, and the cleaners are shrouded, a Kabyl chorus.

The coffin's in, but the car won't start. The Postmaster gets inside, the two younger men push at the open doors and then jump in. The station wagon only jolts to a stop. It was over-heated, the Electrician will explain to me afterwards, 'pa . . . pa . . . pa'. The coffin lid slides off, but there's only a white sheet to be seen inside. They try again, with the Electrician pushing too. The engine fires, and the car rumbles out of the courtyard.

21

REN   ͞E JUDIC͞

Out-Patients with Dr Kostov, and there's a knock on the door: an apparition, from the international capital city, from Paris, Rome, New York or London. Her hair, her clothes, her make-up, her walk – they're like nothing I've seen since I arrived. They command immediate homage. Dr Kostov's on his best behaviour, and offers her his chair, which she gracefully accepts. 'The orderly said you were very busy, and that a lot of people were waiting,' says the apparition in pure Parisian French, 'but . . .' She's right to leave it there. Who is it anyway who's going to be kept waiting? 'Je vous en prie, Mademoiselle,' says Dr Kostov. She opens her bag – it's in red leather and has gold buckles – and brings out Baralgin, a pain-killer that's sometimes used in the delivery room, only this time it's in suppository form for children. 'It's the latest from Hoechst,' says the apparition.

Her eyes are on Dr Kostov, levelly. She's the new breed of

liberated girl from the capital. Liberated to become a representative for a giant West German chemical firm. She has less
insight and more commitment than any representative I've
seen. Anything for a sale. Kostov and me on the gynaecological
table? Why not, so long as Maternity continues to push
Baralgin. She reels off the qualities of the different drugs she
produces from her handbag. A sample each for Dr Kostov
and me. The fake pharmacology is delivered in the pillow
whisper of the announcers at Orly Airport. Winded by the
suddenness of her arrival, by her cool and sophistication, Dr
Kostov's sex grin returns and he manages some sauce to his
'Mademoiselles'. He slips me a wink or two when she's not
looking. She produces one preparation that's designed to
counter 'the aggressions of modern life'. She calls it an
'aggressolytic'. I can't control my laughter, and she looks at
me severely. I think of the women outside, and ask if Hoechst
has anything for the aggressions of traditional life. She decides
to ignore me, and continues with the lesson memorized in
Algiers.

Baya watches her leave. Her eyes had been on the girl from
the moment she came into the room. 'There,' she says to me,
'you've seen a girl from Algiers. I don't like that kind of girl.'
But she keeps the pancreas extract, as she thinks it might help
her anaemia.

The workshops don't open till seven o'clock, and there's no
one about in the courtyard. The first vehicle to arrive: the
green refuse truck back from the dump. The second: the
Peugeot station wagon with the day's bread, French-style
bread but soft, the storekeeper says, because of the patients'
teeth.

The gardener squats among the shrubs, surveying his hose,
his colonial helmet reflecting the sun. He's as permanent a
feature of the garden as the plants he so assiduously waters, and
he's equally silent. He's a psychiatric patient. During the war,
he was with Boumediène on the Tunisian front. Those who
know him, like the Electrician, say that when the President
came on an official visit to Kabylia, it was the gardener's
greatest day.

183

I go down to the kitchen to collect our coffee. Dogs watch from the mound of rubble. The thin retriever gets to its feet, laboriously, like a camel, but refuses to come near. The Econome washes his Panhard outside the garage. The painter, wiry, ascetic and precise, stands in the doorway of his workshop, in beret and white overalls. Rough, unfinished coffins and tree-trunk sawing-blocks lie outside the carpenter's shop next door. The dogs that fight and prowl in the night have left their tracks on the gravel of the kitchen forecourt. Cats jump out of wicker baskets full of courgette ends, ants trail across the kitchen door.

I tap on the window. The Cook unbolts the door. 'Bonjour, Docteur!' He's holding the whisk in his right hand, he offers me his left forearm instead: 'Everything all right, Doctor? Nice weather, Doctor?' He whisks the powdered milk and talks of his brother, a lawyer in Morocco. A couple of summers ago, his brother came back to Algeria on holiday. He toured the oases by plane, he went down as far as Tamanrasset. This summer he's on holiday again, in America. A photograph of him standing by the Statue of Liberty: 'And here I am with my pots! Still, mustn't complain. That's life, isn't it, Doctor?' The cook hands me the milk bottle full of coffee, after wiping the sides carefully dry. He's a big man, like a bear, and old enough to be my father.

There are other men who work in the kitchen. They don't arrive till later, to prepare the lunch. I come over for an iced water from their fridge. They're outside in the shade, squatting round the wicket baskets, tailing courgettes, peeling garlic. We shake hands: 'Bonjour, Docteur', 'Bonjour, Docteur', 'Bonjour, Docteur'. It isn't true, I tell them. I'm not a doctor, I'm a student. They say it doesn't matter. As far as they're concerned, it's the same thing.

But even if I was a doctor, I ask, why use the word? Do I greet them with a 'Good morning, Kitchen Worker'? That's because it's no great life working in a kitchen, they say. To be a doctor is something special. Besides, they're not lavish with their 'Doctors' to the Bulgarians, the Russians and the Czechs. They're least generous of all when it comes to Algerians. Once, says the Cook, he had to see a private doctor in Algiers for something in his chest. He lined up in the surgery with fifteen others, shirts off. The doctor passed down the line with a stethoscope. He wasted no time afterwards, the way the Bulgarians do, writing out prescriptions. He had them ready-stencilled. All he did was sign them, and collect his dinars.

That's why the Algerian doctors won't work in the hospital. By staying in their surgeries in town, they can see eighty private patients a day, at fifteen dinars a time. That makes them £100 a day. 'It's a scandal in a country that's supposed to be socialist,' says the Cook. One of the others says: 'I'd go to a French nurse rather than an Algerian doctor any day.' The Cook explains that you must give the French their due: 'They colonized us, they tortured us, but at least they were proper doctors.'

Out-Patients with Dr Vasilev: there's hardly a woman we see who's not been to one of the private doctors in town first. Dr Vasilev never looks at his colleagues' letters – he reads *El Moudjahid* instead. I used to hold that against him. The town doctors were Kabyls, after all, able to talk to the women in their own language. They could get symptoms Dr Vasilev never could, they could explain to the women what a pelvic examination was and why it was necessary. They could – but they never did.

Instead, they use their Kabyl to charge each woman fifteen dinars before sending her on to hospital. Their letters come on fine headed paper, bearing their name, qualifications (all French, except for one) and surgery hours. The patient's name is an approximation. Sometimes it's only an initial. Age is rarely given. There's no record of the examination, for the good reason that none has been carried out. Each woman is new to the gynaecological table. There's not even the temperature, blood pressure or pulse. 'The town doctors are Kabyls,' Dr Vasilev is fond of saying, 'but they don't care about Kabyl women.' What better alibi for the Bulgarians.

A woman arrives who had a baby in Maternity four months ago. Two months after the birth, she bled for five days, and she's not had a period since. The doctor's letter suggests cancer as the likely cause. Dr Vasilev examines her and finds she's two months pregnant.

Fifteen dinars to see the private doctor, twelve to see Dr Vasilev (paid at the office at the entrance to the hospital), and some twenty-five more to collect the iron and vitamins from the chemist's in town. A few of the women are insured. They pay now, and a percentage is returned to them later. As for those rushed in for a curettage, they're treated free. The others just pay. And they're the upper crust of the population, those whose men have jobs. The rest, the certified poor, the registered paupers, get free medical care at the Dispensary down the road, a shack with an earth front where ultra-destitute children are always playing. It's run by two orderlies, and a doctor from Syria about whom I know nothing except what Baya once told me, that beside him, Dr Vasilev is Pasteur himself. Ever since, I've walked past that shack in awe.

The Cook is quietly spoken and reserved. There's one kitchen worker who's the complete reverse, excitable, gabbling his words and pawing me like a drunken man. Behind him, the others shake their heads, to tell me that this one is a little touched. But he's a clown, and he makes them laugh. One moment he's asking me to get pairs of Levi's sent over to him from London, promising me fantastic sums of money he can't possibly afford, the next moment his face has dropped and he's pleading for tranquillizers. I send him over to the doctors' office, where Dr Vasilev has many samples of Librium stacked in his cupboard.

You shouldn't pay that much attention to him, says the big Cook. Some mornings he'll be the happiest man in the world, other mornings he'll cry like a baby over nothing. Besides, there's no need to give him the Librium, he has a prescription for it already, and for stronger stuff, too, from the psychiatrist in Tizi-Ouzou.

The man's troubles date from the war against the French, when he was in the maquis between Bejaïa and Sétif. He was with some others, taking cover in the Kerata gorge, when they were cornered by some parachutists. They all got away, except for his brother. Then the parachutists flew over them in a helicopter. The commanding officer shouted down at them with a megaphone and just behind, in the open door of the helicopter, there was the man's brother, standing with his hands behind his back. They refused to surrender. The parachutists gave them ten minutes to change their minds. Then they tipped his brother out. He fell on the rocks right near him.

That's all very well, Doctor, says the Cook, but we've each got similar stories to tell and we've not become mad like he has. Besides, the man's troubles didn't begin till two or three years ago, five years after the country became independent. How do I account for that? Or do these things pile up in your brain, Doctor, without you realizing it, till one day they suddenly hit you: 'Pam!'? I say that I don't know, but perhaps they do. 'In that case,' says the Cook quietly, returning to his frying pan, 'we've only got to wait our turn.'

Before the siesta's over, we take a walk into town. Dead eyes in beheaded heads stare up at us from couches of furry hooves, butcher's meat boasting its animal origin. The letter-writers type on card-tables outside the Post Office, watched by clients in rags.

In the only shop that sells wine, or anything made from pork, where the customers are Europeans and the richer Algerians, we find the Econome behind us, with a shopping bag. He watches as we buy a dusty bottle of Mascara. From our excitement, and the way we've counted out the coins, he must have guessed we think it a luxury. He stops us on the way out, and asks us not to be offended. Any time we're short of money, he says, we must come to him: 'I know how it is, you only have to ask.'

The Director's playing dominoes in one of the smarter cafés. We take a coffee on the terrace, a few tables and chairs set out on the pavement. The table we choose is the only one left with any free seats. An old man in rags is already sitting there. The waiter, whose white jacket is grey and full of holes, whose trouser bottoms are in shreds, cries out at the old man to get away from us. The next table joins in. The old man has a festering mouth and a milky eye. He's not drinking anything. From inside the café, the Director looks up, gestures impatiently and returns to his game. The waiter strides over, like Dr Kostov to the labour bed. The old man gets to crumbling legs. But the gutter's not far enough. The waiter shoves him across the main street, between the open trucks from the 1930s with unsteady cattle in the back, to the gutter on the other side.

A man sits on the pavement a few feet from us, in patchwork clothes, pinching, pulling at his sleeve. We down our coffees, and move on. In front of the memorial to the dead of the revolution, the Electrican introduces us to friends. Beside us, there's a man in rags, unshaven and sunken-eyed, standing on one leg like those African herdsmen you see in photographs, except that there's no herd for him to mind. The crowded pavement pushes him this way and that. He always returns to the same position, babbling Kabyl. Nobody listens.

The big Cook touches my arm and says in his gentle way: 'Good evening, Doctor,' as people do when the siesta's over. He's walking into work, and he wants us to have a curdled milk with him. We go to a bar where there are men pouring the milk on to grains of cous-cous, and eating with a spoon.

We sit at a window table. Outside, there's a small round-about, where a gendarme's directing traffic from beneath a shaded platform. Behind him, six or seven storeys high, stands the fortress where he lives. The gendarmerie has battlements, and radio masts that spring skywards from its flat roof. It's surrounded by a high wall, with a gate guarded by armed sentries. There are jeeps in its courtyard, and lines of washing on the balconies of its upper floors, tended by women in veils. From time to time, uniformed men pass through the gate with raffia shopping bags. Even as they shop, the gendarmes are maintaining order. They're keeping their wives indoors.

Our milk arrives in a glass, with sugar sprinkled on top. The Cook tells us of the town as it was during the war. 'By day it was French,' he says, 'by night, it was ours.' In the kitchen, they were all involved. They gave out food and drugs to the men who came down from the mountains in the night. The orderlies would give the patients injections of salt water, and the real drugs would go out to the maquis. Soon they were all arrested and interned. After some hesitation, the Cook takes out his wallet and passes an important photograph over to Calie. It's a picture of him and the others, taken in prison, when they were all much younger – and much brighter. The big Cook puts the photograph back and sighs.

They lost their jobs. The excited one took to the maquis of Lesser Kabylia, in the hills behind Djidjelli. As for the Cook, he preferred to wait before deciding. There was a local guerrilla leader called Amirouche who came from Beni-Yenni, the village where the women's jewels are made. But the Cook found Amirouche 'fiercely Muslim'. He could never have worked with him. 'I'd have preferred the French,' he says.

Eventually, he found a group that suited him. He worked with them for a year or so before being caught again. They spent an unpleasant night bound hand and foot in a ditch, in the company of a drunken parachutist who kept taking pot-shots at them with his machine-gun, seeing how near he could get without actually hitting them. The Cook wasn't touched, but two of the others died before a senior officer arrived to confiscate the man's weapon. Then the Cook was taken away, to a little soap factory on the outskirts of Tizi-Ouzou where the French used to do their torturing. 'It was stupid,' says the Cook, 'because I had nothing to reveal.' It was done mainly with electricity.

A boy comes into the milk bar, without shoes, with a red lump the size of a golf-ball under one eye and a battered sombrero on his head. The waiter seizes him and throws him out into the street. The boy spins over in the dust, loses his sombrero, a Western. 'He's a thief,' explains the waiter. The boy picks himself up, looks at Calie and me with a stone in his hand. He tosses it, not through the glass as we were expecting, but through the open door, and runs away.

'This isn't the Algeria we dreamed of,' says the Cook. He wanted an end to private ownership, he wanted every man equal. He dreamed of work for all, and free medicine. The Cook's for the working class. It was always the poor who'd help the maquis in the hills. They'd give you everything they had. The bourgeoisie only helped at the end of the war, when they could see which side their bread was buttered. The Cook left the Party immediately the fighting stopped, and he hoped that everyone would do the same. He thought the Party ought to be dissolved, to stop it becoming a club for privileged people, each seeking his own reward for having fought against the French. But there were only a handful who thought like him. All the others were fighting for the top jobs. You come up against them today in the offices, you tip your cap to them, you say 'Yes, sir', 'No, sir': 'We live the way we're told to.' 'What's the Party today?' asks the Cook, 'it's the settlers all over again, Doctor. It's kif-kif, it's the same thing.'

We pick up our bottle of Mascara and walk with the Cook down the hospital avenue. The road's white and dusty. Stalls outside the main hospital gate sell fruit and drinks on ice. People come over to shake the Cook's hand.

Torture is a strange thing, he believes. At the time, of course, it hurts terribly. But somehow you can bear it, like a bullet received in the heat of battle, because it's in a good cause. The real pain comes afterwards. The Cook's become very sad. He has a long history behind him. He joined the Algerian Communist Party in 1941. They were very active, he says, holding underground meetings in the town. He used to put up posters in Algiers and Tizi-Ouzou. Once, in 1948, the police surprised him in the act and opened fire. He got away, but he goes 'pa ... pa ... pa' at the memory. Then he felt that the Communist Party had stopped being truly communist, and he left.

'Frankly, Doctor,' he says, 'I regret all my years as a militant.' He used to think the people wanted socialism. He thought so for years. But the present régime has proved him wrong. The people want men like they've got – 'Muslim fanatics like Boumediène, fascists like the men who run this hospital'. The government's 'Islamic Socialism' is a fraud. 'What has Islam got to do with Socialism?' asks the Cook bitterly. Boumediène mystifies the people, but they want to be mystified and in the end they've only themselves to blame. It'll be years before there'll be socialism in Algeria, decides the Cook, he and his children will be long since dead and buried.

There are times when he can't accept that, he says. There are times when he wants to take up the gun again. But what's the point, if the people aren't there behind you? He leaves us outside the stores. He's going back to his pots. He seems to wish he'd never spoken. It's only made him depressed.

There's a woman for Dr Kostov to curette in the afternoon. She's another employee of the Post Office, wearing European clothes and speaking perfect French. She's very weak and has to be carried in on a stretcher. That's usual enough with the women from the mountains, but it's surprising in a town Kabyl like her. Why did she wait till she'd lost so much blood? Why did she leave it till she could no longer walk? She says she didn't, her husband brought her to the hospital soon after the bleeding started. But the gate-keeper with the wooden leg told them to go back into town and get a letter from one of the doctors first. She fainted on the way there and had to lie out in the back. of the car. Her husband took his place in the queue of patients. When the doctor finally came out of his surgery, he took one look through the car window, charged fifteen dinars and sent them back to the hospital.

Dr Kostov's furious. He's furious at a man who's made his own work more difficult, and he's furious at a man who reaps where he only labours on stony earth. He leaves me to put up the drip and storms upstairs to threaten the Director on the phone that he'll leave the hospital if this ever happens again. The Director promises to see the gate-keeper immediately. But he makes no mention of the accomplice in town.

Dr Kostov takes his revenge. He's not impressed by the woman's French, by her job or her European clothes. She gets the full Kabyl treatment. The scowl as he asks her how long she's been pregnant, his resentment that she should ever have come to consult him, his hatred of her cervix which is just too tight for the first dilator he happens to pick up (it's flung back into the instrument box with an exclamation in Bulgarian), his repugnance as he runs dilators of ever-increasing calibre through the cervix, infinitely less gently than a man cleaning his pipe, and finally the curettage itself. The woman, whose face I don't look at, manages extraordinary self-control, which I measure by her hand that comes close to my arm when the pincers are applied, that rests on my arm during the dilatation, that holds me only gently as the curette raises red foam from the raw muscle. A quick swab around, with head half-averted, as if he were poking a fire, and Dr Kostov is out of the room with not a word.

A routine curettage, and I look for some criticism in this woman's eyes. I'm on the point of saying something, to dissociate myself from Dr Kostov. But she's not expecting it. She's accepted the whole thing, like she now accepts her Methergin. And in the office, Dr Kostov gives no more sign than usual that he expects a comment on his work. I ask him, at random, if there's much interest in psychoanalysis in Bulgaria. I repeat the word, and write it on one of the envelopes from the drug firms. He hasn't met the term. Instead, he points to his head and says: 'Electrodes.' Then he shakes, simulating a fit in electric shock treatment. I write 'Freud' on the envelope too, but he hasn't met the name. He says: 'Pavlov', and 'dogs'.

'What would you recommend for a touch of bronchitis, Doctor?' the Cook asked me when I came down for our coffee this morning. He was tipping the steaming black grounds into a wicker basket outside the kitchen door. Cats watched from the bushes for anything of value. There was obviously something on the Cook's mind, and I went away with the coffee annoyed with myself. Saying I knew nothing about bronchitis may have been the truth, but what use was it to him?

At lunch, he tells me he's not sure if it's bronchitis after all. He doesn't have a cough, and he doesn't bring up any phlegm. It was more 'an idea of bronchitis', he decides bizarrely, than bronchitis itself. He fries us a pan of courgettes and tomatoes. He hasn't even begun to set out our tray. Usually, it's all ready, and I just pick it up and go. He talks into the pan, turning the vegetables over in their oil. 'It's the nights that are difficult, Doctor.' He gets to sleep easily enough, but he wakes up early, soaking with sweat and with his heart racing. He can't get back to sleep again. He tries to think of quiet, peaceful things that'll make him relaxed, but he can't. He lies awake, his head full of the most terrible ideas that he knows perfectly well are stupid. But there's nothing he can do to stop them. He imagines he's ill, with a fatal disease of the chest, a heart condition, tuberculosis – sometimes even cancer.

Some days ago, he began borrowing the excited fellow's Librium, but it hasn't helped. He adds some boiled meat, bread and melon to our tray. I stand there holding it, while he tells me that the real trouble these last few days has been gas. He gets a lot of it, he says, and it builds up inside him. Sometimes he's able to pass it out the back passage – 'excuse me, Doctor' – and then he'll feel better. But at night he can't get rid of it. 'The gas presses on the tendons of my chest,' he says, 'and I can't get my breath.'

The Cook's turn must have come. We both agree that it's time for him too to visit the psychiatrist in Tizi-Ouzou.

There's a strange smell and a bustle from the curettage room. Vasileva's hard at work inside, her hair under a plastic bonnet, mopping the floor with a bucket of bleach and scrubbing down the table with Ajax. The excitement's greater still in the office, where Dr Vasilev cries out that . . . he'll be examining a German woman this afternoon! She's the wife of the Kabyl doctor in town who qualified in West Germany. She rang at lunch for an appointment. She's 'very sympathetic', he says, and he'll introduce me to her. He even cries out her name, in anticipation.

The curettage room is shining. Vasileva's taken off her cleaner's bonnet and exchanged it for a nurse's starched cap. She's also changed her coat, and she smoothes out the creases over her bosom. Dr Vasilev's calling me, in his happiest voice. What can it be for, but an introduction? The doctor's in his thirties, perhaps a little overweight, yet cooler than we are in a light cotton shirt and trousers. Blond German wife, Vasileva's delight. Dr Vasilev's overcome with joy: 'We thought you weren't coming!' All this, and more, for a man he's criticized to me so many times. He disappears with Vasileva and the German woman into the curettage room.

Dr Kostov and I stay behind with the doctor in the office. There are some moments of awkward silence. The doctor's manner is agreeable, a little 'ah' as he sits down. But Dr Kostov's fed-up, bored, it's plainly obvious. His day hasn't been made by the surprise visit of his Kabyl colleague. Not for Dr Kostov now a cosy medical chat, a scientific conversazione. I can count on him for that. Solicitously, the doctor asks how things are going. He gets a frank and surly answer. Dr Kostov doesn't like his work. There's a lack of staff, and what staff there is, is hopeless. But he doesn't criticize Dr Vasilev. The doctor puts on a doctor's face: he understands, he understands.

Dr Kostov has no respect for him. Partly it's because he thinks Dr Vasilev has, partly it's because he couldn't respect an Algerian anyway, even a rich one. His contempt is written clearly on his face, in the line of his mouth, in his friendliness towards me. The silence returns, and Dr Kostov enjoys it. The Algerian begins to nod his head profoundly over nothing, from professional habit. I ask him if the situation couldn't be relieved by local doctors abandoning their town practices to work in the hospital. Dr Kostov's so pleased, I can feel him laughing beside me. The doctor moves his lips in plush concern: 'You've raised a most delicate question.'

His wife comes out of the curettage room, hugged by Vasileva. We accompany them down the path to a gleaming Citroen saloon. Handshakes through the window, and the car floats upward on its oil suspension. The shark face points into town, back to medicine. The belly is exposed – soft, white and ripe. Gutted by one savage slash from the big Cook's knife, it would spew its dinars forth. But it slips away unscathed, across the gravel of the hospital avenue, the exhaust whispering into the hot afternoon air: 'a most delicate question, dear colleague, most delicate indeed'.

It's getting dark much earlier. The big Cook's nights are lengthening. When the others have gone home, and he's left alone in the kitchen after six, left with the keys, those thoughts begin to prey on him. He feels better upstairs, where he can see people. He walks to the end of the long, high corridor, takes the goods lift to the surface and stands watching the cleaners bring the kitchen trolleys back from the wards. What exactly does he see? Trolleys, silver shining trolleys, pushed by women in blue, between the hospital cats, licking themselves in the bushes and waiting for the jolt that will bring down a piece of anything, tomato, bread or meat. The trolleys come towards him, past the laundry and the Morgue, over the gravel where the Econome washes his Panhard in the mornings. The mechanics and the morgue-keeper wave good-night. The Cook waves back and leans against the wall in his apron, watching the trolleys come in and trying not to think of TB and cancer.

He's been to the psychiatrist in Tizi-Ouzou and he was very impressed. The man's 'a proper doctor – he spent nearly two hours with me, going over everything'. He's done a lot for the Cook's morale. Nonetheless, the Cook had doubts over some aspects of the treatment. After his experiences with the French, he was reluctant to submit to shock treatment. Electricity to the brain, to treat electricity to the testicles. I used to imagine the big Cook's body, jerking helplessly to the current. He's happier with the drugs, and he's taking them as prescribed. I go with him to the kitchen, snatch a drink of iced water from the fridge and collect our tray. He brings out a little bottle from his apron and asks me, Doctor, for my opinion of the drug he's taking. I recognize the name of Hoechst's 'aggressolytic', and I have to tell him it's exactly what he needs.

'We prefer the woman who gives birth to a pilot, to the woman who becomes a pilot herself.'

Mouloud Kassim,
Member of the Revolutionary Council

El Moudjahid's *day begins at the Post Office, where it arrives from Algiers early in the morning with a brown wrapper around it addressed to Dr Vasilev. At nine it's collected by the Postmaster and stuffed along with the other mail into his old army bag, to be given a bumpy ride back to the hospital on those surgical boots. It reaches us from Paediatrics across the courtyard and it can be expected any time between ten and ten-thirty, hopefully before Dr Vasilev leaves for Out-Patients.*

It's unwrapped, usually in the Postmaster's presence, and its front page is read hurriedly, without being exhausted. Then it's folded and trailed along the walls, snapped over the rungs of the radiators, all the way to Out-Patients. There it's opened out over the desk, to fill the gaps between patients and often to substitute for patients when they're actually there. It's carried to lunch in Dr Vasilev's coat, and brought back to the office after the siesta. It can be used for swotting a fly, for tickling the one-eyed cat, or as a screen if the Supervisor happens to glare in from the courtyard. El Moudjahid's *day is ours.*

22

Today's the day, I'd forgotten. Calie's reminded by Vasileva, who waves as she pulls in the washing from her kitchen window. All week, the excitement's been building up. Dr Vasilev's been promising orange groves and sea, in the fishing village of Dellys. Announced on the day of Calie's arrival, before she'd even got down from the motorcycle, it's the long-awaited 'excursione alla mare'! How many times have I been reminded since? How many times, in the middle of a ward round, or in Out-Patients when we've been together at the sink, has Dr Vasilev tugged on my trouser leg' (so it has seemed to me later) and begun, in a low and tremulous voice, 'On Saturday, you, your nice little wife, Madame Vasileva . . . and me, of course!'? How many times have I stood there, looking down on the top of his head (sparse black hair on leathery scalp, odour of tobacco and oil), waiting for the cycle to complete itself, with the inexorability of one of the donkey's cries: 'in the car of our very sympathetic Bulgarian friends'? Watching him creep up my body in a series of jerks, as if each word were releasing a catch, in a curious clockwork un-folding: 'gently . . . doucement . . . dolcemente'? And at the conclusion, having his eyes staring upwards into mine, full of the same joy, undimmed by any amount of repetition, stethoscope shaking coastwards like a diviner's twig: '. . . to DELLYS!'

The early afternoons, when the dry blades of grass are motionless in the garden, when the heat crushes the dogs on the mound of rubble, when there are just the crickets, and the scraps of silver paper form a little heap on the office desk: 'It's cool', cries Dr Vasilev from the depths of his director's chair, 'in Dellys!' The very name evokes lilies and delight, it's a Garden of Eden. Its l's already ripple for us. Dellys is Dr Vasilev's Pompeii, it's where he recuperates from the uproar of the hospital, it's where he becomes himself.

After lunch, at about three, we hear a car braking on the gravel below. Dr Vasilev calls up to us (not too loud, there are people still sleeping). We collect our swimming things and hurry down. The car's a Peugeot 404, with yellow CT plates. The driver is a young agricultural engineer. His wife is enormous and blond, curls and baby fat. Dr Vasilev presides over the introductions with enthusiasm. We are his 'very sympathetic English friends'. The new couple are as friendly as he promised. The engineer insists that I come in the front with him. Calie sits behind, on one of Vasileva's knees.

We stop in town to buy petrol and lemonade. Picnic baskets in the boot. Small boys watch the car being filled. Dr Vasilev pays. He has a clean shirt, and newly pressed trousers. Men work nearby on the new mosque. Crates of vegetables from the market career down the slope on rollers, chased by boys in rags. Buses with long snouts, prewar Citroens, leave the main square for villages in the hills. We spot the Econome in his Panhard. He waves, and I say that I think he's different from the others. 'Certainly,' says Dr Vasilev, but without conviction. It's not that he disagrees, it just doesn't concern him now. He doesn't want to talk about the hospital, and I drop the subject. Why spoil things for him, he's so happy to be away, riding in the back of the car with the windows down, in the company of all his friends, nursing the small camera on his lap.

'Orange groves!'—rows of small trees with tilled earth between. The fruit are small, and Dr Vasilev says that's a shame. We'll have left before the time comes to pick them. We pass vines and lemon trees. It's all he promised in that first letter to me in England. From the hill above Dellys, we see vast stretches of empty beach. At the entrance to the town, there's a police control point. But it's for Algerians only. The gendarmes see the yellow plates and wave us past.

We drive down the twisting main street. There's a mosque with old men and cripples outside, a main square, a bus station, and there are boys everywhere. We reach the engineer's apartment, in a block at the other end of town. It has a fore-court with giant green rushes, and a view over the sea. The water's calm and little boats float beneath the harbour walls.

The engineer invites us inside, and closes the shutters. The apartment isn't a lot different from the Vasilevs' in the hospital, with the same light sparse furniture and wooden floor. We sit down, a little uncertainly, with our swimming things on our laps. Then Vasileva and the engineer's wife catch Calie by the arms and lift her into the kitchen, female vigilantes.

We men stay in the living-room. On the bookshelf there's an engineering manual in Bulgarian, and a pamphlet in English on folk-dancing, put out by the Bulgarian Ministry of Tourism. There's also a stack of *Paris-Match* and *Jours de France*, a more complete collection than the Vasilevs'. The engineer tells me he used to have them all, every issue of the last eighteen months, but he's lent several of them out. He's fitted his radio with a special aerial. It crackles through the stations, staying for a long while on Rome for Dr Vasilev, who'd cried out: 'Italia!' I work through the magazines and think of Calie crushed in the kitchen. Dr Vasilev sits back on the settee and smokes. And smokes. Suddenly, he sits forward and announces to me with his arms outstretched: 'DELLYS!'

I'm dying to be out there beyond the closed shutters, explor-ing its streets and cafes, and swimming in its sea. But Dr Vasilev is anything but frantic. His adverb for the way he takes his pleasures is 'doucement – gently'. We'd drive to Dellys, he used to tell me, 'doucement', and so we did, at never more than 70 kilometres an hour. 'Doucement' was how we'd spend the day on the beach, 'doucement' was how we'd swim.

Calie's released from the kitchen, her face red. Vasileva and the engineer's wife follow her soon afterwards, and get them-selves ready. They change their shoes and dab powder on their cheeks and nose. Vasileva arranges a white shawl over her shoulders and we step outside, down to the harbour. It's already dark. Pipes and drums reach us from the town. We take an anisette in the restaurant on the jetty, and Vasileva smiles good-evening to her opposite number, also in a shawl, among a party of Russian engineers at the next table. It's an evening out, rather an occasion, and she's looking every bit like a Bulgarian queen mother.

The restaurant owner's wife delivered in Maternity last year. He comes over to shake Dr Vasilev's hand. Then, with a grand gesture and peremptory tone of voice, he calls into the kitchen in Kabyl. A sweating cook comes running out, bearing a magnificent fish, called a 'loup', on a silver tray. The proprietor offers it to Dr Vasilev with a flourish. The loup still glistens from the sea. 'I'll have it grilled for you!', cries the proprietor. But Dr Vasilev shakes a feeble head. The loup is *my* 'Dellys!', and he must refuse. The fish only dazzles him by its excellence, and he's overcome by the celebrity treatment. Hoarsely, without looking at the proprietor or the fish, he mumbles something about his wife having already made his evening meal. The loup is whisked away, and we get meekly to our feet, to eat yoghurt soup and stuffed peppers in the flat, exotic enough for Calie and me, but home food for Dr Vasilev, his shepherd's pie and peas.

He's a scarcely credible picture in the morning. He's like a man rising for the last time. He croaks: 'Good morning', and coughs until breakfast. Calie's spared by the women and we wait, swopping magazines, till French toast and coffee arrive from the kitchen.

During breakfast and after, Vasileva and the engineer's wife work through issue after issue of *Paris-Match* and *Jours de France*. They are a devoted readership. Their interest is deep and genuine, in a way the West has lost. They discuss the pictures, the people, the advertisements. They're as familiar with them as we are, except that they believe in them more. Aristotle Onassis and Jackie Kennedy aren't only King and Queen of the West, they rule over their world too, more securely still, with all their princes and princesses, courtiers and courtesans, counsellors and jesters. It's also the world of Zora and the apparition from Hoechst. Toy women and sparkling cookers, in the court of Queen Jackie. Communist and Muslim alike, swallowed by the universal West.

Green rushes dwarf me in the forecourt outside, and I dwarf Dr Vasilev as we have our pictures taken together by Vasileva.

She fluffs the first, and Dr Vasilev braces his shoulders for the second. Then he takes his wife, with her arm round Calie. We get into the car with the raffia picnic baskets and drive 'doucement', a mile or so along the coast, on a largely unmade road that's full of holes. We come across another engineer and his family, a coincidence that delights Dr Vasilev. He describes them to us as 'a very sympathetic Bulgarian family', and he's just as proud introducing us to them. They have a flat tyre and we help them change the wheel. Dr Vasilev insists on another photograph together in front of the car.

We park and go down to the beach. Dr Vasilev rolls up his trousers and paddles. The older engineer builds a sand-castle for his children. The younger engineer does push-ups on the sand. The wives sit three on a rug and knit, marching through the stitches needles in unison.

For once, the weather doesn't last. The sky becomes overcast and a cold wind begins to blow. We're forced back to the apartment when it actually begins to rain. Others follow. The flat becomes a refuge for all the Bulgarians of Kabylia on their Sunday outing. Every other minute, the door opens on a wet engineer and his family, till the forecourt's full of cars with yellow plates and there are more than thirty people in the living-room, a ghetto of Bulgarian engineers. Vasileva steps across with glasses for everyone. Spirits are high. Toasts and flushed faces – the bad weather's spoiled nothing for them.

Rain on the sea, rain on the Turkish ramparts, and I wonder if there's rain on the hospital, or perhaps it's too far away. It gets dark, and the flat begins to clear. Soon they've all gone, and it's our turn to leave. Relief, disguised as contentment. 'Did you enjoy our little excursion?' asks Dr Vasilev happily. Very much, we tell him.

I wonder, did he? He's silent during the ride back to the hospital in the dark. The boisterousness of the others seems to have left him quite flat. He hadn't joined in their conversation of barks and bellows, thick brown hands punching fleshy knees. After the first couple, he'd even stopped introducing us. Overwhelmed, he'd kept to himself, on the settee, reading the fresh *Oggi* that had arrived on Saturday. And the sea, had he really enjoyed that? The young engineer had called for him to join us: 'Doctor! Doctor!' He kept promising he'd come, like he keeps promising he'll take out the motorcycle. It's sadder to watch him relax than it is to see him work. What was 'Dellys'? Like the hysterography long ago, like the silver paper, like the game of the seven mistakes, it didn't seem to have a point. As we come near the hospital, we're passed by a cortège of hooting cars. 'Eh!' goes Dr Vasilev, 'in nine months, work for us!'

23

Children cry all night in the ward above. As dawn breaks it becomes much worse, and we run the bath during coffee to blot out the noise. It'll stay a background to the whole day, a chorus of tears, with shrieks reaching nightmare pitch. During the round with Dr Vasilev, Baya will say she couldn't sleep. After the siesta, she'll say it again.

I find Dr Vasilev at the desk on the landing. Baya's called him to examine a baby. There's no particular reason for him to be sitting here, but it happens to be halfway between his apartment and the patient's room. He flicks some ash across the desk, sighs, and gets to his feet. We traipse down the corridor to the woman's room. She looks anxiously up at him and speaks rapidly in Kabyl. 'Ai, Madame,' goes Dr Vasilev wearily. He doesn't want her words. But she rattles on, and he pays no attention. 'Dellys!' has done nothing for him.

The skin on the baby's head is flaky and dry. When Dr Vasilev gets closer (his technique being to keep the cigarette in the non-examining hand), he finds the pressure high in the spaces between the bones of the skull. He says there must have been a haemorrhage. 'Why wasn't it noticed earlier'? he asks Baya, his voice a little raised. Baya says the mother only told her about it an hour ago. 'Is the mother a nurse?' asks Dr Vasilev, 'it's your job.' Baya says it isn't her fault, it's Malika's. Dr Vasilev's not going to argue, though the word itself is a gross exaggeration. He and Baya have not been crossing swords, they've been flailing each other with blades of grass. 'Eh,' goes Dr Vasilev, staring into the empty temperature chart, 'you always blame the others.' And to me, he says:

'I'll call another meeting!' We shuffle through the remaining rooms.

The morning belongs to a girl of sixteen. She had convulsions when she delivered, the day we left for Dellys. Now she looks through us, like that woman out of the dark corner in Baya's village. She throws her baby on the bed and bursts into tears. She runs her fingers through her uncombed hair and calls for her mother. She pulls at the other women, wailing for her brother – one moment she says we've killed him, the next she's wanting us to find him for her, to fetch him from work so that he can ask us why we've left her baby naked. She'll be present all morning, wandering distraught through Maternity, her spotty face swollen from convulsions and tears. 'Keep quiet and get back to bed,' cries Malika from the desk, 'or else we'll tie you up.' The girl stumbles on, past the cardboard boxes of the night, returning at intervals to her room to lay her head on the mattress in fits of inconsolable weeping.

Dr Vasilev waits in the office for the mail to arrive. Baya leans against the metal cupboard, blood pressure cuff in one hand, Out-Patients' Register in the other. We all catch the unmistakable approach of those surgical boots. Dr Vasilev brightens up as the Postmaster swings the bag off his back like Santa Claus.
What is it that Dr Vasilev likes most about *El Moudjahid*? The game of the seven mistakes, undoubtedly. But at a deeper level, what he likes even more is getting the newspaper at all. He enjoys expecting *El Moudjahid* to arrive. He greets it with an 'Ah!', and he's never without a smile and a bonjour for 'Mr Postmaster!' He's the only doctor in the hospital with a subscription to the Algerian national daily, and the Postmaster treats him with a gruff sort of friendliness.
Before slipping the wrapper off, he recites it half-aloud: '*El Moudjahid* – Algiers, Dr Vasilev – Maternity.' And then, as he opens it out, he seems to enjoy its familiarity. The unchanging title, white on a black-speckled background, sandwiched between an advertisement for Hoechst every Wednesday and one for Satuca, the nationalized hydraulic engineering company (taps, pipes, canalizations), every Friday. The births

and deaths on page 2. Popeye, Scamp and the crossword puzzle. The jokes in the 'Laughter Corner', the serial on the back page (Vasileva's favourite): 'The Barbed Wire of Life!' with its drawing to illustrate the theme of the day. The bizarre picture and caption that immediately catch his eye: '*Rhinos are not Cows*!' When cows see a train going by, says *El Moudjahid*, we all know how they can't help looking up. '*But these rhinos in Whipsnade Zoo, England, are a different kettle of fish!*' When the little train passes by with all its passengers waving, '*tugged along by Chevalier, the old-soldier locomotive who weighs 20 tons*', the Whipsnade rhinos don't even glance up. Instead, they browse away quietly in their field. Dr Vasilev flourishes the picture before my eyes. It shows a herd of rhinos, turning their backs on a miniature train.

All this is what Dr Vasilev enjoys about *El Moudjahid*, innocence and unexpectedness within a fixed and familiar framework.

The jeep draws up just as we're leaving for Out-Patients, with two different gendarmes. They've picked up a woman in front of the mosque. 'She's got something in her belly, Doctor,' says the senior officer confidently. He hands over the usual form from the Gendarmerie Nationale.

The woman follows us into the curettage room and takes off her veil and shawl. She surprises us by speaking good French. She's no trouble to examine. She's not pregnant, and her womb is even a little on the small side. 'When was your last period?' asks Dr Vasilev. 'Three years ago', says the woman. 'How old are you?' 'Forty-nine,' she says, 'I did tell them, but . . .' Dr Vasilev withdraws his fingers and whistles his sad little whistle.

On the way to Out-Patients, Baya and Dr Vasilev talk about the mosquitoes last night in the doctors' building. There were millions of them. With the mosquitoes and the dogs, how could they sleep? Their sandals drag.

A girl tells Baya that she's vomiting in the mornings. She has a pleasant voice, and pretty eyes above the veil. She lifts her arms and unties the knot at the back of her head. Under the veil there's a huge goitre, a colloid ledge for her chin to rest on. Baya tells her to take off her pants. The girl doesn't answer, she just turns away her head and covers her eyes with her arm. Baya asks her a second time and the girl takes her pants down. She won't look at us and when she gets up on the table, she twists away, trying to leave her genitals far behind. There's an awful moan and a deep nail mark on Baya's arm as Dr Vasilev's fingers go in. Her cervix is soft as a lip, instead of hard as a nose. She's two months pregnant. Baya translates. 'If it's what Allah wills,' says the girl.

Diagnosis is never a problem for Dr Vasilev. Baya pulls a woman's robe from between her legs: 'Ai, ma!' When she carries water, says Baya, the woman gets a pain in her back. Dr Vasilev puts his fingers in and cries to the woman to let her belly go soft. Then he withdraws, and it's my turn. He keeps between the thighs to stop them from closing, until I'm safely in. Then he takes off his glove, goes to his desk, resumes his cigarette and writes out the prescription. 'Retroverted uterus,' he says. But I know better than to ask if that's really the cause of her pain, as I did during my first sessions with him. 'Yes,' Dr Vasilev used to say, and that was all. He had no explanation to offer, not even a bogus one. As for the treatment, it's iron and vitamins. 'In Bulgaria,' says Dr Vasilev, 'I treat retro-version with warm baths. But here . . .' For once, Kabyl women aren't losers. The iron and vitamins can only do them good.

When he's asked to examine a woman, what exactly does Dr Vasilev do? He goes over to the basin and picks up his glove. It's inside out, because that's the way it comes off. He turns it back, but that's not enough. The fingers don't come out, the glove's all shrivelled and wet. There's this little trick: blow into the glove, then twirl it several times between your fingers, like the greengrocer with a bag of tomatoes. The air runs down into the fingers, and they pop out one after the other. Dr Vasilev then dips his right hand into an old powdered milk tin, where there's some cotton wool impregnated with talcum powder. He pulls on the glove, pressing it down between his fingers with his left hand. A squirt from the bottle of alcohol, and the enrobing of the specialist hand is complete.

One woman has been sent in with a Kabyl nurse from a small hospital in the mountains. She's young and very thin. She's so weak she can scarcely walk. But from the nurse, there's complete indifference. In fact there's more, a lack of sympathy in face and manner, a touch of brutality in every gesture, designed to show us her 'professionalism', her 'experience of patients' and how far she wishes herself to be considered from this illiterate peasant. The letter she brings from the Czech doctor says the woman suffers from painful, scanty periods. No other information is given, and Dr Vasilev adds none of his own. He asks no questions about the woman's general health. He examines her pelvis and declares that all is normal. Even the breasts aren't considered part of the examination of a woman. Dr Vasilev's fond of saying to the patients who complain of anything anywhere else: 'This, Madame,' – both hands over his lower abdomen – 'is gynaecology. All the rest' – hands running over his chest and head – 'is general medicine!' We lift the woman back on to the stretcher. She's been married two years, she tells us, and she's very unhappy with her husband and mother-in-law. She doesn't eat, and she doesn't want children. But Dr Vasilev's not interested. It's not 'gynaecology'.

Between each woman, he sits motionless before *El Moudjahid*, face hidden behind his glasses. When he talks, it's the minimum necessary, and he takes a breath between every phrase. He needs the fortifiers he prescribes more than any of his patients.

The last woman of the morning is fifty-five and large. Blue crosses are tattooed on her forehead and chin. She's never been to a doctor before and she doesn't know what's coming when Baya asks her to take down her pants. She steps out of them without a murmur. The crotch is stained where she's been bleeding. She starts by climbing on to the table from the side, causing it to tip over towards her. Baya rescues her in time, and shows her the way up the steps. But instead of climbing them, the woman sits on them. She has no idea what we want from her. She sees no connection between the table and her own body. Baya shows her the stirrups for her knees. But the woman only puts both knees over one stirrup. Baya catches a knee, to pull it away from the other. The woman begins to see what the point of all this might be. She holds down the robe between her legs. Dr Vasilev puts on his glove, but it's practically impossible to examine her. The robe is constantly being thrown in front of his eyes. He has a perfunctory poke, and he begins that infinitely sad little whistle. Drawn face between massive dirty thighs, everything he touches must remind him of disillusion and defeat.

'Olé!' cries the Electrician, clicking his thumbs and launching into an absurd cha-cha-cha round the desk in the deserted doctors' office, 'there's going to be a party tonight!' I've just told him the news: we're on the eve of Bulgaria's national holiday. 'Olé!'

He slumps back into my chair, acutely depressed. 'What a miserable lot they are,' he says bitterly. Take any Kabyl off the street, and he'll tell you more about life than a Bulgarian, Russian or Czech. They come here no better than savages, says the Electrician. They're butchers and peasants, people who don't know how to live. If a Bulgarian wants to enjoy himself, he drinks. It's Algeria that makes them civilized. 'What miseries they are,' he says disgustedly.

He's full of last year's memories, when he was 'bored enough' to attend their soirée in Tizi-Ouzou. 'Put it away!' – when I show him the printed card I received from the hands of Dr Vasilev, inviting Calie and me to tonight's celebration of the Twenty-Sixth Anniversary of the Bulgarian Socialist Revolution. 'Never in a million years!'—when I tell him the Prefect, the Vice-Prefect, the Mayor and the Captain of the Gendarmerie will all be there. He agrees they may all have been invited, but they'd never go themselves. They'll send one of their secretaries instead, he says, if they send anyone at all. Last year there was no food, and there wasn't even any drink, the Bulgarians are so mean.

The Electrician hurries away before Dr Vasilev arrives, brighter than he was this morning. He's showered and changed, and he's left his white coat in his apartment. 'This afternoon,' he tells me, 'you will be the consultant!' He's leaving me in charge. It's my consolation for not being invited to their celebration lunch in Tizi-Ouzou. But that's because it's official, he explains, it's for Bulgarians only. This evening will be for everyone.

His spirits are high. He's looking forward to the meal, to the speeches, to the soirée later on. 'Me,' he announces excitedly, 'I am a Communist!' He tells me he's been a Party member for the last twenty years.

Dr Kostov too has had a shower and change of clothes. But he's not rejoicing. I ask him if he's also in the Communist Party. He's not, and he never has been. The very idea makes him laugh. 'In England, you call it Capitalism,' he says, 'in Bulgaria, we call it Communism. It's kif-kif, it's the same thing!'

He stretches for *El Moudjahid* and stares at the wrecked jet on the front page: 'Look what the Palestinians have done to that Boeing!' he roars, 'millions and millions of dollars – and they've just blown it up!' They must be anarchists, he decides. It's not surprising that Hussein wants to kill them. After all, he's a king. Dr Kostov studies the photograph and begins to chuckle. He has no quarrel with the Palestinians, over there in the Middle East. Their exploits make amusing reading.

Dr Vasilev makes no comment. He'll never discuss anything in *El Moudjahid*, even when we're alone together. He'll only exclaim over a news item from England or Bulgaria – a serious car accident, a third place in the world volleyball championships. Only once has he ever said anything, and that was about Khrushchev: 'That man made many mistakes.' I asked him what they were. Dr Vasilev went 'eh', and that was all. He's no more a Party member than he is a gynaecologist. Like in medicine, he's forgotten almost all he's been taught.

They leave, by separate cars – Dr Vasilev first, in the Peugeot 404 of the very sympathetic engineer from Dellys, Dr Kostov a few minutes later, in a white Mercedes-Benz with CT plates belonging to a friend of his own. The meal they'll be eating won't be cous-cous, he tells me before he leaves. It's being served in an Algerian restaurant, but it's been prepared all morning by Kostova, Vasileva and the other Bulgarian wives of Kabylia. Otherwise, Dr Kostov wouldn't be going.

When he first arrived in Algeria, he came without his wife and he lost 20 kilos before she joined him. He lived entirely on the contents of tins from France, heated in pans from Bulgaria. He's still never eaten out in a restaurant, even in Algiers. If he goes to a café, he's careful to choose a bottled beer from France and whenever he's been invited to eat in an Algerian's house, he's refused, except on the one occasion when the wife was European.

The Electrician watches the cars drive away down the hospital avenue. He asks me which restaurant they're going to. The Baghdad, I tell him. 'Typical!' he cries, and asks me: 'Would you choose the Baghdad for your Christmas?' I tell him I have no idea, I don't know the restaurants in Tizi-Ouzou. He brushes me aside with the assurance that 'of course you wouldn't, you'd go to the Djurdjura. But that's too expensive for them. They're worse than the J . . .' – the Electrician corrects himself – 'they're worse than the Egyptians.'

Dr Kostov's the first back. He didn't eat a lot, and he left during the speeches. He prefers the curettage room, and there are women waiting. One who says she's thirty-five, and so she might be, except that in Europe she'd make an old fifty. She's lifted on to the table, for one of her last curettages before the menopause brings her peace. The next woman speaks excellent French, her husband's an officer in the Algerian army. He's away doing a spell of military training in Moscow, so it's his brother who brings her in. It's her third curettage, she says, she had an anaesthetic for the others. Dr Kostov scoops the black clot from her vagina as if he were doing a manual removal of impacted faeces. So I tell her: she mustn't be afraid, this is Dr Kostov from Sofia, he has a reputation that extends beyond Kabylia, he's known as the fastest, gentlest man with the curette in the whole of Algeria. I say it with such conviction that she believes me. Dr Kostov doesn't relent, he doesn't smile or acknowledge her in any way. But he is quick, and she never even screams.

Then a girl arrives by ambulance from a town 40 kilometres away, bleeding heavily from a torn hymen. Dr Kostov does the stitching, and the technician brings a pint of blood from the laboratory. Minutes after the transfusion begins, the girl's seized by some kind of fit, teeth chattering, shaking uncontrollably, drenching her sheet in sweat, terrifying the other women. We stop the transfusion. The technician swears he made no mistake with the grouping. But I'd never have blood from the laboratory. I'd be happier with Rheomacrodex, like Dr Kostov with his bottled beer from France.

It's marvellous to be in a cinema again, especially such a good one. It belongs to the film club of Tizi-Ouzou, there's an exhibition in the foyer of old projectors and gramophones, there are stills on the walls from famous pictures, including one of James Dean from *Giant*, and there's a letter from Chabrol, the French director, saying it was one of the most sympathetic film clubs he'd visited. We're determined to come back again, but there's an evening of Bulgariana to sit through first.

We sit next to the Vasilevs, with Dr Kostov and his wife behind, nearer the exit in case there's a call from the hospital. He's on duty tonight. No sign of the notables, or any of their representatives. Not even the Director of the hospital is there, though I recognize one of his secretaries at the back. It's almost all Bulgarians, and many of them we've already seen, Sunday afternoon in the apartment at Dellys, refugees from the rain.

Picture a gathering of engineers and doctors anywhere in the world. Subtract the alcohol. Now add that they're from Eastern Europe, come to celebrate their liberation by the Russians in 1944. It's sadder than any funeral. 'They're dead,' the Electrician said this afternoon.

A paper of pitiless orthodoxy is read by the agricultural engineer whose tyre we helped to change on the coast road at Dellys. Fascism has been defeated and socialism achieved, he tells us, thanks to the unfailing support of the Soviet Union. A list of industrial achievements follows. We're assured in an unsmiling monotone that today is an occasion of boundless joy for the people of Bulgaria.

Lights out, and a short on the Black Sea. The credits ripple, and Dr Vasilev points out with pride how that suits the subject matter. Endless shots of waves breaking over Bulgarian rocks.

Churches and monasteries, ecclesiastical treasures that testify to the greatness of Bulgaria's past. Dr Vasilev pulls on our arms, and repeats all the mileages of his motorcycle excursions. He enjoys the film immensely.

He's less enthusiastic about the feature, possibly afraid it might offend us. It's a political fable, about the abortive insurrection of 1923. It opens with a summary execution of partisans on the edge of a river. They cry: 'Long live the Soviet Union!' before the shots ring out. The film has fat, cartoon capitalists, with fur-collared capes and golden telephones. In some hysterical scenes, waxed moustaches twitching. dimpled hands trembling, eyes deformed by intrigue, we see them darkly plotting the overthrow of the workers and peasants who'd been inspired by the Bolshevik revolution. There's a priest, a Greek Orthodox Fagin, hammed up to the skies, flitting silently down the corridors of the palace in his cloak, always ready to bless a capitalist. He's there to signify God's delight when the social-democrat throws in his lot with the palace, revealing himself the social-fascist he always was. There are workers and peasants, with iron faces and iron brains, possessed by an inborn hatred of the capitalists.

And, of course, the routine surprise of any Bulgarian film, stepping out from behind a row of mine-workers, there's: 'George Dimitrov!' As the leader, as the intellect of the insurrection, he can't be dressed in the cap and overalls of the workers. Even in the mountains, he's dressed in a conservative tweed suit, waistcoat, collar and tie. Nor is he ever seen with a gun, only a pen. He possesses unexplained military genius, and all the Party cadres make the correct tactical decisions in the war against the Fascists. The worker-hero's father, an old coachman who'd been shown the light at the end of his life by a strange man in a tweed suit, carrying a fountain pen, who'd arrived to stay the night, dies in battle with the cry: 'George Di-mi-tr . . . ov' on his lips.

On the journey back, the French pediatrician from the hospital, a nice old lady, stuns us by asking: 'Did the old man really die like that?' Dr Kostov has the answer for her. 'That's politics,' he says.

24

I've been thinking of films. On my way down to the kitchen, I catch sight of the Supervisor outside the Morgue, parking his Peugeot. He's Lee J. Cobb in *Twelve Angry Men* – the same physique, the same bluster and, I convince myself, the same fragility behind it all. I dream in my white coat of being like Henry Fonda in his white suit and bringing the Supervisor to the point where he tears up his Party card, like Cobb tore up the photograph of his son.

Things are very quiet, like a Sunday. I'm consultant for the day. Vasileva's away, and the doctors haven't come in. Dr Kostov's left with friends, to visit the Trade Fair in Algiers. Dr Vasilev's resting in his apartment. All the Bulgarians in the country are allowed the day off, it's written in their contracts. Fatma seizes on the opportunity and starts cleaning the office.

She empties Dr Vasilev's wastepaper basket, the only one possessed by Maternity. It's full, but not of screeds covered with drafts of the articles that might have brought him renown in the profession, 'Obstetric techniques of the Berbers of Algeria' (*Am.J.Gyn.Obst.*), 'Muslim custom and gynaecological practice' (*J.Fr.Gyn.*), nor of careful letters from young specialists all over the world, eager for a place on his waiting list for the job of second assistant (whatever must he have thought when he got my letter out of the blue?). It's full instead of the envelopes from his relentless, one-way correspondence with the laboratories of Hoechst, Roussel and Roche. He stores the brochures in his desk. The shiny literature fascinates him. A colour supplement every day. If he had the strength, he'd paper the walls with the sparkling pills and glasses of water, the anguished models in period pain, the fairytale surgeries where women say helplessly to their doctors: 'Doctor!' and then take their daughters out shopping, radiant, their discharges controlled.

I sit on the radiator while Fatma mops around me. 'Sound the alarms!' cries Mouloud Kassim in this morning's paper, 'the critical threshold has been reached!' Algeria's on the brink of moral collapse. Mouloud Kassim joins battle with the danger facing his country. He begins by likening it to an 'erosion', such as swept away the top-soil from the country round Timgad, granary to the Romans during their occupation. Then he sees it in more modern terms, those of medical science, as a 'loss of immunity', where gendarme antibodies are locked in combat with the antigens of disorder. No one expression seems adequate for so complex a phemomenon. It's a crisis of civilization invading the whole world! It's a veritable mal du siècle! Mouloud Kassim writes feverishly, swept along by the 'tidal wave' he's describing, a wave of sexuality and bestiality, alcoholism and juvenile delinquency, engulfing the family unit and every human value on which civilization is based, leaving a multitude of stray women in its wake.

Only the provinces have been spared, he says. 'They remain, God be praised, intact and faithful to themselves.' He pays humble tribute to the 'poor women of Kabylia'. Poor they may well be, in financial terms. But in their antibodies, how rich! They're immune to 'that disease called modern life'. Looked down on by cosmopolitan Algiers, pitied by their colonized sisters in the capital, the 'poor' women of Kabylia are the very wealth of Algeria. In our moral economy, they are our oil and our gas!

And Mouloud Kassim harks back to the time, many years ago, when the cities of Algeria could claim a comparable purity. It was the time of the French, when order reigned. 'The life led in our large towns was beyond reproach', he remembers, 'until we took up the struggle for independence.'

A furtive glance from the Electrician before he enters the office. But once in, he's very much at home, stretching out in my chair while I sit in Dr Kostov's, and taking a cloth from his overalls to polish his dark glasses. He wouldn't have come in, he says, if he'd seen 'them' here: 'It'd depress me for the rest of the day.' Thanks to the Bulgarians, I get off to a good start with every Algerian I meet.

The Electrician's a big talker. The hospital represents only a fraction of his world and he's come in this early so that I should know it. He gives the impression that the hospital's his hobby, that he's only helping out, an Algerian Co-opérant Technique. His real life is spent elsewhere, living it up in Algiers with the Prefect of Kabylia, and drinking into the early hours with the Captain of the Gendarmerie at the Djurdjura in Tizi-Ouzou. One of the ministers in this government is his personal acquaintance. He knows where Ben Bella is locked away, and he has 'information' on the politicians in exile.

I've no way of checking anything he says. But I've seen him at work on the electrical system of the motorcycle. He refused to look at my instruction manual, saying it was for beginners only, and in no time he had it running like a dream. I tell him he was quite right about last night. It was a very sober occasion, and not for one second did anyone allow joy to get the better of them. The Electrician believes it was a useful experience nonetheless. 'It's only right that you should find these things out for yourself,' he says graciously. After all, Algerians have had years in which to get to know 'these people'. The Electrician's only consolation is that the country will be rid of 'them' in five years, or in ten at the most.

But he thinks I should take his word about the Egyptians. He knows them well, whereas I'm unlikely to meet them – they have nothing to do with the hospital, they're only here to teach Arabic in the schools. 'The Bulgarians may be worse than the French,' says the Electrician, 'but the Egyptians are worse than the Bulgarians.' He spent a fortnight with Ben Bella in Cairo. The Egyptians only helped for what they could get out of it. He's convinced that if Ben Bella was still in power, Nasser would be the ruler of Algeria. In fact, it's 'the one thing I thank Boumediène for' – he's cut down the ties with Cairo. In a year or so, thinks the Electrician, Boumediène will have sent all the Egyptians back home.

They came for two reasons. One, of course, was the money. You should have seen them, he tells me, collecting their first

month's wages at the Post Office. The Electrician holds out
the trembling, incredulous hands of an Egyptian schoolteacher
counting through a pile of notes. 'They're so underdeveloped
in their country that they asked: "Is this for the year?" '.
The second reason they came was to get away from the Jews.
They're scared stiff of them. 'They can't run fast enough.'
The Electrician has great respect for the Jews. He's always
admired them profoundly. He suspects that the representative
of a battery firm from Algiers is a Jew: 'I can tell you, I look
forward to each of his visits.'

With a little 'bonjour', a crestfallen Dr Vasilev appears at
the office door – in his working clothes. 'One of us had to
come in,' he says. What would have happened if there'd been
a rush of curettages, he asks, or a Caesarean to do? The women
would have had to be driven all the way to Algiers. The ambulance could never have coped. 'Eh,' says Dr Vasilev again,
'one of us had to stay.' In the battle for the day off, he's no
surprise loser.

There are only a few women for him to see in Out-Patients.
The orderly didn't think a doctor was coming in, he's been
turning patients away. A girl of sixteen complains to Dr
Vasilev of sterility, which means that she hasn't become pregnant after a year of marriage. She can't look at us when she
gets off the table, keeping her head turned away. 'I'm ashamed
because they've seen me naked,' she tells Baya, and lays her
head on her shoulder. Baya laughs and strokes her hair.

Dr Vasilev smiles over the arithmetic of a woman from the
mountains. She looks about thirty-five, but she says she's
twenty-one. Baya asks her when she was married, and she tells
us it was during 'the events', the war against the French,
when she was twenty-five. 'But twenty-five comes after twenty-
one', says Baya, 'and the events stopped eight years ago.'
The woman shrugs her shoulders. She can't explain. Dates are
a man's business.

A girl's sent over from Dr Ivanova's Out-Patients as a case
of 'severe jaundice'. From the height of her womb, Dr Vasilev
makes it a seven-month pregnancy. The baby's heart and position are normal. And that's all he puts down on the form that

goes back to Dr Ivanova. Books have been written, conferences have been held, on how to look after a jaundiced mother. But Dr Vasilev has reached a terminal stage in ignorance. He hasn't an idea of what he doesn't know.

A tiny, doll-like girl tinkles with every piece of Kabyl jewellery there is, ankles and wrists and head, earrings and buckles, a necklace that never ends, with old French coins arranged in chains. Underneath, there's a fine new yellow robe, printed with minarets and doves, embroidered in red and blue. A belt that she spins herself round to undo. Baya admires each item, tells me where they're all from, hugs her. The girl's seventeen, and she wants a baby. 'Of course you do, my daughter,' says Baya. She's so good and quiet, she does everything she's told, she doesn't fight. But she has an operation scar beneath her navel. She had a curettage, she tells us, in the small hospital in the mountains, and then an operation. Dr Vasilev puts his fingers in and tells her she can't have a baby, because her womb's been taken out. The Czech doctor was too vigorous with his curette, he must have pushed it through her womb. The girl nods and leaves as gently as she came.

The cases are routine, the pace funereal. Dr Vasilev opens *El Moudjahid* over the desk. It covers proceedings like a blanket of gloom. 13.8 *kilograms!* – *the 'super-potato'* unearthed by a farmer called Paulo, way further south, in Villa de Macia, Mozambique. A pregnant woman gets down from the table and asks if she's going to die. When we say no, she kisses our hands. For a Kabyl woman, to be four months pregnant, to come to Out-Patients and die, is possible, and acceptable. Dr Vasilev smiles. But it's possible, and acceptable, for him too.

We make our way back, earlier than usual, down the Out-Patients corridor, physical destitution all round us. Dr Vasilev resumes *El Moudjahid* in the office, until a man comes in asking for a stretcher. He's collecting his wife after a curettage, and he's found her still lying in bed in her hospital coat. He needs the stretcher so that he can carry her out to the taxi. 'Do you think we'd let her home if she has to be carried out on a stretcher?' cries Dr Vasilev. 'I don't know, Doctor,' says the husband. He would have allowed us to receive her for a curettage and return her paralysed. 'She can walk,' Dr Vasilev tells him, 'she can walk like you and me.' The husband nods. It's impossible to tell if this colossal change in his wife's health has any effect on him.

An old man asks Dr Vasilev if he couldn't change a prescription made out for his wife. For the last two days, says the old man, he's been doing nothing but going from chemist to chemist in Kabylia. He hasn't been able to find the particular drug prescribed. Dr Vasilev changes it for him, telling me it's Dr Kostov's fault. The chemists send in lists of their stocks, and the doctors are supposed to prescribe accordingly, except that Dr Kostov never bothers.

The drug was no life-saver anyway. It was just one brand of vitamin preparation instead of another. The old man's no wiser, and he thanks Dr Vasilev kindly. What's two days, his whole life's been no different. It's left him with a scraggy chicken's neck, a rotting mouth and mutilated hands from fifteen years' labour in France. The fingers on his right hand are stumps. He tells me he knows France well. I don't take it up. During my first days here, I used to. But it was always a different France, the 18th and 19th arrondissements, the suburbs of Paris and Lille, a France I'd never known.

We wait for the clock to join hands over 12. But then a phone call arrives from Dr Ivanova, asking for an 'opinion' on one of her patients. Dr Vasilev's very pleased, and he invites me along with him. We set off together, the consultant and his intern, over the bridge to the main hospital.

I'm interested, it's the first time I'll have been to another ward, and I want to see how they're managing. But Dr Vasilev's excited, and he's walking fast. It's a special occasion. To receive a call from your colleague requesting your 'opinion' – what your eyes have seen, what your hands have felt, what your experience has accumulated – is one reason why people become doctors. To ask for an opinion, as Dr Ivanova has done, is a salute to the doctor. It's a salute to have a salute back, a salute to the profession. There's a whole ceremony for when you arrive on your colleague's ward. Sister is warned in advance, she prepares the patient, assembles X-rays and notes, in tribute. It may be an irrelevant moment for science, but there's none greater for a doctor.

Dr Ivanova isn't there. She's just left, off to an early lunch. She hasn't even written a note for Dr Vasilev, or any instructions about the patient we're to see. Dr Vasilev's sad. His colleague's not playing the game. There's only an orderly, who takes us into the ward.

I'm almost proud. It's worse than Maternity. There are twelve beds with not more than a foot between each. Some have sheets, and they're a peculiar grey-brown, made of a sack-like material. There's rotten food everywhere, and there's the same débris, and it's worse than Maternity because there's a notice on the wall recommending hygiene. The women wear ancient robes. The anaemia and depression are the same. The eyes follow you, the faces stay fixed.

We come to a stop at the bed by the window. Apart from her notebook, the orderly's empty-handed. She has no notes, no X-rays, no tray of the instruments Dr Vasilev might need. The woman's talking away, but Dr Vasilev's collapsed, back to his everyday self. He's elsewhere, immensely tired. His mouth's a little open, and he's breathing quietly. He's reached the patient's bed, and that's enough. An 'excursion!' is the journey, it's the expectation, it's not when you arrive. I'm thinking: one bedside punch from Dr Kostov, and he'd be out of his misery.

'She was a patient of yours, Doctor,' the orderly's saying. Dr Vasilev doesn't remember. He flicks some ash towards the window, it falls short. 'How long has she been bleeding?' he asks. 'Two or three days,' says the girl. Dr Vasilev goes 'eh', and falls silent. The girl looks at him and in her eyes I see none of the reverence that real nurses have for the birth of opinion. She's not in the presence of the daily bedside miracle, the undefinable process of opinion-making that's peculiar to men with the proper training. She'll have no respect for its pedigree: by acumen, out of experience. Instead, the girl's asking the same question as Djamila the other night across some woman's knees: 'Why doesn't he retire?'

We wait. The patient's stopped her talking, she's looking

from Dr Vasilev to the orderly and back. And still we wait. I'd told Djamila that Dr Vasilev's contract had another year to run. No doubt he'd hang on till the end. 'Do you want to examine, her, Doctor?' asks the girl at last. Dr Vasilev jumps. 'No,' he says. And the orderly waits there, pen at the ready, to take down the treatment, the distillation of twenty-three years' practice of gynaecology.

'Methergin,' says Dr Vasilev. Methergin that flows as water through Maternity! Methergin that I'd forgotten was a drug any more! He's looking out of the window, he doesn't see the orderly close her notebook without writing anything down. There's a flurry of car horns from the street, like a traffic jam in Paris, and Dr Vasilev smiles: 'A marriage!' He resumes his cigarette. He and Dr Ivanova have just buried the ritual and we make our way back to Maternity in pain, two mourners at a pauper's funeral.

After lunch we sleep, it's as hot as the first days. We're woken by appalling shrieks, the worst we've heard yet: 'Doctor, Doctor, aieee maaa!' hoarse, horrible. We look out to Maternity because it seemed they came from there, but we see women at the first-floor windows pointing back to the surgery ward over our heads, Ivanov's ward. If it wasn't for them pointing, we'd think we'd been dreaming. You'd have to be dreaming to hear cries so terrible.

A girl I've just delivered puts her hand on my arm and looks at me with urgency. She pulls me towards her. I bend a little. Her hand runs up my arm, over my shoulder, till it reaches the nape of my neck. She seems to want my head on her chest, by her face, I'm not sure. Her lips are pursed, her eyes fixed and wide, calling me. I press back against her hand, and straighten up. She doesn't know what she's doing. She's not to feel this way, not when she's fifteen, and it's a baby she had no choice in having, from a man she had no choice in marrying. It's reflexes, hormones, it's physiology posing as feeling. She begins massaging my back, in deep, circular movements, and I leave the room.

Dr Vasilev wanders into town, to the Post Office, for the new issue of Lenin centenary stamps announced in *El Moudjahid* this morning. Dr Kostov's still away at the Fair. My only visitor, apart from the Electrician, is a man in red pyjamas who walks in on crutches. He's a truck-driver who broke his leg in an accident. He's been in hospital for months, he says, it's become his home. His leg's in plaster, and it looks horribly deformed. His toes are swollen and blue, and he says they no longer hurt. It occurs to me that when an Ivanov patient takes off his plaster, it must be like one of our women giving birth, one limb in four ripe for a cardboard box.

I point it out to the Electrician, who shrugs. In Eastern Europe, he says, you can become a doctor in three years. You start off in hospital with a broom. If you show promise – if they can see you're good with your hands – they promote you. He knew a surgeon from Moscow who arrived in the first batch of foreign doctors after Independence. The man told him he'd been a sweeper only three years before. 'They call it an accelerated programme', says the Electrician. We go outside into the courtyard and the truck-driver does some practice walks in front of us, swinging fast on his crutches. He's glad of the audience. The hospital has no physiotherapists, no well-bred girls in white to call out: 'Oh jolly good, Mr Ibrahimi.'

The sun begins to cool. The Bulgarian national day, 'their Christmas', as the Electrician likes to call it so that I should understand its importance, draws to a close. I sit out on the parapet with the one-eyed cat in the grass nearby. I've thrown her a piece of steak and she's pulling it to pieces, looking around as she does so like a wild animal. No other cat can come near. There's a dog in the courtyard, a big, stupid dog with its head down guiltily, knowing the cat is watching. It trots towards us without conviction, till the one-eyed cat stops chewing and begins to stiffen. The dog must be fifty yards away still, but it heads off on a tangent, to the shade of the refuse truck.

The white Mercedes brings back Dr Kostov and his two friends from their trip to the Trade Fair. They climb out a little noisily, tinged pink from the sun, and from glasses of French beer. They come up the path together. The two friends are engineers. Their faces take my breath away. Next to theirs, Dr Kostov's is friendly and reassuring. One in particular is huge and pig-like. They install themselves in the office and get down to business, while I sit there pretending to read my textbook. Their conversation hinges on the words 'dinar', 'franc', 'Zurich' and 'per cent'. Their faces are as alert, as alive, as they'll ever be, with a sort of sexual flush to them as they cover a sheet of prescription paper with figures, the only non-medical writing that Dr Kostov ever does, apart from his correspondence with the BMW factory in Munich. My limited understanding of what they're saying only makes it more of a caricature than it already is. It's a scene from the cartoon of *Animal Farm*, it's a re-enactment of the palace stereotypes we all watched in the fairy-tale last night, it's a reunion of German exiles in South America. I notice that Dr Kostov has their respect. He's probably given more thinking hours to money than both of them put together. Besides, he's quicker than they are at the conversions.

Dr Vasilev makes a bronchitic appearance at an early stage of the proceedings, hovering at the office door, showing me his Lenin stamps. The conversation clatters to a halt. The pig-friend is in his seat, and he makes no move to leave it. Dr Vasilev would dearly love to ask them about the Trade Fair. But he mumbles something instead, and goes outside to sit on the parapet with the one-eyed cat. It's not my imagination, the tone of that meeting descends from excitement to contempt. Dr Vasilev is the dinar of humanity.

I follow him outside and sit on the parapet too. He suffers no loss of face at being driven from his office. Perhaps it was always rather grand for him. On the parapet, he has the cat, in the grass between his feet, and he has the newspaper. '*One metre! Three kilos!*' – *the giant lobster caught off the Florida coast.* The photograph shows the happy fisherman pretending to eat his catch with a knife and fork. Kilos and metres, lobsters, rhinos and potatoes, these are Dr Vasilev's units.

A Kabyl, husband to one of the patients, passes and says hello. I remember seeing him briefly at the petrol pumps in town, when the Peugeot was being filled for the trip to Dellys. He accepts a cigarette, and sits between us. He's small and thin, in physique very similar to Dr Vasilev. After the initial greeting, warm and excited, Dr Vasilev runs dry of words

224

for his friend. They smoke in silence, and three sturdy voices rise in the exchange market behind us as bitter argument comes to blacken the Bulgarian day.

The man between us begins a story, much as someone will pick up a guitar and start to sing. His voice is soft and nostalgic. He's back to being a small boy, many years ago, at the end of the Second World War. His family had joined an opposition movement against the French. One day, his father gave him a pile of their newspapers to distribute in the cafés. The boy went up to the Kabyl chief who ran the town for the French, called the 'caïd', sitting in the best café, and asked him if he'd like to buy a copy of the paper. 'Who gave you that?' cried the caïd, who wore two hooded wollen coats, one white, one blue, both in the finest wool. 'Mind your own business,' said the boy. The caïd hit him with his stick, took all the papers and burned them.

Years later, the caïd was one of the first victims of the war. He used to spend every evening in the French camp, chatting to the commanding officer. One night they waited for him as he came home with his French escort. They opened fire, and the escort ran. The caïd was left standing there all alone, in his two hooded woollen coats. They didn't kill him straight away. They took him round the villages, and in each one they forced him to tell the people of his treachery. Then they strangled him and hanged the body from a fig tree, with a sign that read: 'The same fate awaits all traitors.'

'We were fanatics,' the man remembers, 'we were ready to die, we'd take any risks. Revolution came before anything else.' He's wrapped in that past and as his story continues, he becomes fanatic again. He draws me back to those years. His excited whispers recruit me into a conspiracy to plant bombs in the dark. In his lips that scarcely move, I see the forced ventriloquy of prison cells and prison courtyards, the need to conserve strength during hunger-strike and disease. In the hollowness of his voice at the end, I find myself on the balcony of the sanatorium overlooking Tizi-Ouzou.

'Today,' the man says, 'it's evolution, not revolution.' When he was discharged from the sanatorium, he left the Party. He thought its only function had become the stifling of political life. He was entitled to a pension for his tuberculosis, and to a veteran's card that carried various other benefits, but he didn't apply for either. 'The maquis was never an investment.' His friends from those days keep offering him administrative posts, pressing him to join them. But he's always refused. He's become a clerk in a travel agency. 'I'm their guilty conscience,' he says with a laugh.

He looks at his watch, surprised to have been talking so long. He's quiet and unpretentious. It's only my questions that have made him talk about himself. He gets to his feet. 'C'est la vie.' His story's been a lament on Algeria, on his own life. Unwittingly, it's been an anniversary lament on the tragedy of Bulgaria.

It's getting dark, and Christmas day is done. The wheeling and dealing has ceased in the office behind us. The engineers walk out to their Mercedes, and Dr Vasilev's not worth even a Bulgarian bonsoir. A frustrated capitalist from Sofia is left yawning in the office, exhausted by the hard bargaining. Beside me on the parapet, a Communist of twenty years' standing has blended with the dusk, and the stone top glints with balls of silver paper.

25

The same dawn every day. We watch it together. Trucks pulling up the hill into town, dogs barking, a bony cow being driven with sticks on to the field opposite. The swallows fly right by the window. It's Calie's last morning, and there's a gift from the Cook of melon for breakfast.

'The Fair! The Fair!', cries Dr Vasilev, waving *El Moudjahid* in delight. He went to it last year, and he loved it. He draws a little map for me on prescription paper, showing where the Trade Fair's being held: 'Fort de l'Eau!'. The traffic lights, the roundabout, the one-way street, all remembered with affection and marked. This year there's a hovercraft that runs across the bay from the centre of Algiers.

But I know all this because I've been reading the paper too. I've seen Boumediène cutting the tape at the entrance to the Fair, his ministers round him, a phalanx of suited men. I've seen him visit the Palestinian pavilion and receive an ivory mosque from the hands of its director. I've read all the tributes to the Revolutionary Government, from the East Germans, the Czechs and the North Koreans, and I know about the Algerian pavilion, specially designed by architects from China. The Fair's been the proudest moment in their lives for a group of young students from Constantine.

But alas . . . The diesel engines, the irrigation equipment, the date-processing machines are but a façade. Algeria's foundations are riddled with worms! At the very moment that she steps forth to take her place in the front line, she must hide her head in shame. 'What atrocious sights!' laments the Women's Page, 'what appalling scenes!'

Every day, to the gates of the Fair, there come women. Some

are with their children. 'I'm taking Ahmed and Yamina to the Fair,' they tell their trusting husbands as they leave for work, 'I want them to measure the progress of our industrial development.' But no sooner are they inside the gates than young Ahmed and Yamina are bundled into the nursery, and their mothers turn drugged eyes to the arena that awaits them. Other women come alone, or are brought to the gates each morning by an innocent father or brother. These are the hostesses, the young girls who have been carefully selected – and discreetly dressed – to project an image of womanhood that is specifically Algerian. Yet how cruelly do they betray their country's trust! Instead of giving the concerned visitor all the information he requires on the achievements of the Five-Year Plan, these girls haunt the cafés of the Fair, fluttering like so many moths around the fumes of tobacco and the vapours of alcohol, all sense of decency blunted in the dimmed lights. 'Why must these lost souls smile at the first man who looks at them?' cries the Women's Page, 'why must some smile even *before* he looks at them?'

The cry has not fallen on ungallant ears. The gendarmes on duty at the Fair have been erasing each blemish as it appears. But is that enough? 'Women of Algeria, let us remember our past!' In 1870, during the Kabyl uprising, we led our men against the French on the slopes of the Djurdjura Mountains. A decade ago, we played wife and mother to one and a half million martyrs. Our bombs and our grenades ushered in the dawn to the long colonial night. Are we to give up the struggle now, when victory is at hand? We are still at war! Today we wield a new weapon – our morality, and we fight in a new maquis – the Algerian family. Let us watch each other, and above all let us watch ourselves. 'Women readers! Each one of us must become her own gendarme.'

I've been keeping quiet about the Fair to Dr Vasilev. But how could he miss it, it's been all over the paper for days, and here he is, just as I feared he would be, promising that next weekend, me and my nice little wife and Madame Vasileva '. . . and me, of course!', in the car of the very sympathetic friends from Dellys, would all go . . . would all go . . . the

228

excitement breaks over his face in waves, *El Moudjahid* points unerringly along the road to Algiers . . . 'To the FAIR!'.

I tell him that Calie's leaving. He cries 'Ahhh!' in disappointment. Then he thinks again, and realizes there'll be even more reason for us to go to the Trade Fair together. 'You'll be all alone,' he says kindly, 'it will be an excursion for you.'

Djamila arrives two hours late on the bus from Algiers, curved nose diving between perfect white teeth, to find three women waiting for her, three heads in three vaginas. 'Oh là là!' she cries, buttoning on her coat, getting back into the swing of things. 'What's the matter with these women, for heaven's sake? They get on my nerves! Enough noise, do you hear? Oh, I don't know what's the matter with me this morning. If you only knew what I'm really like, I've got a heart of gold . . .' Malika puts her head round the door to say that one of the husbands is outside. 'Give me time,' says Djamila, 'I've only just got here.' 'He was in the maquis,' says Malika. 'I couldn't care less what he was in,' cries Djamila and, as Malika slams the door on us, she says to me: 'In the maquis! Who the hell does he think he is?'

Dr Kostov kicks open the delivery room door and strides inside, eyes and teeth a-glitter, fists itching. He looks around him. Three women in three beds: he can't abide a stagnating delivery room. One of the girls starts screaming, appallingly. 'Toi! – you!' Dr Kostov points at her. He'll take her first.

But she's on the labour bed. It's too soft, there'll be no resistance. A 'Chris-Taylor' will only make the mattress bounce. So Dr Kostov grabs her arm: 'Hey-ho!' and pulls her on to the steel delivery table, which will be so much more effective. It's a grotesque sight, a slaughterhouse worker herding frightened cows: the same apron and long white coat, and the same large brown eyes showing their whites. The girls cross to their new beds, stumbling over the stained floor on hands and knees, pushed and pulled and knee'd by Dr Kostov, with 'Heys!' and 'Hos!' and all the time they're screaming for their lives. 'Why scream?' asks Dr Kostov with clenched fist, 'this isn't Psychiatry.'

The changeover completed, Dr Kostov with his squat, ape-like action swings up on to the delivery table with the help of the oxygen cylinder. First he uses his broad forearms, right across the top of the womb, crying out 'Zidi, zidi, zidi,' like a football coach. Then he switches to both fists, and the girl screams that she's dying.

But the fists don't work, and Dr Kostov decides on a forceps. When they touch the girl's vulva, she lets out the most piercing scream. Dr Kostov walks round to the front and delivers a crashing slap to her face. Her legs tremble insanely in the stirrups. Her screams don't stop. 'Ai, mas' from the girl in the next bed. A tearful pitch creeps into Dr Kostov's swearing, he whacks the thighs on either side of him till he's got the forceps screwed together. The head's quickly down and the baby's out, helped by a jagged tear. Djamila does mouth-to-mouth and splashes alcohol on its chest. Twenty minutes later, the baby feebly cries. One.

In the next bed is a sixteen-year-old with a premature first baby. The delivery's not difficult, Dr Kostov uses only a fraction of his strength, but the baby's small. Too small? I hold it uncertainly, and look from Fatma to Djamila to know where I'm meant to put it. 'In the changing room perhaps . . .', says Fatma, '. . . where he'll do as he's told and die,' Djamila finishes the sentence for her. Two.

Dr Kostov's begun a second forceps. The girl doesn't scream like the last one. She's vomiting and her eyes are rolling. Dr Kostov pulls the baby out. It needs resuscitation too. Djamila squeezes its chest and blows into its mouth and nose. It's a shame about the empty oxygen cylinder. Dr Kostov washes his hands, walks across the sheets laid over the puddles on the floor, from baby to baby, scowling. Three.

Then a sudden arrival, that Fatma tries to push back out of the door. But we have to take her. In she walks, her legs apart. She says she's seven months pregnant. Dr Kostov pulls down her pants and they have a tiny baby girl in them, dead. Four. He hoists her on to the bed, where she delivers a second, a raw, long-since-dead foetus, half the size of the first. Five. Then another, a live baby boy, weighing just over a kilo who'll be dead by the time I get back in the afternoon. Dr Kostov's drawn the babies from her like a macabre conjurer. Six, and the floor's awash.

Dr Vasilev puts his head round the door, he has scruples about coming into the delivery room with a cigarette. The aftermath of their panic is there in the women's eyes. 'Pauvres femmes kabyles,' says Dr Vasilev, 'poor Kabyl women.' It's nothing, but it's nice. It's the difference between him and Dr Kostov.

The day's under way. The Econome's secretary, the one with the mournful face, arrives on the landing with the green Ledger of Deaths. Malika fills in the details and Dr Kostov signs. They're all 'stillborn'. That way, you don't have to write anything under 'cause of death'. What never lived can't die.

'Ce n'est pas pratique,' complains Baya, 'it's not convenient.' For a moment, I wonder if it isn't her French that's let her down. But her French is fine, and 'convenient' isn't an inappropriate word. No more Biotic-Algérie boxes are left, she has to go off to the Pharmacy to get some more.

Two gendarmes ask to see the Register of Births. They could be coming with criminal charges against all of us. Instead, they're inquiring about a woman who's just had a baby here. Her husband has been in France for the last two years. Someone wrote to him what happened and he got in touch with the gendarmes via his nearest Algerian consulate. Malika thinks the woman will go to prison. The gendarmes only stay a minute, as the woman's already left. Young, moustached and ugly, they're soldiers in the service of Islamic Socialism.

Malika accompanies us on the round upstairs. She and Dr Kostov share a definite rapport. She likes anyone who'd look good in military uniform. No fair hand ever flits across Dr Vasilev's shoulders when she does a ward round with him. Dr Kostov's sex face when she kissed Baya twice on each cheek this morning: 'Mademoiselle Malika, how can you do that in front of me!'

A woman's protesting that she's been given someone else's

baby. She's sure she had a boy in the night, and what's in her cot is a girl. But Zora's gone off home and since she filled in none of the charts, there's no way of checking. The other mother in the room seems happy with what she's got. But the woman's not satisfied, she's going to speak to her husband. 'It's only natural,' explains Dr Kostov coarsely, 'she speaks a little French, she has some culture. The other's from the mountains, she'd be happy with anything.'

And we stride on, past boxes of Russian sugar alive with red ants, between anaemic patients walking unsteadily from wall to wall, holding their heads. Dr Kostov stops to examine a woman he did a forceps on yesterday. But she won't let him rip the sheet off her. He bends down and shouts in her face, hand threateningly raised: 'I've seen it already, I've seen your vagina, you prostate!' But she won't let go. A growl, and we're on to the next, a diabetic I remember seeing a long time ago in Out-Patients with Dr Vasilev. He'd admitted her then for 'observation', and since he's doing the round downstairs today, he won't even be 'observing' her dead baby. 'We will wait!' I remember him telling the woman, as if waiting were a policy, a deliberate course of action, and not the solution of a man who lives according to the chance events of the outside world, from one 'excursion' to the next, who's long since abandoned any claim over the simplest things, let alone disease. Dr Kostov never uses the word 'observe', it wouldn't suit him. If the baby's alive, get it out. If it's dead, embryotomy. At least you know where you are.

His routine at each bed is to ask Malika: 'Is the baby alive?' If the answer's no, then he puts down pills on the temperature chart to stop the milk. If the answer's yes, and the delivery was more than twelve hours ago, then Dr Kostov asks the woman in his Kabyl: 'Atsforat? – Home?' When she says yes, as she always does, Dr Kostov goes: 'Hey!' and gives a great slap on an imaginary rump, to say 'Off you go then!' If the answer is: 'Yes, it's alive, but . . .', as it often is – as it was just now – Dr Kostov will lean over the cot at the end of the bed and take a look at the old shrunken man inside, at the wizened face in its grey cotton wool bonnet. But it's only for the form. There's nothing to be done for an ailing baby. If it doesn't pull through on its own, it dies. This one hasn't a chance, it'll be in its card-board coffin before the day is out, and Dr Kostov gives it the thumbs-down scowl.

By Out-Patients, Dr Kostov's mood has settled into its rest-ing state, sarcasm and resignation, over the girl who speaks perfect French yet insists on giving her symptoms to Baya in Kabyl. Dr Kostov pulls on her arm: 'I'm not here, Madame, I'm only the doctor.' The girl won't acknowledge him, and Dr Kostov turns to me to ask: 'What can we do?'

The girl's not had a period for two months, and she gets sick every morning. Dr Kostov tells her she's pregnant, and the news makes her wince. Her father took her away from the lycée for the marriage. She doesn't like her husband and she doesn't want a baby. But most of all, she says, she has no one to talk to. She begins to cry. 'Au suivant!' shouts Dr Kostov.

'Next!' is a father. He wants a certificate of virginity for his daughter. He married her three years ago to an impotent husband, and now he's found her another match. It prompts Dr Kostov to tell me of a little operation he used to perform in Bulgaria. Women who weren't 'intact' would come to him before their marriage. He'd put two stitches across their vaginas, where their hymens used to be, and on the wedding night everything would go to the husband's satis-faction. Dr Kostov did over thirty of them, with never a complaint. He laughs: 'I've had lots of gifts from grateful women!'

The pig-friend comes in while the last women are being examined. He's not in the least interested in what's to be seen between the stirrups of the gynaecological table, the way you might expect a pig to be. He talks business with Dr Kostov as if they were back in the doctors' office.

Dr Kostov steps up his pace. An old woman drags her legs, and looks at us out of white eyes, she's crippled with anaemia. Once on the table though, her legs come together with sur-prising force. 'No strength to walk,' cries Dr Kostov, 'but plenty now! No nonsense, Madame!' Elbows into each thigh, face contorted, he prises the legs apart and plunges inside. Then he realizes the absurdity of having called a prostate such a grand name as 'Madame'. So he draws his left hand across her belly in a sarcastic sweep, a manservant bowing to his mistress, and goes: *'Madame!'* Then his right hand's out in a flash, and he's crying: 'Hospitalization! Curettage!' They're in a hurry, he and his friend. Before washing the glove in the sink, he opens the door to beckon the last woman in with a blood-stained rubber hand.

Dr Vasilev comes to meet us on our way back from Out-Patients. Dr Kostov strides on with his friend. I stop, and Dr Vasilev hands me some Sahara sand in a plastic envelope, a goodbye present to Calie from Vasileva. I won't be alone when she's gone, he promises. He and Vasileva are going to look after me. They'll be making me suppers, they'll be taking me to the Fair.

Fatma runs up to us: 'Come quickly!' We hurry back with her across the bridge to Maternity, down the stairs to the curettage room, where there's a woman on the table entirely naked, only her jewels on her. Dr Kostov's bending over her ankle, watched by his friend, as he cuts through the skin in an attempt to find a vein. The gallows is beside him, with a bottle of Rheoma-crodex upturned on the hook, ready. He finds the vein, threads the plastic tube up it, but when he connects the bottle, the fluid won't flow. 'Hold them!' he shouts, and I keep the different pieces of the apparatus together to try and minimize any leak. But there's something different from the other times. There's no vomit by the woman's head, no blood between her legs. Her pupils are fixed and wide, and Dr Vasilev has begun to pump on her chest.

The inevitable's happened. After so many near misses, after so many woman have been brought in on the very brink, here's one who won't be brought back, not even with Vitamin C. Her lips are white, and blood can't be drawn from any vein. Whimpers now, echoes of the night of the mole, as Dr Kostov tries another cut-down on the other ankle, cursing the heat that's causing his glasses to slip off his nose. This time, he can't even find the vein. Dr Vasilev gets a syringe with an extra long needle and pushes it between the woman's ribs, adrenalin for her heart. I catch some flutters through the stethoscope, then

234

nothing. 'Her heart's fine,' shouts Dr Kostov, 'she just hasn't any blood.' He grinds his syringe into the drug trolley and strides from the room with his friend.

They sit round the office desk, as the family stands in the door. Baya's there to translate. 'She's dead!' cries Dr Kostov, 'who's the husband?' He isn't there. He's away labouring in Algiers. 'Who's the mother?' She's not there either. These are only the in-laws. The mother-in-law tells how yesterday morning the girl was well, how she'd stayed at home to make cous-cous while the rest went to the fields to gather figs, how she'd eaten a big lunch with them, how she'd been happy and well, as strong as a lion. Dr Kostov's turned to his friend, bored by the whole thing. Baya doesn't respond. She's always distrustful of mothers-in-law.

Everyone's quiet. The relatives stare into the floor. Baya looks away. Dr Kostov's in a huddle with his friend. There was nothing more we could do. The woman was dead on arrival. For once, our record in the affair is immaculate. 'Dead!' says Dr Kostov to the father-in-law, a peasant with a stick and straw sombrero and white moustache, who can speak a little French.

Dr Kostov leaves with his friend. It's past noon, Calie's finished at the laundry, and I go to collect her farewell lunch. It's cous-cous, masses of it, with at least a litre of sauce, and water-melon to finish. 'C'est bon, mon cous-cous', says the Cook, and I admit: 'Eh, oui' that his cous-cous is indeed very good. I carry it back towards the room, but my hands are shaking and I have the headache I expected. On the way, outside Maternity, I come across the old man with the straw sombrero. I stop. I think I ought to say something – walking back with this lunch, life going on – but what? He's squatting outside the main door, against the wall. He stands up straight, painfully still and aged, the tattered woollen coat thrown over his shoulders. He salutes, says 'Doctor', and then something I can't catch. I get him to say it again. He wants me to tell him where there's a urinal.

Farewell from the laundry girls: a necklace from Beni-Yenni. Calie says goodbye to the Econome, in an office that's as chaotic as ever. 'You're leaving us, Madame,' he cries, 'so soon!' He makes her promise to come back.

The Electrician loads the motorcycle for us outside the garage. We watch the truck-driver practising his turns. He's getting resigned to a life on crutches. Almost anything could remind the Electrician of the Egyptians, but this time it's the truck-driver's pyjamas. It so happens that the Electrician has a friend, a Kabyl, who's a fighter pilot in the Algerian air force. He was sent over to Egypt in the six-day war to help the Arabs. He didn't get out of his uniform for a month and a half. But the Egyptians made a point of sleeping in their pyjamas, so their planes would be destroyed by the time they'd got dressed.

A hot mid-day road that's virtually empty. One level crossing, one traffic light, between us and Algiers. A roadside stall sells orangeade and sausages. We join the main road, with signs pointing behind us to the South, Ghardaïa, Touggourt, places we'll never have seen. We reach Algiers on the wide magnificent road, between the palms, food for the colonial fantasies of governor-generals. Complicitous nods from gendarmes, on the same motorcycle as ours. Dust in the air, cobbles by the bay.

The Palace, the Forum, the rue d'Isly, the Milk Bar, Bab-El-Oued – our heads are full of the names of the Algerian war, names that have changed. We decide to see one thing only and, in a street of colonnades like the rue de Rivoli, we ask a gendarme for the Casbah. We climb and get closer. We stop again and ask, and people say: 'It's right here,' and we still can't see it, until we park high above the town on a street where buses run, and see gaps between the buildings below us, no wider than staircases. Streets like Kabyl mountain tracks, as crowded as Baya's courtyard. 'Visit the Casbah,' says the same man in English, French and German. We ask him for the streets of the Battle of Algiers, the rue de Thèbes, the rue Caton. He doesn't know them, and nor does anyone else. Men bend over sewing machines in miniature shops, children run with us. We eat curdled milk in a tiny shop. The man's making butter in a wooden churn that's spinning on top of the refrigerator. He climbs up the ladder to get some for us. It's white, unrecognizable, like nothing we've tasted before, a new food. Children press against the window, faces squashed, laughing, waiting to join us when we came out. And all the veils and shawls. Djamila Boupacha, Zora Drif, Djamila Bouhired and the others. Girls who took a greater step than it's possible to imagine, put on European clothes and walked alone into the bars of the rue d'Isly to blow the cream of settler youth to pieces. Where have all the bombs gone? They've been buried in street names, rue de la Bombe, plaques like funeral stones.

We watch the hovercraft leaving for the Fair beneath Che Guevara boulevard, and the same treacherous idea occurs to us both. We jump back on to the motorcycle and race to the Fair. Pleased gendarmes signal our way. The roundabout, the traffic light, the one-way street – they're all there, just as Dr Vasilev had marked them in his little map. Over the vast sandy car park to the main gate. There's just time, the plane leaves in an hour. We run to the window, buy our tickets and rush inside.

On the right, the Algerian pavilion stretching the length of the Fairground, shipped en bloc from Peking, monolithic and industrial, flattered by those grey pictures in *El Moudjahid*. The Spanish pavilion at the other extreme, trendily, blatantly Western. The Palestinian stand, a sad shack. North Korea next door, and a gigantic portrait of a waxen Kim Il Sung. And way over in the far corner, where the hovercraft comes in, an anonymous concrete cube – Bulgaria.

We tear towards it, over the grass and down the steps, pushing people aside in an enthusiasm that exceeds anything shown by *El Moudjahid* itself. Inside the pavilion, across one wall: a photograph of Jivkov and Boumediène in diplomatic conversation. Across the other: the beaches of the Black Sea. We ask for a brochure. They've not got one. Panting, we ask to sign the Visitors' Book. There's no such thing. We look desperately around. Tractors and water pumps and other industrial equipment. It's all heavy, desolate, dead. There's absolutely nothing to take away. I'll have no evidence to show. He'll never believe I've been. There's not even a list of the hotels in the picture on the wall. There's nothing. They're

terrible salesmen. We rush back to the motorcycle and Calie
flies away, with henna still on her feet from the marriage.

'You went!' exclaims Dr Vasilev. My feeble proof is there,
in the ashtray on his desk, torn scraps of paper like cinema
tickets. 'You went!' he cries, as open in pain as he is in joy,
'ahhh!' I needn't have tried to commit details of the Fair to
memory, he's not going to test me. The day was all planned!
We'd have gone in the car of our very sympathetic friends from
Dellys and after the Fair, we'd have driven into Algiers and
he'd have shown me the Casbah. I tell him we saw that too.
I feel bad, like the day the report went astray.

26

We have a new doctor, Dr Nikolenko, a Russian woman. It's Dr Kostov who gives me the news when he arrives in the morning with his bottle of water for the fridge. He knew nothing about it until just now, when he had a phone call from the Director's secretary. Dr Vasilev's gone off to welcome her. Apparently, she's come with her husband, a general surgeon who'll be lending a hand (an ungloved hand?) to Ivanov in Theatre. But it's unfair of me to feel like I do, prejudiced from the very outset. Ivanov and his wife have defined the Russian doctor for me. But that's only two, and there are hundreds of thousands of others. Dr Nikolenko's new, everything's possible. Let's begin afresh.

Perhaps I'll like her face when I see her. That would be nice. Perhaps she'll speak a little Kabyl, and be gentle and kind, with a weakness for taking temperatures and giving anaesthetics. That would be very nice. But perhaps, in the intervals between patients, during those empty afternoons when I'll talk to her about her country, she'll betray just one-millionth of the loathing and contempt I myself feel when I see a picture of Party Secretary Brezhnev. Perhaps she'll give Tamara-style thumps on the desk in the doctors' office to denounce a man so oafish, reactionary and distant from socialism that it would be flattery to suggest he could ever have betrayed it. Perhaps she's the Red Gynaecologist that Kabylia needs, a Pasionaria, come to expose the fake socialism of the Algerian state. Her message will be anarchy and atheism, her programme arson. Fired by her teachings, bands of women will make torches from *El Moudjahid*, burn down the mosques and the buildings of bureaucracy, they'll dangle genitals from gendarmerie washing-lines and turn to each other instead.

But here she is, with her official escort, arriving by the bridge from the main hospital, on the landing of the first floor. There's the Director, portly, a little pompous. There's the Supervisor, cuddling dimpled Malika close. What a mistake I made that day! There's Dr Vasilev, happy as anything over the new arrival. There are the Nikolenkos themselves, the husband a smiling astronaut, the wife large and smiling too. The Director introduces us, Dr Kostov first. He's not warm when he comes to me, referring to me as 'the student whom we have allowed in the department for two months'. 'Allowed' is a word the Econome would never have used. Then he sends Malika off to fetch Baya the orderly, 'but not the cleaners, there's no point'.

Dr Kostov's smiling beside me. It's amused contempt, partly for ceremony, which he has no time for, and partly for the hospital officials themselves, who are hardly less prostates than their women.

He exchanges a few words in Russian with his new colleague, but without the warmth he can use with me. I already know which of us he'd choose. He'll always defend Russia in arguments with Algerians (he refused to admit to the Electrician that cholera had broken out in Astrakhan, and he told the Postmaster that the print in *Pravda* never dirtied your hands as much as *El Moudjahid*'s) but to me he never bothers.

The arrival creates a line-up, between me and Dr Kostov on the one hand, and the new woman with Dr Vasilev on the other – reinforced by Dr Vasilev's absence for the next two hours and by a plague of curettages that Dr Kostov takes very personally. We've hardly begun the first when a violent quarrel flares up between him and Vasileva. It lasts for two curettages more and smoulders for the rest of the day. Dr Kostov's being persecuted by all the miscarriages of Kabylia while his chief plays blissful escort to their new colleague. And Vasileva's not looking happy at the prospect of working with a woman doctor. She snaps ampoules with extra viciousness, Dr Kostov curettes with a scowl, angry words fill the room and the women on the table get the worst of it. Vasileva doesn't look at me – respectable women don't engage in slanging matches. Dr Kostov has no such scruples concerning gynaecologists, and he looks at me to enlist my support at the end of every round. But it's all in Bulgarian, and I have to show him I'm just bewildered.

The last woman for curettage wears European clothes under her veil and shawl. She arrives with her two teenage daughters in the family Peugeot, driven by her teenage son. The girls could almost be French, except for their skirts which are a little long. They sit on either side of their mother on the bench in the hall.

Their brother comes on into the office. He's younger than his sisters. Yet he's very sure of himself as he gives the symptoms to Dr Kostov. He knows his mother's dates, he's familiar with her miscarriages, he's brought her in for a curettage before. Dr Kostov listens surlily. Then the son goes off into town, to buy grapes and melon for his mother's stay in hospital. As he leaves, without a word to her or to his sisters, he takes care to close the main door of Maternity behind him.

Dr Kostov beckons the mother forward. She gets to her feet with a heavy 'ai, ma'. But her daughters stand up too and come with her into the curettage room. Dr Kostov closes the door on them. Still they come on forward. 'Hey!', roars Dr Kostov pushing them back, 'prostates!' The eldest girl says: 'We don't want to leave our mother.' But the sentiment doesn't sway Dr Kostov. He forces the door shut and tells me to make sure they don't come in. I find them standing just outside. I explain that their mother's going to have a curettage, without an anaesthetic. It's a very thin door and they'll hear everything. It would be much better for them to go back and sit in the hall. But they won't move. The eldest girl says: 'We mustn't leave our mother.'

Then I realize what's happening. It's not to comfort their mother that they must be with her, it's not to make things easier for her. Despite the high wall surrounding the hospital, despite Maternity being deep inside, invisible from the street, despite the main door that's now closed – despite this protection three layers thick, insulating these girls from the outside (my imagination up to this moment was equally enclosed) – they need their brother's permission before they can sit in the hall. My incredulity is no argument. The girls won't move. The curettage box clatters. I watch their faces. Their mother screams, and Dr Kostov roars. I'm almost pleased. But the girls don't seem to mind.

We do Dr Vasilev's ward round for him. 'It's not another doctor we need,' says Dr Kostov darkly. Yet he relaxes during the round. Things go smoothly, and nothing rouses him. He never reaches his peak. The last woman we see needs a curettage. Her pants are full of old blood, her cervix wide open. We walk with her down the corridor to the curettage room. Dr Vasilev and Dr Nikolenko are back from their tour of the hospital, and they come inside after us. I get the woman installed on the table, legs up, thighs and vulva cleaned with antiseptic soap and alcohol.

Dr Vasilev invites me to go ahead. I wonder if it's an honour. Or am I more of a scapegoat? Dr Nikolenko's about to witness her first curettage in her new hospital, and it's me who's been chosen to break all the rules in front of her, her and two others with something like sixty years' specialist experience between them. I go ahead and scrape, aware of the new presence. The woman squirms and moans. There's that matador-like moment at the end, when I hang up the rubber apron on the hook, put my hand on the woman, I'm sweating as much as she is, and she takes my hand to kiss it. Dr Nikolenko strokes her head and says in French: 'It's all over now.'

I go outside to speak with her afterwards, in case there's something she has to say to me. But there's nothing. She doesn't think we're a madhouse. Perhaps she thought that the first time, but now she's used to it. She's been in Algeria a year already, working in Constantine. She tells me about her contract. She regrets she ever signed it. She hasn't stopped working since the day she arrived. Fortunately, it has only another six months to run. 'On 1st April,' she says, 'Algeria and me . . .' – she washes the country from her hands.

She offers me a present. It's a postcard, a 3D view of the Kremlin, taken from across the river. I protest, but she insists that I keep it. We go up to the delivery room together.

'Take her away to the shower!' Zora's crying, and Fatma leads a woman down the corridor who has a pile of bay leaves stained in henna strapped to her belly. The delivery room's full. On the far bed, on the world's most encrusted mattress, lies a toothless woman eight months pregnant and bleeding into a yellow pan. Zora thinks it's a case of a badly positioned placenta, and she tells Dr Nikolenko that she's already sent for Dr Kostov.

In he comes. He's in magnificent form, a ringmaster, with hearty 'Heys!' and 'Hos!' to the women on the other two beds, and a word in Russian for Dr Nikolenko. He reaches the far corner and with one sweep of his hand, he sends the woman's robe flying off her knees to flutter back over her toothless face. With some vigorous tickling, he excites her womb into contraction. Then, as he feels it harden, he says to her: 'N'ki! N'ki! Push so hard you'll send the baby BOOM! through the wall, like a rocket!' Roars of laughter, and both fists on top of her womb, driving the baby out to the accompaniment of 'Hey! Hey! Hey!' The old woman screams for her life, her hands pull at Dr Kostov's fists, there's a growl from him in warning and I'm afraid – from jovial to vicious, it needs only this. The contraction's over.

The baby's come further down. More tickling, and another contraction. The mattress bounces up and down as Dr Kostov kneels beside the woman, a delirious horseman, both arms extended in front of him, his full weight in those fists and you can't believe the womb isn't going to burst. The head's out, Zora grabs it, pulls down, then up. A girl. The heart's not beating, and it doesn't take a breath. Zora fetches a cardboard box and in it goes, head first. The old woman points to the yoghurt carton, Fatma gives her a drink of water.

I come away with Dr Nikolenko, down the stairs. She's off to attend Out-Patients with Dr Vasilev. She's shaken, there's no doubt. 'That baby was born too fast,' she says, 'it was a scandal. In Russia . . .' But then she stops, and decides: 'Each doctor has his own way of working.'

The Electrician pushes open the office door with a look of deep suspicion on his face. He sidles to the desk, and picks up

El Moudjahid, as yet unopened, still in its wrapper (so busy has Dr Vasilev been with the new doctor). He fingers it, he pulls at it, turns up his nose. 'How much?' he asks aggressively, following his question immediately with an indignant: 'You're a thief!' He leaves the office, slamming the door behind him.

The door reopens softly. In comes the Electrician on tip-toe, with a sweet smile and nod of the head to the proprietor and the other customers: 'Bonjour, Messieurs.' He minces to the desk with wonder on his face, and alights on *El Moudjahid*. He turns it with delicate hands and exclaims: 'Isn't it pretty?' He asks: 'May I know the price, Monsieur?' and cries: 'How reasonable!' He pays, and leaves as he came in, with a nod and a smile: 'Au revoir, Messieurs.'

The Electrician's purpose: to demonstrate to me the mean-ness and rudeness of the Egyptians, even in the simplest things like shopping, compared to the exquisite 'politesse française' he once saw displayed by a colonel's wife entering the jewel-ler's in Tizi-Ouzou.

We're all sitting in the office before lunch. Dr Vasilev and Dr Nikolenko are back from Out-Patients, and they've brought an extra chair with them. There are crickets in the garden, and the shouts of the caretaker's children playing with the hose. Dr Vasilev talks contentedly to Dr Nikolenko. *El Moudjahid* lies in its wrapper on the desk. Dr Kostov gives loaded sighs, and studies his nails.

The pathetic gendarme, the one with the hanging lip, comes up the path with two women behind him. He gives us a limp handshake, and I find myself thinking: what a colleague. Dr Vasilev introduces 'our friend, Monsieur Gendarme' to the 'very sympathetic' new doctor. Then he takes the two women into the curettage room. Dr Nikolenko asks what they're being charged with. 'Prostitution, Doctor,' says the pathetic gendarme. Sex grin from Dr Kostov, who tells us of the thirty brothels in Oran, and the 150 women he had to examine weekly during his first appointment in Algeria. Of course, there are no official brothels in Bulgaria. He seems to regret it. 'In Oran . . .', he remembers. I say: 'You didn't have to force their legs open there!' and he roars with laughter.

But the pathetic gendarme scarcely smiles. He has problems, and in the new lady doctor he searches for a sympathetic audience. He's unhappy in his job. Here we are, he says, at the end of September, and he's still not had a day's holiday. He won't be surprised if it's going to be a repeat of last year – in the gendarmerie, people are beginning to forget what holidays are. 'Work, work and more work,' he says, 'frankly, Doctor . . .' He tells her about his contract. There are times when he regrets he ever signed it. 'Ach, Monsieur Gendarme,' Dr Nikolenko sighs in sympathy.

There's a girl born during the siesta, to a thirty-eight-year-old woman who's had eight normal children, and one abnormal. This one's abnormal too. It's large, for one thing, close on four kilograms. It also looks like a Mongol, or a 'trisomy', as they're called. The mother's already back in her bed. They won't be giving it to her. It's already been entered as stillborn in the Ledger of Deaths, and now it's just a matter of waiting. It's in the coldest place, lying in a blue cloth in the scales in front of the air-conditioner. It's got plenty of black hair and a wet face, with a lot of the yellowy, cheesy material that babies are born with on their skin. It has a strange cry, a squawk. Its limbs seem to have extra joints, one in the forearm and one in the calf. They're floppy and rubbery, you can do with them what you like. Its lips and the inside of its mouth are raw, without the normal lining. Actually while we're looking at it, some blood starts to trickle out the side of its mouth. Yet it's breathing well, and its heart sounds fine.

I show it to the doctors when they arrive. It's perverse of me, but I ask each of them separately the same question: what is the cause of Mongolism? Dr Nikolenko says: 'Marriage between cousins. We forbid it in the Soviet Union, but you'll find a lot of it in Algeria.' Dr Kostov says: 'Syphilis, X-rays, and severe bouts of 'flu.' Dr Vasilev cries: 'I've forgotten!' Yes, I say to each, but what is Mongolism exactly? Shrugs from all three shoulders. 'It isn't known,' says Dr Kostov. But, I say, isn't it something to do with chromosomes? They frown, and I have to write the word on prescription paper. And then, so there can be no mistake, I draw a little picture of a cell, with a nucleus, and 'chromosomes' inside it. They shake their heads. The concept is new to all three.

A cleaner looks unhappily at the Mongol on the scales. She's eight months pregnant herself. Delivery day's only round the corner, she says, she always tends to be early. At two months, she went to see Dr Ivanova with the urinary troubles that pregnant women get. Dr Ivanova gave her no fewer than five X-rays, all to her pelvis. 'Perhaps I'm going to have a Mongol too,' she says.

Dr Vasilev's mood of the morning hasn't left him. It's been a day of introductions, a day doing his favourite thing. He's been with Dr Nikolenko constantly (the name is Ukrainian, she says, it doesn't take the ending in 'a' like the other Russian names in the feminine). He's hardly spoken to Dr Kostov and me. He continues his introduction in the office, talking to her fluently in Russian, with no time for either *El Moudjahid* or the silver cigarette paper. Dr Kostov's Russian is almost as good, he understands all they're saying, but he won't have a part in it. He's on the seat next to mine, and he puts his hand on my knee: 'Are you emigrating to Canada when you qualify?' If I open up a gynaecological practice there, he says, he'll come as my partner. Again, that great laugh. I'm not sure what it means. Nor perhaps is he. Maybe he's having restless sleep on the skyscrapers of Montreal.

So we have an extra doctor on our hands. What to do with her? Perhaps she's the Director's solution to the Maternity problem – inject another doctor into the department, like Dr Vasilev steps up the dose of Vitamin C in the severer cases of shock. 'I might as well stay here,' says Dr Kostov with a yawn, 'because if I go back to the flat, what can I do?' 'Read about chromosomes' might have been an answer, but only for an absent audience.

I go over to the garage, and Dr Kostov strolls after me. The Electrician, the morgue-keeper and the mechanic are adjusting the timing on the motorcycle. The crippled truck-driver offers advice from his crutches. They're all expert, and I take it for a ride round the courtyard to show how well it's running. First I offer it to the Electrician. He's taken aback, and I have to ask him if he's ever ridden them. But he recovers quickly. He goes 'pa . . . pa . . . pa' that such a question should ever have crossed my mind. 'Triumph, Norton, BMW,' he says, 'I could drive them in my sleep.' So, to Dr Kostov's distress, I hand him the key. It's the first time I've called the Electrician's bluff. Not only do I have to start it for him, but before he's even got it into gear he's let it fall over on its side. It's my turn to be magnanimous.

Dr Vasilev comes over to join us, with Dr Nikolenko. She watches me circling the courtyard in my white coat. She's big, with great calves. She's only a few grams lighter than Tamara. I'm wondering what she's thinking of us all, engaged on this typical afternoon's activity.

A shock for Dr Kostov. He's on his way to supper when he hears me talking English, with a survivor from that plague of curettages this morning. The girl has her baccalaureat, she used to go to the lycée in Tizi-Ouzou, until her father took her away to be married. Dr Kostov puts his head through the window, sees what she's doing, and goes 'Ah!' in sudden respect. The girl's translating a passage from one of Vasileva's *Life Magazines*. He asks her if the bleeding's stopped. She says it has and he doesn't reach inside and tear back her robe to check. The Kabyl animal's a person. To be able to read *Life* in the original is what he'd want for his son. He admits the girl must be very intelligent. But he reminds her to listen to everything she's told. 'You weren't listening this morning when we told you not to move!' He roars with laughter, and swings his water bottle in a good-night wave.

At six, regretfully, Dr Vasilev takes his leave of Dr Niko-lenko and goes off to his supper. She stays on in the office, waiting for her husband. It's the first time we've really been alone together. For a while we don't talk. Then she gets to her feet and asks me if I'd like to see the two Russian curettes she's brought with her. I say I would, and I follow her next door into the curettage room. She takes a cloth and lifts the lid of the sterilizer. The curettes are bigger than the ones we already have, and they have a spoon at the end, instead of a loop. She says they're much safer that way, they're less likely to make holes in the womb. She closes the lid, and we return to the office.

I ask her about abortion in Russia. She tells me how it's done. A local anaesthetic, a curette, and it's over. It's nothing, she says, she's had three herself. You come in during the morning, and you're out by lunch.

She gets up again, and goes to the window. She stands there for a while, biting her lip, and pulling at loose threads in her white coat. She goes back to her seat. She speaks in short, staccato sentences. Her smiles seem to vanish the moment they're formed. It's as if there was something on her mind. Probably it's her contract, or it could be a problem with her husband. Or perhaps even it's the day she's just spent – I remember her coming away from that Kostov 'Chris-Taylor'. Tentatively, I say that Maternity doesn't have to be the way it is, there are things that could be done. 'Ach,' she says softly, Dr Vasilev and Dr Kostov are both men, they're from a different country, what can she do. She can't interfere. Besides, she'll be going home in six months.

But that's still time to change things, it's still time to use those forms piled up in the Stores. 'No, no!' cries Dr Nikolenko under stress. She sits on the edge of her chair and almost shouts at me. Yes, she knows that's how it should be; yes, that's how it is in Russia, but now that she's here, one temperature chart per patient is going to suffice. That's the decision she's made, and she's not going to be shaken from it by anybody. She spells it out to me, word by word, to prove her strength of will: 'While I am here, I want to work as simply as possible!'

She sits back, ill at ease. She'll conquer herself in a sudden outburst, only to fall back into the same fidgety state. Without something to do, without Dr Vasilev to talk to, she's unable to keep still. She's nervous, or she's shy, or she's both. She gets to her feet again and asks abruptly: 'Will you walk with me, please?' We cross the hall. We go down the corridor and took through the doors at the women in their rooms. We climb the stairs to the landing, where Dr Nikolenko admires the plaits of the pregnant cleaner, sitting there placidly knitting for her baby, with a blind trust in the shape it's going to be after that dose of X-rays in its second month. We go to the bridge over the courtyard and gaze through the window. I point out Paediatrics, the kitchen, the operating theatres. But the light's fading, and it's difficult to see. Dr Nikolenko drums her fingers along the ledge. Suddenly she turns away from me and forces an 'I'm fed up with obstetrics!' through her clenched teeth.

27

An immensely long day, and a black one for Kabyl women.
An insight at last into Dr Kostov, and even an invitation to
coffee.

I don't know what time Dr Nikolenko arrived in Maternity
this morning, but I find her at seven o'clock in the curettage
room with Vasileva. She's in a worse state than yesterday.
Dr Vasilev's chosen this morning for introducing her to
Theatre – she's going to assist him in an operation. Dr Nikolenko's holding a startled Vasileva by the shoulder and wanting
clear answers to her questions: is she sure that the patient has
eaten nothing this morning? that she's had an enema? that
she's been shaved? Dr Nikolenko insists on the woman being
properly prepared for the operation. Vasileva answers yes to
everything, how could a respectable nurse not. But at least
she does go down to the woman's room afterwards with a
razor and bowl of water.

She didn't sleep all night, Dr Nikolenko tells me. There was
no point lying awake in bed, she decided to come in early.
She doesn't know the woman who's due to have the operation.
She doesn't know what's the matter with her. She doesn't
know what operation she needs, or even if she needs an operation at all. She's been down to her room to look at her temperature chart, but there's no information on it. It's all stored
in that fallible structure, Dr Vasilev's head. 'I'll be operating
in the dark,' she says.

She's shaking her head, sighing, tightening her lips. She
may be talking to me, but I feel her to be far away. With her
husband, she wouldn't be worrying so much. But operating
with Dr Vasilev is going to be different. 'He's tired,' she says,

'he should retire.' And here he comes, the man we've been speaking about, down the steps of the doctors' building, buttoning his white coat over his singlet and calling good morning to the one-eyed cat among the bushes. He sees us in the distance and waves. 'I didn't want to operate here any-way,' Dr Nikolenko's telling me. In Russia, everything's clean and sterile. Here . . . Just to take Out-Patients, to do ward rounds and deliveries: that was all she wanted. She tells me she's a physician at heart, not a surgeon. I ask her what speciality she'd rather be doing. 'Skin diseases,' she says, and disappears with Dr Vasilev to Theatre.

It's all so rushed. Baya says Dr Vasilev made the decision to operate yesterday evening, and called Dr Nikolenko at her flat. I'm sure he means it kindly, a sort of 'excursion!' for her, but she's obviously terrified.

I go down the corridor to fetch the woman from her room. I find her in the lavatory instead, shampooing her hair under the cold tap. She dries herself on a towel. Her eyes are full of tears. She asks me to promise that everything will be all right. I promise. She puts on the special dressing-gown and the green plastic sandals. I'd like to walk beside her, it would even be nice to take her hand. But there's no question of anything like that. She walks two yards behind me, blowing the tears from her nose with her fingers.

She's been with us nearly two weeks. She looks about five months pregnant, and she's been losing blood at irregular inter-vals. Her womb has never felt right, and Dr Vasilev's sure it's a mole. First, he gave her injections to help her womb push it out, but they didn't work. Then, when he heard there was a simple test that would prove if it was a mole or not, that only needed the woman's urine and some frogs, he remembered a pond he'd seen near Dellys. We've always been about to go. But somehow, 'The Frog-pond!' has never assumed the pro-portions of 'The Fair!'

'What's going on?' shouts Dr Kostov as we pass the office. I tell him I'm taking the woman to Theatre. 'What do you mean, to Theatre?' 'Dr Vasilev, Dr Nikolenko . . .' 'That prostate!' roars Dr Kostov, smashing his fist on the desk as he realizes that an operation is taking place which he knew nothing about. Now he has both ward rounds to do, then Out-Patients, plus any emergencies in the delivery room. It's payment in kind for that morning he took off for the deal in Algiers, currency in Kabyl women. 'Prostate!' – and I hear his crashing fist again.

The woman sits for a moment on the bench in the Theatre corridor. The daily circumcisions pass by, boys in ceremonial clothes still asleep from the anaesthetic, being carried away by their fathers. The woman's inconsolable. A cleaner talks fast in Kabyl, trying to make her laugh. She only shakes her head. 'What's the matter, my girl?' cries the cleaner, 'look at me, I've had two operations,' and she slaps her belly with both hands.

We go into Theatre. She seems too stunned to panic, it must look as foreign to her as the moon. Dr Nikolenko's still washing. Dr Vasilev's already gowned and scrubbed, smoking a cigarette from a sterile pair of forceps. The woman takes off her dressing-gown and sandals. Underneath, she has a hospital blouse. She climbs on to the table, as if she were mounting an altar. They give her a blue sheet to cover her lower half, while she takes the blouse off. Then she lies back, pulling the sheet over her breasts. 'Ai, ma,' she sighs.

The anaesthetist slips a long padded crosspiece under her shoulders and straps her wrists to the ends, crucifix-style. He tightens some rubber tubing round her arm, rubs alcohol over her elbow, shows her his fist, clenched, and commands her in Kabyl to do the same. The vein pops up, blue. 'Pa . . . pa . . . pa,' says the woman as the needle goes in. Valium and atropine premedication. The anaesthetist keeps the needle in the vein with his thumb and changes the syringe. This time it's the real thing, thiopentone and curare. He pushes the plunger down and the woman's nerve goes, the sacrifice begins to talk. 'Telegraph my brother in the village,' she says, 'telegraph him that I'm having an operation.' 'Yes,' says the anaesthetist with a smile. 'I'm going to die,' the woman says, 'I'm going to die. Allah. All . . .' The thiopentone cuts the holy name in half, and a tear falls on the woman's blue headscarf.

'There,' chuckles Dr Vasilev, closing his eyes too, letting his head fall sharply to the side in imitation of her sudden sleep, 'now you know what to do if your wife talks too much!'

'I'd never manage,' says the anaesthetist with a laugh, as he tapes a slow Rheomacrodex drip to the woman's arm, 'she has such terrible veins.' Theatre chat, banal, cosy and comfortable, the same the world over.

But one who's anything but relaxed is Dr Nikolenko. Dr Vasilev hands her a sterile cloth, and she puts it on the wrong way. Then he makes a straightline incision down the woman's belly. It isn't smooth, blood vessels jump up and surprise him, it's difficult to believe he's cut open hundreds of bellies before. But Dr Nikolenko's so agitated that she catches her fingers in her clamps and Dr Vasilev has to reapply them for her. From behind her mask, she keeps up a non-stop, self-critical commentary. Dr Vasilev tries hard to soothe her. The anaesthetist's retreated into the background with staring eyes. 'Where did they dig this one up?' he whispers to me.

Dr Nikolenko settles down markedly with the arrival of her husband, already without cap or mask, conforming to local custom. The Supervisor follows him, puffed and absurd, with some crucial information for the anaesthetist. They talk urgently in Kabyl. He leaves, and I'd like to know the anaesthetist's opinion of him. But I hold my curiosity back. I don't know the line-up. Perhaps they're in the same faction. I'm too rarely in Theatre to have the anaesthetist's confidence. Above us on the wall, there's a discoloured and pathetic note from the hospital's first director after Independence: 'I appeal to all staff to take hold of themselves, to forget the old squabbles and eternal quarrels that can no longer be tolerated inside a hospital, I appeal to them to devote themselves entirely to their noble and magnificent duties, and to discover the joy there can be in working in unison.' It's dated 1963. It's like that 'Come back to France' on the lonely ruin off the road to Bejaïa.

Dr Vasilev's through the peritoneum. If it is a mole, I have no idea of what he plans to do. But underneath, there's no womb at all, only a pale firm skin blown up like a bladder, with blood vessels running across it. 'Ovarian cyst!' he cries. No wonder all his injections never worked. It's a nice surprise. A cyst is so much better to have than a mole. He punctures the bladder with a needle, puts in two stitches to hold it, and begins draining the fluid into a bowl on the floor.

We all watch. There are litres of it, and there's nothing to do but wait till it's finished. It's pale and yellowy in colour, and it makes a sound we're all familiar with as it splashes into the bowl. Dr Vasilev's the first to succumb. After a minute or so, he cries that he can't control himself any longer. He pushes the needle into Dr Nikolenko's hand and bends himself double, crossing his legs as hard as he can. Everyone's laughing, Dr Vasilev too, but he's in real trouble. Go in the bowl, the anaesthetist tells him, none of us'll mind. He pushes it over towards him with his foot. But Dr Vasilev jumps away and goes hopping round the table in circles. Then the flow slackens off, and he's able to straighten up. It's always the same with cysts, he tells us, he should have gone to the lavatory before. 'Eh! But then I didn't know!'

He whistles through the stitches. He's in a good mood, the operation has not gone badly, and Dr Nikolenko seems happy enough with her performance, after that poor start. I wheel the woman along to her room. She's groaning, already awake. No one's about, it's the weekend. Baya and Malika must have left early. There's only the pregnant cleaner who's been dragged up from somewhere. She helps me lift the woman off the trolley, and promises to stay with her a while.

I join Dr Vasilev and Dr Nikolenko in the office. They're chattering away happily. *El Moudjahid* lies ignored, straining inside its wrapper. With my thumb nail, I release it. The pages spring apart, and the centre fold envelops me – in *the* problem. It's the problem that no revolutionary needs to name. It climbs into bed with him at night, it wakes beside him at the beginning of every day. It forms the stuff of his daydreams and nightmares. It's how he sees, and how he hears. Any name he finds for it can only be the lamest approximation. *El Moudjahid*'s editor must make do with: 'THE MORAL DECAY OF ALGERIA!'

But to discuss it in his office he's summoned a veritable brains trust, a committee of concerned experts drawn from every field, journalists and university professors, representatives from the police force and from the National Union of Women. He describes the range of their knowledge as 'remarkable', and their mastery of the subject under discussion as 'incontestable'. He foresees 'a brilliant debate'. When he invites his guests to begin, the policeman and the professor stumble over questions of precedence, each overwhelmed by the other's competence. The editor's a reluctant referee. He rules for 'our brother from the Sûreté Nationale', as being the man with 'the facts' at his disposal.

The policeman recalls *El Moudjahid*'s glorious past, as the mouthpiece of the liberation struggle. He pays tribute to its leadership today, in the campaign for moral health. And he confesses to a feeling of inadequacy, at being invited to speak first in such company. He humbly presents his graphs, fresh from the Sûreté drawing-boards. Dotted, starred and continuous, his lines climb relentlessly through the eight years of Independence. Adultery, homosexuality and suicide, the parameters of decay. Only the official brothels and prostitutes have not increased in number. They remain at their pre-Independence level. But for every one 'professional', projection studies hint at some fifteen 'amateurs', part-time prostitutes in the working class, filling out their budget in the way they find easiest. The policeman prefers figures to the untrustworthy impressions gained from everyday life. He calculates the overall decay at 'eighty per cent'.

Djamal Baghdadi runs the Schools Programmes on Radio-Algiers. He's also been an eager prompter of the policeman's opening speech, always one step ahead of the rest of the class. His next question crystallizes the thoughts swirling murkily through the others' minds. He has a further 'interpolation' to make. 'Have you no figures on prostitution in the upper classes?' he asks the policeman, 'I mean on those women who practise this thing without an exchange of money, but purely out of vice?'

There are two pictures on the centre fold. One shows two girls in Western clothes, seen from behind. The caption says: 'The slavish imitation of the West.' The other shows a man in Western clothes, seen from in front. The caption to this reads: 'Djamal Baghdadi.'

I put the paper down. I've become uneasy, sitting here like this, me reading, Dr Vasilev chattering, as if there were an army of well-trained staff to take care of everything. Dr Kostov's away in Out-Patients, and there's not a soul about. I go back to the woman with the cyst. She's well, and the pregnant cleaner has fallen fast asleep on the next bed. I start up the stairs. There's a Bob Dylan song coming from inside the delivery room. It's loud and strong and nasal. Zora's inside, her radio's full on, and there's a woman on the table with a look about her that hits me immediately, that's absolutely unmistakable. She's dying.

It's not that she's deathly still. Her head's thrashing from side to side, her lips are drawn back over her teeth and she's trying to free herself from the bandages that hold her to the bed. She's naked, and her belly's enormous. The baby's still in there. I shout to Zora to know what's going on. She tells me to tie down the woman's feet while she puts up a drip. Instead I ask her why she hasn't got help. You must get help! 'I'm fed up with the lot of them,' says Zora, 'if they can't care less, then I can't either.'

She's totally out of her depth, and she can't see it. She has no insight or imagination. She wants me to tie down the feet of a woman who's dying. I rush out, rush down the stairs, where Dr Vasilev's chatting in the office with Dr Nikolenko, the old reflex at work in me, the reflex of the general population: get a doctor, and all will be well. Better still, call two doctors, call upon 40 years' obstetric experience for a strictly obstetric problem, and all *must* be well. At the office door, I cry: come quickly! there's a woman in the delivery room who's very bad!

They hurry up the stairs after me. Dr Vasilev looks at the woman, takes in the scene. Please make the magic presence work! 'Is she grouped?' he asks. The right question! Go on! 'Yes,' answers Zora, who's still searching for a vein for her drip. 'Is the blood on its way over?' asks Dr Vasilev. Right again, it's the question doctors always ask! Go on, please! 'Yes,' answers Zora. But oh, oh can't he see she's lying? Can't he hear the lie in that 'yes'? Shrink, collapse, of a myth born of panic. The woman is to be received into nobody's arms. She's on her own and she's going to die.

Dr Vasilev takes over the needle from Zora, he's found himself a little job. He gets into the vein. The drip is Rheoma-crodex. Is there anything else in it? Zora says yes, of course. But if that's true, where are all the ampoules? I run down to the curettage room, collect hydrocortisone, coramine (even Vitamin C, my faith can't have gone completely) and inject them into the drip, while Zora goes off to fetch the blood. She's happy to get away.

Two bottles of blood arrive, 250 ml each. One's A+, the woman's group, and she gets that first. When it's through, she gets the other, O+. Something goes wrong during the change-over, and the giving-set jumps under pressure, to spurt blood on to the wall like an artery.

Dr Nikolenko holds the woman's arm to keep the drip in. The woman opens her eyes, looks at us for a moment quite consciously, and says the Kabyl word for water. But before I can get the carton to her lips, she's fallen back again, giving great bites to the empty air, teeth clicking, gnawing the oxygen tube so savagely that all my strength can't get it away from her, reaching back with open jaws for the cake-cover so-called oxygen tent, and cracking her teeth down on its filthy Perspex again and again, without feeling a thing. She tears her hands free of the bandages, and scratches and pinches anything within reach. 'It's a psychosis,' says Dr Nikolenko. 'Ai, Madame,' says Dr Vasilev, and hits her with the stethoscope.

Dr Kostov arrives back from Out-Patients. He's just found a woman on the floor of the curettage room, he says. He put her on the table, set up a drip and came here. He thought we were still in Theatre. He first set eyes on the woman in front of us an hour ago, before he went off to Out-Patients. He guessed her placenta must have come away too soon and he told Zora to get her grouped and transfused. There's no comment, no word even, from Dr Vasilev. I suddenly realize he's no longer with us. He's left the room.

Dr Kostov feels the woman's belly, keeping away from her savage hands. It's stony hard. He doesn't bother to listen with the stethoscope. He says there's no point, the baby must be dead. Then he leaves the room too.

Dr Nikolenko and I are on our own. What a team. Neither of us knows what to do. I put a cuff round the woman's arm.

The pressure's good, and I wonder if it isn't time to stop the drip, in case we're giving her too much fluid. Dr Nikolenko doesn't know. I run out to ask.

The landing's empty. I rush down the stairs, into the curettage room, and stop short. Dr Vasilev's there, with that woman Dr Kostov spoke of; he's sitting between her legs with a needle and catgut and he's sewing up a tear that the mountain maternity had been unable to repair. 'But Dr Vasilev . . . !' He doesn't look up. Yet he knows I'm there. I rush out, and in the hall I find Dr Kostov, incoherent with rage, kicking at the bench, slamming his fist against the wall. I run back up the stairs, pull out the woman's drip myself, and find I have to keep cotton wool tightly over the hole because the bleeding won't stop. It doesn't stop till she dies.

Dr Kostov flings open the door, beside himself. He'll do an embryotomy. I get the special box down from the top shelf. His embryotomy exceeds anything that's gone before. He's never been more brutal. The woman feels nothing. She's even become quieter. Her pressure stays the same. Dr Kostov drives through with the perforator of Blot. He's into brain first time and he opens the arrowhead. Out the stuff comes, white and curdled, with a little blood. Now for the four-pound cranioclast. But he just can't get a hold. The thing keeps slipping, bringing out more brain instead, sending Dr Kostov reeling back to the basin, his glasses spattered with blood, crying 'Algeria!'

The cranioclast slips out of his fingers and falls to the floor, an immense clatter. He switches to the basiotribe, a similar sort of thing, the same size. But the woman's cervix is only four fingers dilated. 'I can't get through,' whimpers Dr Kostov, 'I can't get a grip.' No hold from its serrated edges, only black blood all over Dr Kostov's face and clothes. Then suddenly there's a gargle, liquid in the woman's throat, her blood pressure drops to nothing. Stethoscope swinging in my ears, I'm bending over her arm saying there's no pressure, no pressure at all, Dr Nikolenko's pumping her chest and Dr Kostov's throwing the basiotribe down and pulling off his apron and washing his face and hands in the basin and saying: 'Leave her, why should we bother.' The pregnant cleaner waddles in with a cardboard box, but we never managed to get the baby out. Brain and thick black blood between the woman's legs, flies on the drips, I'm shaking all over.

In the curettage room, from that heap Dr Kostov had to revive on his way back from Out-Patients, Dr Vasilev says in a strange voice: 'Ah, she's dead, that woman.' It's strange because it's not really a question, and I've said nothing. Dr Vasilev knows perfectly well what's happened. He sews on, neat catgut stitches. 'Only us doctors are here,' he says, 'you, me, Dr Kostov, Dr Nikolenko . . .' And so on. Why bother recording all he says. It's the same old stuff, the foreign doctors who'll stay into their lunch-hour if need be, the Algerian orderlies who won't. It's never been more bogus. It's no longer just petulant, it's become a whine. He calls me over, but I don't want to hear him. He calls me a second time, using my name, to come and watch him put in his final dedicated stitch. But before I can move, I fall towards the wall. My shoes have stuck to the floor with the blood from the woman upstairs.

Dr Vasilev goes back to his apartment, to get ready for his long-awaited trip to the Fair, and Dr Kostov goes home to lunch. Dr Nikolenko too. The pregnant cleaner and I load the dead woman on to the trolley and wheel her into the babies' changing room. The Mongol from yesterday is there in its cot, still alive and still with that trickle of congealed blood from its mouth, but one eye's now closed and the other's open and fixed, staring back over its head.

The woman with the cyst has been sick, all over her head, shoulders and pillow. She asks me if I'd move her further over on the sheet, as she's passed urine all over it. She doesn't even expect the sheet to be changed. She vomits again, green elastic strands towards the floor. I call upstairs to the cleaner for a fresh sheet, pull the old one out and fetch some water, soap and cotton wool. I clean her back and thighs and between her legs. She groans but there's nothing she can do about it, she's so weak it's pathetic. There must be a life of good works to be spent, going round the hospital washing urine off patients. But why bother. Her husband's getting rid of her, she tells me, if she doesn't have children after this. She has no strength, she

259

says, 'oulesh forsa'. 'Forsa' is the French word 'force'. It's what all the Kabyl women say. They don't seem to have their own word for strength.

Zora invites me to have lunch with her in the midwife's room. It's cous-cous, and she's collected my tray too. She's eating well. 'They just let that woman die,' she says, 'it's shameful. It's not their country, they couldn't care.' I say yes, but vaguely. I know she's not feeling entirely blameless herself, and she wants me on her side. This lunch is for getting my approval. 'She was perfectly well this morning', Zora goes on, 'her blood pressure was 120/80.' That has to be a lie, I've never seen her take a blood pressure yet. But I don't bother to argue. She's seen the husband, he's around somewhere. 'Such a nice old man,' she says, oozing feeling. Djamila comes over from her room and has a little cous-cous with us. She crosses herself, a habit she must have picked up from the French, and hopes that she'll never have a death while she's on duty.

They eat for a while in silence. Djamila asks brightly: 'Remember Farida?' Zora looks up, immediately interested. Well, it seems Djamila was in Algiers yesterday, looking up her friends, chatting of this and that. Guess what: Farida's got married! To a fellow doing medicine, no less. He's even qualified already, and specializing in surgery at Mustapha. On top of which, he's fabulously rich, with a lovely car and a maid for everything. You couldn't ask for more. 'Not bad,' Zora has to admit, 'not bad.' The only thing, says Djamila, is that he's 'terribly' jealous. He's stopped her working. Farida was trying to get a job in one of the private maternity clinics of the capital, but her husband soon put a stop to that. He won't let her out of the house. Once she wanted to take the car and visit her parents. But he wouldn't let her, not until he had a day off and could drive her there himself. 'He's really terrible,' says Djamila.

But it's just another lie. She's all too fascinated by the male force that pervades her story. I ask them if Farida's life isn't exactly what they'd like. 'Well, yes,' says Djamila, blushing like a little girl, 'it can't be that bad!' And Zora says: 'It proves he's very fond of her.' I leave them to the cous-cous, I've eaten nothing of it.

The pregnant cleaner and I wheel the dead woman to the Morgue. She's loose still, and one arm keeps falling through the sheet. We fix it with sticky tape. The heat outside is appalling. A dog crosses over towards us from the green refuse truck. It's the dog with the thin, uneven coat and the missing paw. It limps beside us until we're in the main hospital building. The cleaner says we must go the long way round. The Morgue is only across the courtyard, but the trolley jolts too much on the gravel and we can't keep the woman on. We go the long way round and the dog's there waiting for us when we come out the other side.

The morgue-keeper arrives with his keys, and opens up. There are eight coffins on rollers, and the cooling unit's by Frigidaire. We slide the woman in and pull away the sheet. At the tap outside, the cleaner produces an unused bar of Palmolive soap from her overalls. She washes like a surgeon before an operation. The morgue-keeper watches. 'It's the tradition,' he says.

A Peugeot 403 draws up at the end of the path, with two men inside it. One gets out and comes into the office. He says he's the cousin of the man outside, who's the husband of one of the patients. Why can't he come in himself, I want to say, but don't – it's always like this, a brother or a cousin instead. He's come to collect the wife. I check on the register and remember the girl well. She came in bleeding, but with her cervix still closed. She's resting in bed. The bleeding's stopped, and with a little more rest she should be able to keep the baby. I remember her because of the nasty wound on the inside of her leg – a raw area about four inches by two, very painful and leaking fluid. An old woman had done it up in the village with burning wood, as treatment for her bleeding.

So I tell the cousin that she should stay in a little while longer. Take her back to the mountains now, and to her daily routine, she'll almost certainly lose the baby. The cousin goes out to the car and comes back with the husband, who's younger, poorer, shabbier. He's taking his wife home, he says, there are children for her to look after and a home to keep. If she stays in hospital, he can't go out to work, he's in danger of losing his job. I explain it all again, and ask how far he is from the hospital. He's four hours away, he says. Supposing she miscarries, I tell him. By the time he's found a car and got her here, she could be already dead, especially as she's so weak already. 'But there's water to fetch,' says the man, 'figs to pick, fields to look after, the house, the children . . .' Aren't there people nearby who can help? There's no one, says the husband. The cousin says that's true. But then, I say, it'll only be worse if your wife does die, you'll have no one to help you at all. I ask him if he has another woman he could marry if this one dies, who'd be able to do her work. He shakes his head: 'There's no one else.'

He hesitates, perhaps he's going to change his mind and let her stay. I've conducted the conversation like a doctor, like one of those grey-haired humanists on the brochures from Roche. I've even gone so far as to draw a pair of scales on the back of one of their envelopes, with a few days of lost work in one pan and a dead wife in the other.

But suddenly, the husband shakes himself. 'I don't care!' he cries, 'I just want her back, she won't do any work.' 'That's not true,' I say. 'Oh let her die, let her die!' he shouts, 'give me that paper to sign!' 'Bastard!' I shout back. 'Why am I a bastard?' 'Because you couldn't care less if your wife dies.' 'If my wife dies, OK. If I die, OK. If the children die, OK. We'll all die!' It's the cry of absolute despair. He tells me again about the water, the field, the donkey and the figs. . . . The hospital's an intrusion on his life, it's no aid to it. I know he's right, I know in a way he does care, but I can't stop saying 'salaud' instead of 'monsieur' – 'Go upstairs, salaud, and get your form . . . Sign here, salaud,' and so on, it's terrible. He signs with his whole body, a contorted, associated movement that involves his trunk and both legs. The biro goes twice through the paper as he engraves the initials 'BJM' on the bottom of the form.

'At least I tried, Doctor,' says the cousin with an apologetic shrug of the shoulders but, over the crippled handwriting of

262

the other, there's something insinuatingly obsequious about the remark, and I don't respond. I'm fed up with them both, with the whole place, with myself most of all. The husband puts out his hand. I don't shake the hands of salauds. He insists, I end up shaking the hand of the cousin instead. Why should I bother – Dr Kostov's expression is coming naturally to me now. 'Thank you, Doctor,' says the husband, 'we're very grateful.' The wife follows them to the car, in veil and shawl, limping from that burn on her leg. I hate Algerian men, Algerian women, Bulgarians, Russians, I hate them all.

They've no sooner driven away than the Econome's mournful secretary arrives in his grey overalls, with the heavy, green-speckled Ledger of Deaths. No prizes for guessing who's with him. The husband of our death today is about fifty-five, tiny and shrunken, in blue overalls patched many times. Hollow, unshaven cheeks. A lower jaw that moves with a kind of tic. White canvas shoes full of holes, a tattered sombrero. He stares in front of him with tears in his eyes. 'He has a few fields of figs in the plain before Dellys,' the mournful secretary's saying.

Dr Kostov must sign the Ledger, and we go out together to look for him in his flat. But we meet him on the way, on the path outside the Maternity windows. He's not paralysed by this kind of encounter. Finger plonked on the frail husband's chest. 'You the husband?' He's saying 'tu', but I don't think that's deliberate. 'Yes,' says the shrunken man. 'I saw your wife this morning at 10.30,' says Dr Kostov, 'she was very ill.' 'Yes, Doctor.' 'What time did she come in last night?' 'At three in the morning, Doctor.' From the hopeful look in the man's eyes, you'd think he's expecting Dr Kostov to bring her back from the dead. 'Was she well then?' asks Dr Kostov. 'Yes, Doctor, very well. She started getting the pains in the night. We walked two kilometres together along the road to Dellys. She was strong.' 'Why didn't you go to Dellys hospital?' 'We did, Doctor, but they were closed. She was strong, Doctor.'

We're back in the doctors' office. Dr Kostov in his white coat, sitting behind the desk, the husband with his sombrero, standing in front: it's the very picture of underdevelopment. Dr Kostov fills in the Ledger. I don't see what goes down as the cause of death. 'Your wife's case was very interesting,' says Dr Kostov, 'very interesting indeed.' The man listens. The sombrero passes through his fingers like a rosary. The humiliation defies belief, I can hear the gasps of the world behind me. Yet Dr Kostov's deaf, and the peasant too. 'It was a very interesting case, because we think it was a premature detachment of the placenta (in French 'un décollement prématuré du placenta').' 'What did he say?' asks the man of the mournful secretary who's taken back the Ledger, 'displaced lungs (in French 'poumons déplacés')?' 'No, no,' says Dr Kostov, taking the other side of the envelope from Roche to draw a womb, a baby and a placenta. 'Blood pressure . . . haematoma . . . placenta . . . detachment. You see?'

The man falls back on the chair opposite me. It's as if his wife has died again. If only he'd say he'll get another. But no, his distress has given his hands, his legs, his head, a lolling, flopping movement that's almost effeminate. He looks over to me, both hands out: 'But what am I going to tell the children? What am I going to do? Tell me!' Is there no family, are there no friends to help? 'We have no one, Doctor, I'm all alone. Why didn't you see her when she came in the night?' He asks the question a second time. I turn away, Dr Kostov hears it too, ignores it too. Instead, he's explaining the detached placenta to the mournful secretary.

'It's sad, of course,' says Dr Kostov when we're alone afterwards, 'but it's all the fault of the head of the department.' During the next hour or so, Dr Kostov's soul appears, deprived like a Maternity baby, and to be marked down in the Ledger as dead, but with a few jerky movements before it actually disappears.

Objective, opening his defence: 'When I first arrived in Algeria, I replaced another Bulgarian. It was a one-doctor department, so I was the head. I held a meeting of all the staff on my first day there. I was nice and gentle with them, because that's what I'm really like.'

Character witness: 'In Bulgaria, I'm calm, I never shout,

I never throw things. I'm the quietest of all the doctors I know.'

Self-righteous: 'But here I'm becoming neurasthenic. I shout, I scream, I throw things. I don't like my work. How many times do you think I shouted at people when I came here? I even shouted at Tamara. But then I saw that nobody cared. The head of the department didn't care. The Algerians didn't care. Only I cared. So why should I bother?'

Thwarted reformer: 'How many times do you think I said to Vasilev: "Everything's going wrong here, call a meeting"? He used to say yes, and he'd "call a meeting". You've seen yourself how he does it. That's why I never helped you. I knew there was no point, I knew how it would end. After his "meeting", he says they refused to turn up. But he does nothing about it! Zora, Djamila, Malika – he lets them do what they like. If it'd been me, I'd have dragged them to the Director. I'd have gone all the way to the Ministry of Health. Only if they did nothing would I say: "I wash my hands of the whole business, I let everything go on as it is" .'

Unimpeachable: 'I've actually said that to Vasilev, you know. I announced it to him one day, officially. I said: "You know what I think about this place. You know what I've tried to do. Well, from now on I'm just going to carry out your orders, and I refuse to take responsibility for anything that happens." I said it again this morning. When he ran out of the delivery room, I went after him and grabbed him by the shoulder. He knew that woman was going to die, we all did. I said to him: "Look, idiot. What do you want me to do with her? You're the Professor. Tell me, and I'll do it. But I warn you, I'm taking no responsibility for what happens!" He told me to do an embryotomy, and that's exactly what I did. I knew it would only kill her quicker.'

Mean: 'And off he went downstairs to stitch up that tear! Have you ever seen a head of department doing that? It's the student's job, it's your job. He was so pleased to blame the orderlies, but that was his fault too. He's supposed to know when they go off duty. He's supposed to check up on things like that before he starts his operations. He didn't even warn *me* what he was going to do. He left me to do the lot! The

Professor shows the new doctor how to operate – when it's his weekend off and it's not going to be his job to look after the woman! I should let her die for him!'

With his Kabyl-vagina face, Dr Kostov yanks open the biggest drawer in the desk, takes two handfuls of the pharmaceutical brochures that Dr Vasilev's been hoarding ever since his arrival in Algeria and hurls them into the wastepaper basket: 'Prostate!' With the brochures goes a piece of prescription paper with a dozen Kabyl words in Dr Vasilev's handwriting, their Bulgarian equivalents opposite – relics of the early days.

Inconsequential: 'His trouble is that he's ruled by his wife. She's only got to say "do this", and he'll do it.'

Disinterested: 'But what can I do? If I put in to be head of the department, they'll say it's because of the extra money. But what do I care for their extra hundred dinars a month?'

Patriotic: 'Think how it would look if I went to the Director to complain about Vasilev. Vasilev's a colleague of mine, a doctor from the same country. It wouldn't look good. What do I want to go to an Algerian about him for?'

Last of all, vulnerable: we sit together in silence a little while longer, except that Dr Kostov sighs 'ai, ai, ai,' several times. It's nearly six, and getting dark. He invites me back for a coffee in his flat. He's friendly and gentle, his Bulgarian self. I say that no one's around and I'd like to keep an eye on the woman whose cyst we took out this morning. And because that doesn't seem sufficient, I invent an exam I'm preparing for. Luckily, my textbook is on the desk. He turns its pages, for the first time. He should be helping me, he says, answering my questions, explaining things for me. But he doubts if his French is good enough. Then he picks up my notebook and leafs through that. But it's all in English. 'Write, write,' he says, 'you're always writing. I wish my son worked as hard.'

Dr Vasilev appears immediately afterwards. Has he been waiting for him to leave? I think so. He looks in too poor shape to take on Dr Kostov. The afternoon in Algiers was catastrophic. With a little 'eh', Dr Vasilev admits he didn't even go

to the Fair: 'There were a lot of cars, it was very hot . . .'
Serve him right. I'm fed up with him, I can feel no sympathy.
He's come to tell me that supper's nearly ready.

I've been thinking of going into Tizi-Ouzou tomorrow
morning and bringing a law suit against the hospital in the
name of the fig-farmer from Dellys. I mention it to the Cook
on my way over to the Vasilevs, but he isn't keen. I'm only
here for three days more, I'd get nowhere. What would it
prove, he says, as if everyone doesn't know what's going on
already. And the judge must be the same as the Director, Lenin
and two telephones in the service of feudalism.

Cool meatball soup with parsley and lemon, stuffed peppers
and curdled milk, Mascara wine. I know the food's delicious,
but it's tasteless to me. I know they're taking care of me, but I
feel nothing for either of them. Vasileva's disappointed by my
appetite. She puts her hand on my shoulder and calls me their
son. Later, as I leave, she tells me how bad things have become
in Sofia, with all the foreign students who are there. Some are
from Africa, black Africa, and they mix freely with the Bulgarians. How much better they do things in Moscow, where
'these people' are kept at Patrice Lumumba, their own university. Some of the students she's seen in Sofia are 'black,
black', and she gives a civilized shudder.

I escape, back to Maternity, and to some sickeningly hectic
hours of curettages and births. Sticky shoes, blocked drips,
the single bowl for urine, faeces and vomit. Four births in
under an hour, Djamila and I doing two each, with more women
crawling round the walls on the landing waiting to deliver.
Names, ages, villages unknown to me and to anyone else.
Being forced to call in help from Dr Kostov, and glimpsing
him astride an unconscious woman in the hall, pulling her
head back by the plaits and flicking cold water in her face.
Running from drip to drip, their veins hurting, their arms
aching, bottles to change. Sticky tape that won't stick, saline
all over the floor. The woman who arrives six months pregnant,
cervix wide open and pushing well, a baby long since dead,
'So much the better,' she says. It falls to pieces into the enamel
bowl and the whole lot goes down the lavatory next to the
woman with the cyst. She has a sheet drawn over her like a

shroud. I'm scared, I pull it back a little: 'Lebess?' 'Lebess,' no more than a whisper.

Then it all stops. I stand in the office, brush the ants from my coat, kick them off my shoes. It's the first moment I've been alone all day. Fatma locks the main door behind me. It's early morning outside. I hear her pushing the bolt home, and I suddenly feel awfully exposed, there in my white coat, with the courtyard just a blur before my eyes. A firing squad's out there for me, and I've nowhere to flee. But I'm not going to run anyway. I'm going to stand and let the bullets come.

28

It's Dr Nikolenko's first full day on duty. She's going to be entirely on her own. Dr Vasilev will only drop in from time to time to see how she's getting on, and Dr Kostov won't be appearing at all.

She begins with a round on the ground floor, attended by Vasileva, Fatma and me. The language confusion is the same as with the other two doctors. In the course of the round, I see her face the problem and solve it, in the same way that they've done.

Her French is very poor, her Kabyl non-existent. The same goes for Vasileva, who's also very weak in Russian. The patients speak Kabyl only. So an interpreter's needed. Best would be Malika, but she's always got urgent paperwork to do. Next best would be Baya, tired but at least available. Her languages are Kabyl and French, with a few words of Arabic for the odd patient from outside Kabylia. She's also used to interpreting for Dr Vasilev and Dr Kostov on their ward rounds. But Vasileva insists on having her in the background. She's suspicious of Algerian girls. She's happier with Fatma the cleaner, more her own age and with all those years in the service of a French colonel to her credit.

Fatma's fluent in Kabyl, French and Arabic and she's been interpreting all her life. But it so happens that Dr Nikolenko's new, and Fatma finds my French easier to understand than hers. Therefore, if the doctor wants to ask the patient a question, the basic route has to be: from Dr Nikolenko to me in French, from me to Fatma in clearer French, and from Fatma to the patient in Kabyl. For the return journey, Dr Nikolenko understands French from me better than from Fatma, or perhaps she just needs things repeated before they sink in.

But all sorts of auxiliary routes may be required, depending on the circumstances. Baya can come in from the background, only trying to help, in Kabyl to Fatma and the patient, in French to Dr Nikolenko, Vasileva and me. Or Dr Vasilev may intervene, in Bulgarian to his wife, in Russian to Dr Nikolenko, and in French to Fatma and me. Or Dr Nikolenko can prod the patient herself and look for the answer in her face, breaking the whole circuit. Messages get lost on the way, they're hopelessly garbled. Dr Nikolenko waves her hand brusquely and writes down any drug on the temperature chart: 'I'm prescribing blindly! The patients are in the hands of God!' But she'll get used to it. The others have. And by the end of the round, she's asking no more questions.

But something else is the matter with her. Her mouth's tight, she's as cold as ice. Only her lack of confidence could have made her sympathetic. But now that she's decided to take a firm line with herself, there's not even that. When I heard of her arrival, there were an infinity of people she could have been. When I saw her, the range shrunk. When I heard what she had to say, it narrowed still further. That's what happens anyway when you meet new people, except that with Dr Nikolenko, only the nicer things seem to be getting excluded.

How she slaughters all those possible selves, once and for all! She's found her feet now, heavy and discoloured feet with knotted veins. That first time, under Dr Vasilev's supervision – when she'd been so on edge, remember! – she'd actually replaced the sheets over the women she examined. Now she's found the Kostov pendulum technique: one hand holds the temperature chart, the other tears down the sheet on the backswing, throws up the robe on the front swing, and then prods the thighs open with the biro. Woe betide them if there are pants underneath: 'Allez, Madame, a hospital isn't a cinema!'

The wretched cry is uttered with a snarl, a twisting of the lips not so different from Dr Kostov's. She catches hold of the pants, commands Vasileva to do the same, and they pull them off together. Vasileva adds reprimands of her own – 'You've been told' – designed to save face. With Dr Kostov and her husband, she wouldn't need to. But Dr Nikolenko's still new, and in the old country, in the old ethic, nurses were supposed to prepare the patients for the doctor's round.

Dr Nikolenko passes on to the next, with the warmth of a prison warder. Smart blows to the inside of this woman's thighs. No wonder she's opening them so slowly, she's the one whose tear was mended by Dr Vasilev, albeit with such care, while the fig-farmer's wife lay dying upstairs. Dr Nikolenko looks at the stitches. The thighs and pubic hair are covered in blood. 'Has a genital toilet been done?' she asks. Great embarrassment from Vasileva. 'It must be done every day,' insists Dr Nikolenko. 'Of course,' says Vasileva, but she makes no note of it in her book. The new rota system will ensure that it won't be Dr Nikolenko doing the round here tomorrow morning. Besides, she'll soon understand that there's something 'impossible' about such things as genital toilets in Algeria – the lack of trained staff for one thing, their couldn't-care-less attitude for another ('we have more concern for their people than they do themselves'). She'll understand before the week is out, she's shown such promise already. But it's still worth Vasileva saying to her as we leave the room: 'I was off duty over the weekend, Dr Nikolenko.'

Dr Nikolenko takes Malika off to Out-Patients with her. While she's away, the Electrician calls in with the anaesthetic orderly, down briefly from Theatre to find out if it's true that Dr Nikolenko's alone on duty. When I say it is, he goes 'pa . . . pa . . . pa'. He remembers the day Ivanov arrived. He killed a boy of eight. 'It was murder,' says the anaesthetist, 'but never mind the details.' He sent them off in a report to the Ministry of Health. From there it went to the Soviet Embassy, and he heard there was an inquiry. But no one ever came to the hospital. All that happened was that the anaesthetist was called in by the Director and told he'd lose his job if he didn't drop the matter. 'It's blackmail,' says the anaesthetist, 'if we criticize them, they'll all leave.' There's nothing for it but to appreciate the Eastern Europeans for what they are – 'cheap foreign labour, like us Algerians in France'. Meanwhile, he says, 'we keep our mouths shut, we hold on to our ideals, and we work in total disillusion.'

I reassure the anaesthetist by telling him that Dr Nikolenko's no murderer. She's just the most nervous surgeon I've ever seen.

The Electrician's in my chair and I'm in Dr Vasilev's, behind the desk. We're rather like two examiners after the candidate's left the room. The Electrician removes his dark glasses and polishes them thoughtfully. He thinks highly of the anaesthetist, deeming him 'un type évolué'. He's one of those whom the Electrician talks to in the hospital. I receive advice to do the same. The anaesthetist's not backward, in the way that some of them are who've never been outside Kabylia. The Electrician puts his hands beside his eyes, to indicate the blinkered vision of some of his compatriots.

I ask him if he's read this morning's paper. He hasn't. He never buys *El Moudjahid*, he tells me, for much the same reasons as he likes to keep to himself in the hospital. He finds its outlook too provincial. He's a *France-Soir* man himself. I choose a piece by Mouloud Kassim, on the 'problem' of education for women, and begin reading it out to him: 'Though it may be necessary to send girls to school, as the Prophet suggested – even ordered – fourteen centuries ago . . .'

The Electrician claps his hands over his ears. Kassim's a caveman, he tells me. He belongs to prehistory. Nobody takes him seriously. He's the laughing-stock of the country. The Electrician smiles pityingly as I read on aloud. Girls who go to school must not be left to themselves, on a loose rein, to come and go as they please . . . A strict watch must be kept by fathers and brothers . . . Why tempt the devil that slumbers in the best of us? To the hesitant among his readers, Mouloud Kassim recommends a maxim of Lenin's on Bolshevik Party discipline: 'Vertrauen ist gut, Kontrolle ist besser – Trusting is good, checking is better.'

The Electrician asks me to read that bit about the devil again. For a while, after I've done so, he makes no comment. Then he says, with an excitement out of place in a man whose whole style is to be blasé: 'They say there are women who like it so much they'll do anything to get it.' It's half a question. 'They say,' he goes on, 'that there are men in Europe who become impotent if the woman doesn't enjoy it.' I can't think what to answer. 'With us,' the Electrician tells me, 'it would be the opposite.'

Dr Nikolenko comes back from Out-Patients, almost relaxed. There's been no major catastrophe. Ward rounds, Out-Patients, it's been routine stuff. She knew what it was going to be, and she was ready for it. But there's still an hour to go before lunch. And after that, there's all the afternoon, all the evening, and all the night until nine o'clock tomorrow morning. They're pure unknown. Anything can happen. How she must envy Dr Vasilev his peace of mind. We sit in the office and wait. The day may dribble to a close on a forceps or a curettage, as it tends to with Dr Vasilev, or the emergencies may strike in any form or order. Enterprising obstetricians could find that exciting. But Dr Nikolenko's a dermatologist at heart.

Her resolution begins to flag. It's not long before she's pacing up and down the Maternity hallway in sandals that sound like boots. Clenched fists, 'achs!' of despair, 'achs!' of anger at herself – suddenly drowned by the brakes of a mountain taxi screeching for help outside.

I run out there with Fatma. The driver opens up the back, we hurry the stretcher down the path and into the curettage room. Seven months pregnant and bleeding furiously and when Dr Nikolenko's trembling fingers cross the cervix, they go straight into soft placenta. 'A Caesarean! Immediately!' She crumbles. It's Malika who phones Theatre to warn them we're coming, it's Malika who calls the laboratory for more blood, she does it all for her. And all the time Dr Nikolenko's standing over her saying: 'You must find my husband, you must find my husband . . .'

Waiting at the lift to Theatre, she fumbles into her bag and takes some pills. She speaks of depression, and of epilepsy. Her mouth's twitching, her hands are hysterical. She's sweating furiously, she's living a nightmare. 'Five years ago . . .', she begins. Then she stops herself and says: 'There are things you don't know, things you will never know.' I become as terrified as her. I'd never imagined we'd be reduced to this. I never thought I'd actually have to operate on my own. But now it's a distinct possibility. I catch her by the shoulders. I tell her I'm stopping the lift, I'm going to fetch Dr Vasilev. 'No,' she begs, 'he mustn't know either.' But as we go into Theatre, she tells me she hasn't operated since 'that event' five years ago.

Mercifully, her husband's there, and he's so calm in comparison that he appears immobile. He's just the sort of partner I'd want if I was in her state. Short hair, face you forget the moment you've stopped looking at it, no knowledge of the extremes of happiness or despair, a technician – like those 'Doctors on duty' on the delivery room wall. He'll do the whole operation for her if she breaks down completely.

They put on their gowns and Dr Nikolenko handles all the instruments laid out on the blue cloth, talking to herself non-stop, as if she's trying to remind herself what they're for. Only then does she realize that she hasn't yet put on her gloves. The orderlies have said nothing, of course, they're too used to that 'mistake' by Ivanov. More cries to herself in Russian. She puts the gloves on, her husband too. He makes the incision for her, and splits the muscle underneath. He speaks in short, decisive sentences. Then he opens the peritoneum and makes the horizontal cut across the womb. Dr Nikolenko puts in both forefingers, pulls sideways, and reaches for the baby. It's a little girl, who cries and kicks immediately. But two months premature, she has no future, and Djamila takes her away to a cot in the babies' changing room. The husband stitches, Dr Nikolenko follows. Good solid work, rhythmical and practised. Dr Nikolenko's forehead is dripping wet. The anaesthetist says: 'I thought we'd seen everything.'

The way she operated, Dr Nikolenko tells me afterwards, was 'terrible, terrible. You must forget what you've seen.' The tension subsides when she leaves for lunch. Maternity closes for the siesta. I sit beside the air-conditioner in the delivery room. Fatma sleeps near me on the labour bed, Djamila in the midwife's room next door. There are no women about to deliver, no screams. Maternity's quiet. No screams means no work. There's no routine for us to be getting on with. The only work we do is in response to emergencies.

Every so often I take a walk round the rooms. The Caesarean's comfortable, and most of the women are asleep. But each time there seems to be something, one woman who wants to vomit, another who's still bleeding from a curettage this morning (I give her Methergin, not because it's right – I don't know what's right – but because I know it's what she'd get from Dr Nikolenko), another with a temperature (aspirins and antibiotics, again for the same reason).

Fatma rubs her eyes, and asks me the time. We've reached the very end of September. Ivanov's begun wearing a singlet in Theatre, the anaesthetist told me – perhaps in December he'll be wearing gloves. I've only two more days to go. I think of all the things I'll not have done, almost all of the country that'll remain unknown to me, cous-cous I won't have seen made, the Turkish baths in town I won't have visited. I've never even seen a baby being born, at least not really. It's always been a matter of technique and I've kept the event itself outside me. Here I am, having done a hundred births and I'm no different from when I arrived. My enthusiasm's gone. Whole days have gone by recently when I've done no births at all.

The door opens, and a tall, slender girl comes into the delivery room. She wears her flowered robe the way the maxi's worn in the West. Her face is simple and gentle, she's from California, not Kabylia. She comes up to me without a word, puts her hands on my shoulders and kisses me on both cheeks. I feel her pregnant through her robe. It's a beautiful salute. What a way to come and have your baby. But here? I ask Fatma to find out why she did it. When the girl tells her, Fatma laughs so much that she slips on to the chair and has to throw out her hands to stop herself falling. The girl thought I was the midwife! She can't have seen foreigners before, says Fatma, she can't have seen a man with long hair. The girl's red with confusion. Malika arrives, the story's retold to her and in minutes it's all over Maternity.

Fatma goes out to fetch Djamila. But this is a delivery I want for myself. The girl's pushing well, she looks healthy and bright, her baby sounds good. I say to Fatma: let Djamila sleep awhile. I get things ready, and I put on a pair of gloves.

The technique takes care of itself. I don't even think of it. I allow the habits developed over the past weeks to do the birth for me, while I concentrate all my attention on . . . on what? What is it about a birth that I've let pass me by? What is 'the event itself'? My mind's only a disturbing blank.

The Electrician comes to change bulbs in the delivery room. He's still in there when a woman arrives in the throes of labour. She's crying from the pain and her 'ai, mas!' echo through a Maternity as still as night. 'Sussem!' hisses Malika from the desk. Fatma shows the woman a sheet. She can go into the delivery room with it over her, she says, the baby can be born underneath. But the woman refuses, and Fatma has to hold her up till the Electrician's finished. Then we help her inside and on to the first table. Her legs are open, the head's in the vagina and she's past caring if the whole world sees.

'That's women for you,' says a worldly Electrician in the office afterwards. As if he hasn't seen a hundred deliveries! He's even done them himself. You did a bit of everything, up in the mountains during the war. He spies Dr Nikolenko approaching across the courtyard. 'Pa . . . pa . . . pa.' He's begun referring to her as 'Madame Barnard'. The anaesthetist's spreading word of her performance in Theatre.

He invites me over to his own office instead. We cross the courtyard and he pulls back the heavy sliding doors of the boiler room. It's vast. I like the whole way the hospital's built, with great workshops for the carpenters, painters and plumbers, and a garage that has everything. It's a small town, self-contained. And now the boiler room, finer still, with massive equipment from Paris, Nancy and Strasbourg that the Electrician keeps cleaner than Theatre. He takes me up a metal ladder to a platform where there are wheels and dials. He wipes the tail of my coat over a pipe, and it comes away clean. He shows me where he's put the motorcycle battery on charge, and then he takes me down again, to his office on the side.

Sparking plugs on his desk, girlie calendar on the wall from a copper wire manufacturer in France. He says the boiler room is nothing like it used to be. He doesn't even use half his equipment. 'Why should I bother?' For instance, there's a

276

machine in the corner for pumping sterile air into Theatre. In the old days, the French surgeon would be down to check it every week. But the only thing that'll bring Ivanov to the workshops is if he needs a ride to Algiers in the ambulance or work done on his car. He doesn't even know the machine exists, and the Electrician's never bothered to tell him. Nowadays the Theatre windows are open all the time. But if ever there was one open 'in the time of the French', says the Electrician, out you went and no mistake. This was a hospital then, a real hospital. 'Ah,' he says, 'that was the time.' He looks out of his office window at the machinery all ready to work at the touch of a switch, as immaculate as in any museum. This is how he'll want me to remember him in Europe, custodian of the monuments of a bygone age.

I find Dr Nikolenko in conflict with a foul-tempered Vasileva. A woman has arrived for curettage, her legs smell rotten, her pants and robe are stiff with blood. She must have miscarried days ago, probably weeks. 'How many days has this woman been at home?' cries Vasileva, 'and why does she have to arrive when we're in the middle of cleaning?' The woman has a great bush of pubic hair. Dr Nikolenko's dismayed: 'She will have to be washed, she will have to be shaved! Have you a razor, Madame Vasileva?' 'There's one in the cupboard, Dr Nikolenko.' 'Would you mind shaving her for me, Madame Vasileva?' 'I'm not touching that woman, Dr Nikolenko.' 'But Madame Vasileva, we can't curette a woman in this state.' 'I don't care, Dr Nikolenko. She only had to come earlier.'

I do the shaving. It's a nice way out of the stalemate, for everyone, including me. I'm at my best doing this sort of thing. So long as you don't catch her with the blade, and I don't, nothing can go wrong. Dr Nikolenko scrapes the woman clean with her Russian curette.

Maybe the Vasilevs have been quarrelling.

Djamila has a problem for Dr Nikolenko. A woman's come in from a mountain maternity with a letter from one of the Swiss midwives there. Labour began at eleven last night, it says. The membranes ruptured at four this morning, the cervix has been wide open since but there's been no progress. The Sister ends by suggesting a forceps.

Djamila tries a desperate 'Chris-Taylor' in front of us. But she's no Dr Kostov, and her fists make no impression on the woman's womb. Dr Nikolenko examines the woman for herself, and listens to the baby's heart. She appears more in control of herself, as if the siesta's done her good, though I can't believe she can have slept. She decides there's no cause for alarm. All is well. A forceps won't be necessary yet, because there's a chance the woman will deliver on her own.

While she waits, Dr Nikolenko curettes a girl who's miscarrying in her room. The girl climbs on to the table and begins to cry as soon as she sees the big box being brought down from the cupboard. Dr Nikolenko uses the safest curette, her own. A few scrapes, and it's over. The girl swallows her Methergin like a child and walks back to her room. The others are at their doors waiting for her, and they're giggling as if she'd just been caned by the headmistress. The girl begins to giggle too.

Dr Nikolenko listens again over the belly of the woman from the mountains. The heart's much slower now. She does a nervous, clumsy forceps. Djamila and I are no substitute for her husband. The forceps have to be withdrawn and replaced. The woman begins to struggle, and Dr Nikolenko strikes her on the thighs many times with her bloody glove. The baby's a good three kilos, a boy, but white and dead. Djamila lifts it into a cardboard box, and can't stop herself from saying (with the inevitable wink to me): 'And to think the heart sounded so good when I called you, Doctor!'

Dr Nikolenko leaves the delivery room immediately, shaking her head. She goes to look at her Caesarean from this morning, standing by her bed and watching her breathe. The woman's doing well, and her baby's already dead. Dr Nikolenko comes downstairs to the office. She's borrowed Tamara's picture book and she turns its pages. But soon she passes a hand over her eyes, and puts the book down. She delves into her handbag for another pill.

She sees the taxi that draws up outside, but I tell her not to move. I'll bring the patient in. Fatma comes out with me. There's an unconscious girl in the back of the taxi. Her face is yellow and bloated, and she seems to be snoring. She had a baby this morning, says the taxi-driver, and she's been having fits ever since. We lift her out, the driver at the head of the stretcher, me at the feet. She actually has a fit as we start down the path. I've never seen one before and I almost drop the stretcher. Fatma keeps the jerking arms together. 'That's the Kabyl man for you,' she says as she runs alongside, 'when their wife's ill, they say: "What's the matter with you? Stop your complaining," and they wait till the last minute, because there's the taxi-fare, the children to look after, the water to fetch . . .' She shouts to Djamila to step aside. 'An eclamptic!', cries Djamila in dismay, 'just my luck!' When she hears the girl's already delivered, she crosses herself in relief.

The woman are all at their doors on the ground floor. They see the shaking robe and the swollen Chinese face. They flutter their hands, 'pa . . . pa . . . pa', and run back into their rooms. We lift the girl on to a vacant bed. Her limbs stop beating, she takes an immense breath and begins to snore again. Dr Nikolenko comes to look: 'What must I do? Oh, tell me what I must do!' She stands there wringing her hands and she's enormously comforted by me, hand on my shoulder, thanking me incessantly as I stolidly take the blood pressure for want of anything better. Then she runs upstairs to telephone her husband.

The girl's heavy breathing suddenly stops. It's been loud and insistent, like those bellows that keep the polio victims alive. Her breath gets cut off in the middle of being taken, as if the bellows had suddenly failed. Her puffy eyelids start to flicker as though there's a nightmare behind them. Her mouth writhes. Her moon-face shakes, her teeth bite hard and her lips curl away. The fit invades her arms and legs. It shakes her for a full minute, and there's no sound but the beating of her limbs on the filthy mattress. Then she starts to breathe again. Only a minute, but it has seemed impossibly long.

Dr Nikolenko's back, with a needle, a rubber tube and a plastic bedpan. Djamila's come along to watch, bored by the action in the delivery room. I hold the girl's arm while Dr

Nikolenko applies the tourniquet. Then she punctures a big vein in the elbow. Dark blood flows out of the needle, down the girl's forearm and drips off her fingers into the plastic bedpan. Dr Nikolenko is bleeding her. She looks up at us, so unsure of herself. 'This is called eclampsia,' she says, 'and no one can explain it.' Djamila asks 'innocently': 'It can be treated in many different ways, can't it, Doctor?' Dr Nikolenko says: 'This is the Stroganoff method.'

When there's about a pint of blood in the pan, Dr Nikolenko releases the tourniquet and pulls out the needle. She administers 'Stroganoff's mixture' – magnesium sulphate, penicillin and Largactil – injecting it with the same nervous brutality that she had on her ward round this morning, plus no less than six ampoules of Vitamin C. Then she beseeches me, hands joined, to fetch the oxygen.

The cylinder in the delivery room is empty again, and it takes me an hour to find a new one. Dr Nikolenko's so glad to see it. It'll make all the difference, she says. She fixes the tube up the girl's nostril and opens the tap a little, to provide her with a constant supply. But the interference only sets the girl off again. We jump back as she lurches into another fit. Her tongue's so thick that it's pushing the airway out. Dr Nikolenko forces it back in before the jaws tighten. The fit shakes the girl mercilessly. From her face, you'd think she was being throttled. Her breasts hang sideways. She's sixteen but she could be twenty years older.

Dr Vasilev looks in at supper time with a French woman doctor I've never met. She's a general physician, and Dr Vasilev's brought her along as a second opinion. She takes one look at the girl's eyes and lips and points out how pale they are. We've been bleeding a girl who's anaemic! She'll need a transfusion right away.

Dr Nikolenko follows her advice word by word. She gets Malika to phone the laboratory. But Dr Vasilev disagrees about the transfusion. He says it'll be too much fluid for the girl to cope with. He thinks it'll be a strain on her heart. The French doctor explains that she's only recommending blood for its red cells – she'll prescribe another drug to take away the fluid. 'But those cells,' says Dr Vasilev, 'they'll cause haemoly-sis!' 'No they won't,' answers the French doctor, 'because we'll make sure they're the same group.' 'Eh!' cries Dr Vasilev, 'then she'll only get a Cushing syndrome!'

The French doctor looks at him in utter amazement. As for Dr Nikolenko, she says nothing. She hasn't understood, or perhaps she feels this discussion is above her. It's impossible to give more than an idea of the irrelevance of Dr Vasilev's remark. But imagine a conversation between two engineers. The Vasilev one says: 'But the bridge will fall down!' The other one tells him it won't, because they'll put pillars under-neath to support it. The Vasilev one then cries: 'But that will only make it more magnetic!' What Dr Vasilev has just said wasn't simply wrong. Credit him with being more than an ordinary doctor. His thought moves in a new plane, defying belief. The relics of a medical education agitate randomly in his brain, to pro-duce what is even more than the opposite of the truth. He hands me *El Moudjahid – 1·4 metres 9 kilograms!, the giant runner bean* held up to the camera by a Mr Bortz of Pottsdown, Pennsyl-vania – and fades into the corridor, one of his profession's most remarkable men.

Dr Nikolenko waits with me for the results of the tests. She's asked Malika to stay behind too, into her supper-time. We prop the girl up on some pillows, till she's half sitting. She's better immediately, breathing more easily. Dr Nikolenko dips cotton wool in water and cleans the mucus from the girl's mouth and tongue. Then she steps back, chewing at her lip, unable to drink the carton of L'Antésite that Fatma's brought for her. The breathing stops again. The girl's eyes swivel to the left, and the fit arches her back in the same heartless pattern. It's impossible to tell what she really looks like under that puffed Oriental face. Beni Yenni earrings, blue and red coral set in silver. Hair parted down the middle, two plaits at the back bound in green cloth. She looks like all the others. This fit's been so long. 'She's going to die!' cries Fatma. But then the girl gives an enormous gasp, a drowning person coming up for air.

Cries from the neighbouring rooms. The women all want

pills. No one can get to sleep who's in earshot of the steam breathing.

Malika brings the results of the tests. She says the news is bad. Dr Nikolenko's reluctant to take the paper from her. In the blood there's more than twenty times the normal number of white cells. 'Leukemia!', exclaims Dr Nikolenko. Oh leukemia, leukemia! If that's the diagnosis, then she can't go wrong. Nothing can save the girl now. Dr Nikolenko won't be responsible, it'll be a pure tragedy. She cries for joy, she squeezes Malika's shoulder, and they go out for a walk together under the hospital lights, arm-in-arm. Poor Nikolenko. Leukemia's been the only bright spot in her day.

29

I drink my coffee on the windowsill, watching everything below. Maternity, garden, gardener. Doctors' building, stone steps, washing. Hills, olive trees, mosque. Cows on the fields opposite. Baya banging on Maternity's door, henna on her nails. Vasileva coming down the path, her hair in curlers under a white plastic bonnet, to find rotten melon beneath her feet. If yesterday's anything to go by, she's feeling rotten herself. The melon fits in nicely. She cries out in her sad French against the culprit, who understands the language even less.

The girl with the fits died at five in the morning. It's the first death there's been in public. The others have been out of sight, behind doors. During the round with Dr Vasilev, the women look away. It's strange, but there's the same hush, the same unwillingness to look you in the eye as there is after a death in the teaching hospital in London. Those deaths are genteel in comparison, dying ladies in pink dressing-gowns sipping morphine, cocaine and gin from petalled cups, Brompton's Elixir, the cocktail with the Knightsbridge accent that brings a quiet life to a quiet close. This death was harsh and ugly. They saw the girl fitting as we brought her in, they were kept awake by her breathing. But I'm sure it's not the cruelty of it that's struck them. Their own lives are cruel. It must be the fact of death itself.

Eight girls in white coats, and with jasmin flowers in their nostrils arrive laughing and chattering in Maternity, their summer holidays over. They're student midwives, on the same course that Zora and Djamila went through. They're a labour force in Maternity, and they get a grounding in practical obstetrics at the same time. 'From now on,' declares Malika, 'every baby will be washed once a day!'

Dr Kostov comes up the stairs with his water bottle, and greets the new arrivals with a sex face. Their reflections in his metal teeth. The attraction's mutual. Dr Kostov's broad chest, his heavy features, his strong voice – he's a man. The girls are immediately captured by his cavalier style, his military swagger, and when he asks for two volunteers to interpret for him in Out-Patients, a girl from the oasis town of Ghardaïa offers herself even though she can speak no Kabyl. But Dr Kostov's not taking Out-Patients today anyway. 'It was only to see who wanted to work hardest!' A leer hammers his innuendo home.

He does a jovial round upstairs, to a gallery of four of the student midwives. 'Hey-hos!' and whistles and great roars of laughter, flashing teeth and knowing eyes and 'Mademoiselles!' that go straight to the girls' hymens. He marks in the drugs with generous flourishes of his pen, drawing great smiles from the women in their coloured robes and crumpled sheets. Malika – they call her 'Mali' for short – finds the atmosphere contagious, and she hangs on his shoulder. He gives me a wink: 'I must be careful, her fiancé's a gendarme!'

There's no doubt that Dr Kostov's rejuvenated, no doubt that his mood's taken a turn for the better. Things are more like what they should be, a proper doctor–nurse relationship. Contented hierarchical inferiors, whom he can count on to be sexually mesmerized. There are vestiges of this relationship with Malika – the plump hand on his shoulder, the wiggle she'll sometimes give when she pronounces his name – vestiges too with Zora and Djamila, especially when Zora, helpless girl to hero man, will ask him sweetly: 'Won't you come and do a "Chris-Taylor" for me, Doctor? You do it so well.' But their professional abilities mar things between them. Each side has too low an opinion of the quality of the other's work. The beauty of the student midwives is that they have no real work, and they're too inexperienced to judge that done by Dr Kostov.

But Dr Vasilev, oh dear! Here are four girls, Algerians, the midwives of the future when all the foreign missions will have left, who need to be taught what obstetrics can be, four girls with whom all is possible. He shuffles in. He doesn't welcome them. He doesn't introduce himself. He refuses to see them. He does a round on the ground floor during which he ignores them totally. Because I'm expecting at least something, just some kind of positive reaction from him, however slight, he appears to have withered away entirely, to have left behind a consultant ghost. It raises him from nothing, which he was, to something, the something of nothing, a new sort of hero. A girl starts to giggle. 'Mademoiselle!' says Vasileva sharply.

No one likes to give a welcome more than Dr Vasilev, I know from my own experience. But with these young girls, he can't cope. They threaten what life is left in him. We make our way over to Out-Patients with Baya. The student midwives carry Zora's *Paris-Match*, Dr Vasilev carries *El Moudjahid*, statements of intention. '*A hen with teeth!*' has been discovered in his backyard by M. Brière, bistro owner in Avesnes, northern France.

We find a salesgirl from a French drug firm in the waiting-room. She's altogether plainer and nicer than the last one from Hoechst. She even offers to wait till we've seen all the patients. Dr Vasilev takes her samples and copies of her literature. She gives me some sleeping pills, of a kind that have fallen out of favour in England. Sales may be going down in Europe, she says, but they can still be got rid of here. The same applies to contraceptive pills with too much oestrogen in them. The doctors from Eastern Europe are about ten years behind, according to her sales manager in Algiers. And that's why, when she presents her products to Dr Vasilev, she leaves out all the 'science'. I think she's making a mistake. He may not understand it, but he likes to hear it all the same.

Dr Vasilev receives one doctor's letter that's remarkable even by his own standards. It comes from the Czech in the mountains, and it reads: 'Dear Colleague, I am sending you Madame Chader, who is eight months pregnant. You performed a Caesarean section on her seven months ago. Thank you. Dr . . .'

The prettiest Kabyl girl we've yet seen in Out-Patients needs to know that she's not pregnant, and she wants a certificate from Dr Vasilev to prove it. She's in a fine red robe but her French is fluent, with a Marseille accent. She stands there waiting, till Dr Vasilev says he can't tell just by looking at her. 'I'm indisposed,' she says awkwardly. Dr Vasilev doesn't mind, he'll still examine her if that's what she wants. 'I know I can't be pregnant,' says the girl. 'No one with a period can be pregnant,' agrees Dr Vasilev. But there's nothing absurd he won't do. The student midwives look up from their copy of *Paris-Match* as the girl removes her sanitary towel and gets on to the table. 'The certificate isn't for me,' she tells Dr Vasilev.

She's only been in Algeria a month. She's lived all her life in Marseille, going to school there, wearing European clothes and living just like the other girls except that she couldn't go out as much. Then her father arranged a marriage with a man from their home town in Kabylia. She left France, and got married in the mountains. For the first two weeks, all went well. She was getting to know her husband. She was beginning to like him, and she was sure he liked her. Then suddenly, at a circumcision party, he turned against her. He told her he wouldn't be wanting her again, and he hasn't touched her since. He's sending her back to Marseille, and he wants to make sure she can't claim against him for a baby.

The girl's bewildered and hurt. She thinks it's a case of what's called 'eshkull'. She'd heard about it in Marseille, but she'd always thought it was old wives' tales. But now she's convinced: 'He's been bewitched. My mother-in-law gave him a potion to drink.'

The student midwives return to their copy of *Paris-Match*. Nothing else arrives to excite their curiosity. They yawn, they don't attempt to hide their boredom, just as Dr Vasilev doesn't try to pretend he's teaching them anything. If the whole world were present, he'd be no different, shuffling through his routine in exactly this way, whirling his glove, squeezing out the fingers, dipping his hand in talc, squirting the alcohol, giving his little whistle and then turning to face his umpteenth vagina on the table. The woman's not ready, she's still standing in front of Baya with her pants on. Dr Vasilev sinks on to the stool, his rubber finger limp, the alcohol drying on its tip, as he puffs air through atonic lips. If you know

'Delilah', your imagination can help him through it. Then he takes his stand between the thighs. Right hand in, eyes to the ceiling. Down comes the woman's hand, and Dr Vasilev pushes it away: 'Ai, Madame! We don't need your hand as well.'

And then, between patients, from the mouth of the mournful secretary, news arrives that's very welcome for a man like Dr Vasilev, who lives from peak to little peak. It's not a surprise. Dr Vasilev's been preparing for it for weeks. In fact, he's been preparing for it since the day I arrived, when together we read a newsflash in *El Moudjahid* announcing the epidemic. But it's been the moment, the precise moment of its arrival in the hospital, after a journey westwards across Asia, the Middle East and Africa, that Dr Vasilev has been unable to predict, and there lies all its charm.

We've had disputes in the doctors' office over the epidemic's origin. 'El Tor' has been a name on everyone's lips. Dr Kostov believed that Calcutta was responsible, with its contaminated water supply. *El Moudjahid* published a picture of Indians drawing water from an infected river, that had Dr Kostov's lips curling in disgust. But in the Electrician's opinion, the epidemic had arisen in the plain towns of southern Russia. *El Moudjahid* provided him with some important evidence. The first cases were reported in Astrakhan. *Pravda* suggested they'd been imported by Soviet technicians returning on leave from Egypt, but this was hotly denied by Al Ahram in Cairo. Then sixty-three cases were discovered in Odessa. Travellers returning from the Crimea told of the towns of Kerch and Veyptoriya that had been closed by the Red Army. Even Kiev was rumoured to be threatened. Flights from Moscow were suddenly cancelled – purely to reduce congestion on the beaches of the Black Sea, reported *Izvestia*. Then the Moscow City Council ordered the disinfection of all its streets and squares, to be carried out within five days. 'El Tor' had begun to grip the capital itself.

In fact 'El Tor' has been a relatively harmless vibrio, killing in twos and threes, a shadow of its ancestors. No one has been following its progress westwards from Astrakhan more raptly than Dr Vasilev. There was talk of an outbreak in

Syria. But Radio-Damascus declared that 'contrary to the news put about by . . . the Zionist enemy, there is no epidemic in Syria, and no case of an infectious disease'. As for the 'suspicious death' that had occurred in a Damascus hospital, autopsy had shown that it was a case of self-poisoning with insecticide.

Vaccination certificates have been made obligatory in the Congo, in Gabon, Dahomey and Tchad. In Dakar, the Minister of Health has invited the population to remain calm. Guinea was visited by a World Health Organization inspector. When he published his report on sixty deaths that had occurred in the country, Radio-Conakry, the Voice of the Revolution, accused him of bias and threatened to leave the Organization. There may well have been deaths from an illness characterized by watery diarrhoea, but to pretend that it was anything more was to slander the name of Guinea.

The epidemic's been creeping closer. It's broken out . . . 'in Libya!', announced Dr Vasilev the other day, and more recently still . . . 'in southern Tunisia!' Algeria's borders have had to be closed. Two thousand people have been vaccinated in the frontier towns. *El Moudjahid*'s called on everyone to exercise personal hygiene. Dr Kostov's threatened the women that the epidemic will spread like wildfire through Kabylia if they don't change their ways. This morning, at long last, those yards of newspaper print come alive, 'El Tor' comes home, to an emotional welcome from Dr Vasilev: we're all to have 'the vaccination!' During the remaining patients, while he's washing his glove at the sink, while he's writing a prescription or waiting for some woman to take down her pants, I'll catch enraptured little cries from Dr Vasilev to himself: 'Eh! Cho – le – RA!'.

He stops the Electrician on the way back to Maternity to ask if he's heard the news. He asks the storekeeper if anyone's had the vaccination yet. Where do they give it, he wants to know, and is it true that it hurts? He arrives back at the office, so contented. It's become the event of the month. Dr Kostov stays dumb behind his Bulgarian paper.

Dr Nikolenko appears briefly, in tears. Her train of disaster continues unabated. Her husband has fallen seriously ill. He has a temperature of 42°C. She sobs on the office desk that he's going to die. She embarrasses Dr Kostov, who puts down his paper. Everything has gone wrong for them in Algeria, she says, they were so much happier at home. Dr Vasilev comforts her in Russian and says she must take the day off to be with her husband, two days if necessary! 'Everything must be done!' he says. 'Dr Ivanova is with him,' sobs Dr Nikolenko, 'we can do no more.'

The telephone rings. This is the moment! Dr Vasilev collects his male staff together, and that includes his wife because foreign women are considered as males for the occasion. It also includes me, but not for the pure pleasure that Dr Vasilev wants to believe. I'll need to show the vaccination certificate when I get back to Europe. That, too, has been in *El Moudjahid*. But he's refused to see it. Not since I arrived has Dr Vasilev accepted I must leave. He's never spoken of my departure, however indirectly.

We march off to Dermatology, to sit backs bare on a stool in the closed ward and receive an injection of Swiss-prepared cholera vaccine in the left shoulder, a site decreed in a circular from the Minister of Health. Ivanov's there, and the French paediatrician. The Supervisor, too, posing as a doctor. He blusters, he swirls his regal coat, and at his heel there's that faithful servant-superior of his, the plump assistant director, washing priestly hands and mouthing wretched 'preciselys' at every opportunity. He looks to his master when the enemy clan arrives from Maternity. The Supervisor salutes none of us, except, peremptorily, Dr Kostov, to 'inform' him that his vaccination is due for tomorrow instead. As for Vasileva, she ignores his invitation to step inside a cubicle. She remains in line with the men and insults him by pulling down her dress before his eyes.

'We've had the injection!' Dr Vasilev cries out to the Electrician, who asks: 'Where?' 'Here,' says Dr Vasilev, turning round and pointing over his shoulder. The Electrician pretends to give him a slap on the spot. Dr Vasilev's delighted, and he attempts to rally Dr Kostov to the spirit of the event. Excitedly, affectionately, the first time that either of them has ever said anything to me about the other in their presence, Dr Vasilev cries: 'Dr Kostov hasn't had his yet! Dr Kostov's having his tomorrow!'. Dr Kostov examines his nails.

Fatma wheels past the lunch trolley. Baked green peppers without stuffing, fried potatoes, lettuce and dry biscuits. There's no meat, no fish, no egg, no cheese. 'In the time of the French . . .', remembers Fatma. There'd be fresh fish from Dellys as long as her forearm, one for each woman. There'd be meat every day. Says the Electrician, watching: 'It was the misfortune of the French to be colonizers. We understood them, we didn't blame them. Anyone in their position would have acted the way they did.'

He takes me into town, for a farewell apéritif. On the way, he buys me a Kabyl blanket – in return he wants my Levi's, though they're already two years old. He invites me to *the* café-restaurant. We climb a flight of steps to a large terrace overlooking the main street. Then we cross to the restaurant half of the establishment, where there are tables laid in white, with cutlery and glasses – all unoccupied. The Electrician pulls out a chair, explaining that he doesn't like to drink with 'the others' on the terrace. When he comes here with his friends – the Prefect of Police in particular – they like to be 'discreet'.

The Electrician's sorry to see me go. I've been someone he could talk to, I've not been like 'those people' from Eastern Europe. In a way, he says, I've reminded him of the French: 'We got on well with them in Kabylia. It wasn't as bad as people say. We went to school and we worked as we wished.' The Electrician calls for another round of fried sardines from Dellys, and more aniseed. 'It was the drink of the French', he tells, me, raising his glass.

This was the café I came to the day I arrived, to wash and change before making an appearance at the hospital. At that time, I remember, the first thing I used to say to each new person I met was that I wasn't French. I'm still embarrassed to walk into a shop expecting them to understand the language and answer me in it. But on the contrary, they'll serve me first and call the dinars 'francs'. I walk back to the hospital, a little heady from the aniseed. At times like this, 'the events' can seem further away than the Second World War in England.

Dr Kostov's just finished an operation, on a woman with a burst womb. But it was not from a 'Chris-Taylor' of his own. He's always said that half an hour with a burst womb was nothing for a Kabyl woman, and I've never believed him. But while I was out in town, he removed a womb that had burst up in the mountains more than twenty-four hours ago. He shows me the baby in the changing room. It's in a cot, there isn't a cardboard box big enough. It's enormous, with a great chest and head, its limbs lying out like an adult. It weighs over five kilos. The mother's next door. Malika asks her if she wants any more babies. She has nine already, and a large goitre. 'You must ask my husband,' she whispers. She's very still. Malika tells her that she can't have any more babies now anyway. The woman whispers: 'Yes.' I ask her how it happened that her womb burst. She points down at her knee and says: 'Toubib – Doctor,' and then something I can't catch. 'Ai, ma,' says Malika, 'they go a bit far in that hospital all the same.' The midwife used her fists, and the Czech doctor his knees, to drive a five-kilo baby through a pelvis that just wasn't big enough. Malika draws the line at the use of knees in a 'Chris-Taylor'. But then I've always felt the Czech doctor was something special.

Married last night, a girl arrives bleeding from a torn hymen. Dr Kostov puts in a speculum. It fascinates the student midwives, and they ask if they can have a look too. Dr Kostov obliges. He's in an earthy mood. The hymen is themselves, their mirror, their essence. 'I'm a jeune fille,' one of them tells me.

I take them afterwards into an empty room on the ground floor, for a little talk on aseptic technique. I've read it all up in Zora's textbook of surgery for nurses. A couple of the girls, like the one from Ghardaïa in the Sahara, are the kind *El Moudjahid's* afraid of. Jimi Hendrix has just died, and they want to hear about him. They listen to me, as if aseptic technique were a way into his world. The others want to hear about medicine. They're duller, slower to laugh, and less attractive. Overcome by premature middle age, they're the ones behind those letters to the coyly entitled 'Forbidden to Parents!' column in *El Moudjahid*.

'I couldn't sleep!' announces Dr Vasilev, back from the siesta. But he doesn't mind. In fact, he's cheerful. 'The vaccination!' lives on in his aching shoulder.

We sit in the office with Dr Kostov. If it weren't for the student midwives (Dr Kostov always has a grin ready for them as they pass the open door), it would be like one of the old days. Malika and Fatma passing in and out, the cat cleaning herself at the door, with a vigilant eye on Dr Kostov, the chain of cigarettes, Dr Kostov yawning and pruning his nails, the full weight of the afternoon heat, the Bulgarian paper and *El Moudjahid*. '*Four tons! Five metres!*' the cachalot whale washed ashore on a beach near Boulogne-sur-Mer.' *What a surprise!*' – for the three Parisians in bathing trunks photographed round it, and for Dr Vasilev. *The old sea-dogs of Boulogne forecast rich shoals of mackerel and one of the warmest autumns yet!*

I ask if it's all right for me to go and clean the motorcycle. Dr Vasilev says of course it is. He actually comes with me to the garage, and we clean it together. I do the wheels, Dr Vasilev polishes the handlebars, the mirror and the petrol tank. He points out a nut that needs tightening. He's content, like the day I arrived with Calie. Yet I choose such a moment as this to tell him when I'm leaving. I've no sooner uttered them than my words echo back to me as cold and blunt. They sound a betrayal, though I didn't mean them to be. They've surprised me. I must be angrier with Dr Vasilev than I realized. He draws in his breath sharply 'Ahhh!'.

In the evening, a woman arrives from the mountains in a Peugeot station wagon. I bring her to the curettage room. She says she's three months pregnant, and so does her husband. A baby's dangling out of her vagina, feet first and back towards me. It's raw and purple, long since dead. I get a glove and put my hand over its shoulders, with its neck between my fingers. The head's still caught inside the womb. My face must look like Dr Kostov's. I pull down on the shoulders as gently as I can, but it's no good, it's all too soft and I've beheaded it. The body comes away in my hand. I turn round, try to be sick but can't, and with a curette I bring down the soft and featureless head. There's no blood from the withered cord, and hardly any from the womb.

So far I've done the right thing. All that remained was to give her some Methergin and put her to bed. But I go all wrong, I don't know what comes over me. I'm covered in sweat. I overlook the fact that the woman's rather hot too, and I take her word for it that she was three months pregnant. If a pregnancy has lasted longer than that, you don't curette them, there's no need. You just give them Methergin and leave them be.

I start curetting her, and I don't even use the safest curette, the one brought by Dr Nikolenko. And I go on curetting, because there's something in there that won't come down, something firm in the middle that I can't bring out. I scrape away and think that the womb's a strange shape because the curette keeps going way in almost to my hand on the left and right, but baulks up against something in the middle. I suddenly realize that what's in the middle is normal, it's the roof to her womb, and that I've simply been making holes on either side.

I put the curette back in the box and wish that I'd never come to Algeria. I'd do anything to make it not have happened. After all my criticizing of others . . . I'd gladly go back and praise them all, if it could erase what I've just done. What a thing to have happened at this point, it's like getting killed on the last day of a war. It serves me right. I was becoming as blasé as the Electrician. There have been times when I liked to feel I've had a curette in my hand all my life. No longer. 'He perforated a woman,' they'll say. He did, and there's no argument against that.

I call Dr Vasilev and ask him to come over as soon as he can. He'll have to take out her womb. He arrives in a minute or two. I tell him I've perforated her. He spots the woman's temperature right away, and says: 'Never curette a woman with a temperature, unless she's bleeding very badly.' He's mentioned that to me before, it's in the book, and he mentions it to me again. Then he looks at the baby in the cotton wool. 'Four months, this baby! Perhaps four and a half months!' How could I not have seen that, and her temperature too? I just don't know. And that small curette I've been using: 'Ahhh!'

He takes the big Russian curette instead, and sits down carefully on the stool. He slides the curette gently into the womb and follows it even more gently with a smaller one. He's become the doctor for me at last, I'm absolutely in his hands. Eventually he says: 'There's no perforation.' I trust him totally. And for the other side, he says a second time: 'There's no perforation.' The woman was born with a two-horned uterus, and that's why she miscarried. I've been saved by a chance in a thousand.

They say mistakes are how you learn. The great men tell you of the great mistakes they've made. Everyone learns medicine for himself, making the mistakes that have been made a million times before and are going to be made a million times again. But it shouldn't happen in a science, and I can't take it. I'll touch nothing again till I leave, neither a clamp nor a curette. I sit with Dr Vasilev on the parapet outside. I say I'm sorry. He says: 'It's nothing.' We stroke the one-eyed cat between us. He says: 'She loves you too.'

30

Flocks of swallows, and a dawn chorus of crying children. An old man, sombrero and little Citroen van, limps over to one of the ground-floor rooms and swings a pannier of provisions through the window to his wife. Vasileva comes down the path, to step on soft melon. 'Every day I say the same thing!' she cries shrilly. And so she does, but each day in French, and each day to a different woman.

She's earlier than usual. She's preparing something for to-night. There'll be a meal, certainly. She knows what I like. And Dr Vasilev's got something up his sleeve. A grand send-off. 'Bulgarians know how to say goodbye,' he told me, 'to their very sympathetic friends.'

I needed a blanket in the night for the first time. It's going to be cold on the way home.

'Nasser's dead!' Dr Vasilev announces the news as he arrives in the office. He's just heard it over the radio. He's not pleased, he's not sad. He's excited.

The Electrician comes running into the office, breaking all his vows, but what matter, this is a special occasion. For Dr Vasilev, Dr Kostov and me, he plays a distraught Egyptian schoolmaster such as he's just seen in town, tearing at his over-alls and running his hands down his cheeks in floods of tears. Boumediène has given them the day off. They've gathered grief-stricken in one of their villas, crying together over their great leader who couldn't lift a finger for the Palestinians. 'He was the best they ever had,' says the Electrician, 'only Egyptians could mourn a man like that.' No one's sad, except *El Moudjahid* in a hypocritical editorial.

A present of figs for me, from Fatma.

Before his round, Dr Vasilev performs some of the last curettages I'll ever see him do. He does no fewer than five, without a complaint. His resignation is infinite. He may look moribund, but he will curette till the end of time.

For the first woman, there's Baya, Vasileva and me, and Fatma too. For the second, Dr Nikolenko arrives with Tamara, they've come in from town together. Her husband's better, she tells us, he's over the worst. It was malaria. She's more relaxed. When she's like that, Russian can sound nice, for a moment it becomes the language of *The Cranes are Flying* (it's on in Algiers this week). For the third curettage – there's no break between them, one's rolling over for her Methergin while the next is taking down her pants with an unhappy face – four student midwives arrive. There's nothing for them to do, they stand in a bunch, talking and laughing in French and Kabyl. When Dr Kostov joins us – during the fourth curettage – he wags his finger at them: greying hair and lustful grin. They lose some self-control, they flap like pigeons when there's a hawk about. Vasileva cries at them in Bulgarian, Fatma gives advice to the woman on the table, it's contradicted by one of the girls, Dr Kostov intervenes in French, which Fatma translates . . .

Dr Vasilev sits on the stool, curette at the ready, smoking the cigarette that goes on the trolley when he's got both hands full. Once, he bangs on the trolley with his curette to quieten the noise, another time he says: 'Mademoiselle!' petulant reminders of his position. During the fifth curettage, when there are twelve people in the room beside the woman on the table, talking in French, Kabyl, Arabic, Bulgarian and Russian – the woman staring from one to the other – we reach Mouloud Kassim's image of hell, the Tower of Babel, and Dr Nikolenko shakes both hands to heaven and cries in French: 'It's a market, I can't stand it!'

Baya gives me prickly pears, in a raffia box her mother made.

Women and babies, familiar Kabyl clothes. It's our last round together. Heavy breasts hang from dull brown eyes, babies in rags lie among blood-stained sheets, Crimean scenes.

Sticky floor, flies. Dr Vasilev switches the lights on and off in every room. They're both depressed, him and Vasileva. It can only be the thought of tonight that's carrying them through the day. Weary phrases in Bulgarian over the occasional patient, long pauses between question and answer. 'Nothing goes right in Maternity,' says Dr Vasilev, 'nothing at all.'

I wonder why they ever came. With Dr Kostov, the answer's clear. He wanted to get his son through medical school somewhere in the world – even if it was Algiers (but they have French professors) – and he wanted the money. It could be that with the Vasilevs too, with her at least. She's told me they're having a villa built. She wants me to send her some *Good Housekeeping* magazines, and *La Maison Française* if I go back through France. They already own two apartments and if I understood her right, that's unusual, because in Bulgaria nearly everyone rents. But Dr Vasilev's not villa-conscious. He's never spoken about money or possessions. He's only ever told me about his motorcycle. Perhaps he wanted to travel a little before he retired. New things to photograph. Perhaps, from Bulgaria, Algeria was an 'excursion!' like the one to Dellys, and he's been living a long weekend ever since. But that wouldn't fit. Algeria from Bulgaria is *my* 'Dellys!'. It's something, it's worth all the excitement you can muster. It's a big step, whereas the whole point about Dr Vasilev's 'Dellys!' was its utter uneventfulness.

Perhaps he was simply feeling the heat in his provincial hospital in Bulgaria, with all the students and newly qualified doctors talking of things he'd never heard of.

Or perhaps Dr Kostov and the Supervisor are right, and Vasileva pushed him into coming.

'Lebess?' he's asking a woman. She doesn't answer. She stares back, appearing stunned. He pulls back her sheet. Her bed is soaked in blood, and there are black clots between her legs. 'Madame Fatma!' cries Vasileva, 'bring the trolley!' We wheel the woman down to the curettage room. There, Dr Vasilev pulls her cervix into the open air, the better to get into the womb. Embryo, placenta, membranes, and more blood. Under the curette, the woman comes alive. The Kabyl spills from her without a pause. She calls on her mother, she regrets she ever got married, her voice rises and falls to the curette, not in the long, piercing shrieks that make the women in their rooms grip each other's arms, but in a kind of song, with Kabyl words and sounds, that I find myself listening to utterly detached, as I hold the gutter for Dr Vasilev, a recital of concrete music. She pulls our hands towards her when it's over, and kisses them: 'Merci, merci.' 'Ai, Madame,' says Dr Vasilev, holding his cigarette in one hand and her pulse in the other.

Goodbye to the Director (a ritual politeness, over in seconds, he's not sorry to see me go), goodbye to the Econome (a breathlessly friendly handshake, as warm as with Calie).

Out-Patients is a final parade of Kabyl clothes, different for the different villages. Baya knows them all, and smiles when they come in. 'Ai, ma!' she exclaims over one woman, 'you should see her village. It's so high up that every time I go there I'm scared I'm going to fall off!' The robes are yellow, orange and blue. They're gaudy, corny, chintzy, gypsy. They're decorated with flowers, minarets and doves. They're never clean, unless new. They soak up the periods and the miscarriages, and they're worn, says Baya, until they fall off.

There are photographs to take, pictures to be painted, of the attitudes of Kabyl women, how the one to come looks at the one who's just been, collecting her prescription at the desk, how they meet and whisper and touch, how they pull on their pants, gravely, and how they leave the room, not knowing what response to give if you hold the door open for them.

A haggard and tieless man in his twenties comes in to tell Dr Vasilev that he's been married three days, but his wife's deformed. He's brought her in for an operation. The student midwives put down their *Paris-Match*. The man leaves the room for Dr Vasilev to examine the girl. She's sixteen, pretty and fat, like Malika, except that she's from the mountains, with henna all over her from the marriage. The mother-in-law insists on being present, but Baya pushes her out the door. Then she asks the girl gently to tell the doctor what her deformity is. The girl prefers not to say, she'd rather we saw it for ourselves. I'd been thinking she might have been born without a vagina, but she says her periods have always been normal.

We get her on to the table, it's surprisingly easy, and she opens her legs for Dr Vasilev. She's been entirely shaved for the marriage. From the outside, all looks normal. Baya holds her hand. The student midwives lean forward. Inside, there's an intact and normal hymen. Everything looks pink and fresh and virginal. Dr Vasilev can get one finger through. Then he examines her via the rectum, and again he can find nothing abnormal. 'Madame,' he says, 'you're a virgin.' Baya asks the girl if her husband gets 'hard'. She shakes her head: 'He's weak.'

She gets dressed and goes outside. Dr Vasilev calls the man in. He has absolutely no idea what it's about, and he's quite unembarrassed. He's anxious to know what Dr Vasilev's found, when the operation will be and how many days it will take. Dr Vasilev smiles and catches the man's forearm. He tugs him close to the desk. 'What's the matter?' he asks affectionately, 'can't you do this thing?' The man doesn't answer. 'Listen to this story,' says Dr Vasilev, giving the forearm an encouraging shake, 'me . . . in my country . . . I had a very great friend! Eh!' He's slipped into his nursery rhyme voice, he's looking into the man's eyes the same way he looked into mine in the garage yesterday, to promise me a 'Goodbye!' I'd never forget. 'My friend was a Doctor! . . . After his marriage, he came to me . . . He said: "I can't!"' Dr Vasilev gestures with the man's forearm as he would with his own. 'And now . . . he has four children!'

Despite the happy ending, and all Dr Vasilev's efforts to make himself clear, the man is none the wiser. At least Dr Vasilev's doctor-friend knew what it was he couldn't do. 'Wait a few days,' advises Dr Vasilev, 'doucement, gently.' Everything will be all right, he promises, and he pulls over the pad of prescription paper. The name of the drug is Yohimbine. 'It's an aphro – di – si – AC!', cries Dr Vasilev, who's never shown such enthusiasm over a prescription before. Yohimbine is good, he says, he's taken it himself. But I know better than to ask him how it works.

Half an hour before doing 'this thing', he tells the man, take this medicine. The man thanks us and joins his family outside

in the waiting room. He's behaved so well that he can't possibly
have understood. He'll be giving the Yohimbine to his wife,
I'm sure. The orderly comes in immediately afterwards to ask
what the girl's deformity was. He can't believe it when we
tell him. Baya leads the girl away, saying to her over and over
again, in Kabyl and French: 'You're a normal girl, you're
made the same way as all the others.'

Yohimbine is a plant extract made by a French firm, Houdé.
It increases the motility of the gut, and in women it stimulates
the secretion of milk after delivery. It also acts on the 'erectile
centre' in the brain and opens up the blood vessels in the penis.
That would make it an aphrodisiac. But this particular property has never been subjected to proper clinical trials. So says
Louis Vidal in his *Pharmaceutical Dictionary* that was published
in Paris in 1960 and that's kept (or rather, that happens to be)
in the top lefthand corner of Dr Vasilev's desk.

I've left Out-Patients early, and I've spread the office desk
with old brochures and put glasses and iced water from the
kitchen on top. I'm offering a farewell whisky. Before the
others arrive, I take some up to Zora, so that she can taste it
behind the door of the midwife's room.

The Electrician is the first to arrive. He tells us that the Director decided on a dog offensive this morning. They made meat-
balls and injected them with a poison from the Pharmacy.
Then they threw them over towards the heap of rubble. That
ought to have raised suspicions in the mind of any Algerian
dog, but my bits of steak must have been providing some
counter-conditioning.

The Electrician puts his glass down and plays the ugly dog,
with half a foreleg, the one who limps. He provides a commentary at the same time. Whisky bottle becomes meatball, and
the Electrician sniffs and limps around it, keeping on his dark
glasses with a finger. Dr Vasilev watches goggle-eyed, like a
child at a puppet show. 'Sniff-sniff', goes the Electrician,
'limp-limp'. Then he opens his jaws and the bottle cap disappears inside. An 'Ahhh!' from Dr Vasilev. 'It was immediate!' cries the Electrician, fired by his captive audience. His

four limbs go stiff and straight like a scarecrow. He begins breathing very quietly through his mouth, and staring straight ahead. 'That dog knew,' he says dramatically. 'Ahhh!' comes the spellbound echo. The dog stayed in that position for half an hour, the Electrician tells us. Then: 'Pam!' it rolled over dead, and the Electrician falls into a chair. The retriever met an identical fate. The Electrician's laughing. But Dr Vasilev looks shattered. I know what's on his mind. He's afraid for the one-eyed cat.

The kitchen workers come, the storekeeper, the anaesthetist, the morgue-keeper, the painter, the carpenter, the mechanic. Dr Kostov sips his share approvingly. Dr Vasilev keeps in the background. He's been hurt by the Electrician's story, and he's also keeping himself in reserve. This may be my goodbye to the hospital, but it's not his 'Goodbye!' to me. The Electrician takes his glass away with him, untouched. I come across him afterwards, playing cards in the night-porter's office with the Director's cousin, whisky beside him. 'I don't like drinking with Bulgarians around,' he explains unfairly, 'a party with them isn't a party.'

I clean out my room and empty my rubbish over the dogs inside the green refuse truck. Vasileva waves from her kitchen window. She asks me not to eat too much for lunch. It's a very quiet afternoon. I do no curettages, and no births. I want to keep my record clear. I do the little things. I walk up and down the stairs with Dr Vasilev's ovarian cyst, with Dr Nikolenko's Caesarean, as amateur physiotherapy. I suggested a gentle walk in the garden, but the women waved their fingers at me. It has to be done indoors, away from the sight of men.

Goodbye to Djamila, knitting in the midwife's room with Arab music on the radio. She's off in the morning too, to a job on the Moroccan frontier, a thousand miles away. 'I've no regrets,' she tells me, 'Kabylia and me never got on.' No regrets, for me included of course. I was miles from getting to know her.

'This evening,' announces Dr Vasilev after his siesta, 'you will meet . . . two friends!' Their plane from Sofia landed in

Algiers only this morning. My last evening is to be their first: 'Goodbye! – Welcome!' The symmetry is part of Dr Vasilev's plan. I'll be able to give them my experience of Algeria, and they will answer my questions on Bulgaria. They'll have the latest news. 'With my two friends,' Dr Vasilev promises, 'you will discuss!' They're Party members, too, he says, from the same province of Bulgaria as his own, and he tells me the number of kilometres they live from his home town. He seems to like them more than anyone he's spoken of yet.

He takes a phone call from the Director's office. It's brief, and Dr Vasilev's brought down like a bird in full flight. For a moment, he doesn't speak. I wonder if his two friends haven't met with an accident. But then he tells me Maternity's moving to a whole new floor in the main hospital that's been empty for the last three years. The Director wants him over there to give the necessary instructions.

We all go – Dr Vasilev, Dr Kostov, Vasileva, Malika, Baya. For me, it's an 'excursion!' into things as they'll be when I'm gone. It's a trip into the future. It's a moon-walk, through empty wards as echo-chambers, cobwebbed windowsills, gutted mattresses, stained baths, a fantastic voyage through Vasilev country, led by himself, unintrepid.

Dr Kostov and I bring up the rear. Winks, grins and elbows – he's having one of his best-ever days. We're back in Montreal, and I'm 'tu': 'Toi et moi – you and I – we'll put up our plates in Canada, we'll do consultations together, we'll earn lots of money, we'll have cars and houses . . .' Roars of laughter, and an invitation to have supper this evening with him and his wife. I tell him I'm already invited by Dr Vasilev. Another roar of laughter, and a pressing invitation for drinks instead (a business cocktail?). We walk on, and each wink's become a putdown of Vasilev the party-giver, each elbow a dig at Vasilev the Communist.

We find the painter on his ladder, with a small brush and a pot of blue paint. Beneath him, there are two small rooms. They have to be marked DOCTOR'S OFFICE, and CONSULTING ROOM. It's for the head of the department, it's for Dr Vasilev to decide which is to be which. These are the instructions the

Director spoke of. It's not a stupendous problem, nothing's at stake. The two rooms are identical, and empty. They'll serve either purpose equally well. The painter, alert and practical, suggests tossing a coin. But Dr Vasilev stalls him, with inconclusive 'ehs'.

The painter doesn't insist. He shifts his ladder to a third door, and begins writing TOILETS. We stand in a group beneath him, watching him space the letters with his pencil and ruler, and then paint them in.

This is an excursion Dr Vasilev never wanted, never planned. A lined and beaten face, a hoarse voice: 'The Director told me nothing!' He's been turning handles, swinging hinges, clicking switches – the little things as always. An explorer creating his own discovery. He hasn't really seen the two big wards, the thirty extra beds, the proper Theatre for curettages with the proper Theatre light. It's virgin territory, a present for any gynaecologist. But not for Dr Vasilev, not now. Two extra wards will only be a new mould for his depression, he has such a colossal fund to draw on. Bleary-eyed in the glare of the possibilities offered by the new department, overawed by the painter's brush, Dr Vasilev's not for resuscitation. Heart massage will only crack his ribs, tear his lungs. It's best to leave him be.

There's a beginning of a storm at dusk, a storm that never breaks. A hot wind brings on the evening faster. Dr Kostov comes to the main door of Maternity in his sandals, holding his bottle of iced water, scowling at the dust and feathers being raised in spirals from the courtyard. Doors swing and slam throughout the hospital, trees are forced over to show the white undersides of their branches, nurses run down the corridors of Paediatrics, banging windows shut.

Drinks at the Kostovs: we talk of medical school and England. He wants to come and visit. The wine's Mascara, and he's charming. He has to be. After all, I've seen the worst of Dr Kostov. This is his higher self. But it's no revelation. Ivanov and the Czech doctor in the mountains would pour Mascara with just the same smile.

Goodbye to Zora. She's on duty with the new midwife, come

to take Djamila's place, and she's telling her how hard night work can be, with as many as ten deliveries sometimes, plus all the patients to look after, especially those who've had operations in the day. The new midwife looks impressed and wonders how she'll cope. Zora reassures her magisterially. Then Fatma arrives from cleaning downstairs, to spoil everything by saying, and not so naïvely: 'Still up, Mademoiselle Zora?' It's not even nine o'clock.

The wind's dropped. In my room, I collect all that belongs to the Vasilevs. The *Life* and *Paris-Match* magazines that I still have from that first evening, dusty from the storm that never was, a 100-page report from Roche on *The Uses of Hormones in Gynaecology* – Dr Vasilev had passed it on to me, no longer a brochure but almost a book – and a salt-and-pepper set that Vasileva had bought in the souks of Tunis.

Dr Vasilev answers the door a little anxiously. They've been waiting for me. I don't like to say that I've been having drinks at the Kostovs. Instead, I tell Dr Vasilev that I wanted him to have time to be with his friends. 'But you also are my friend,' he says, taking me inside.

They've rearranged the furniture. The table's been brought from the wall into the centre of the room. The two friends: they get up, their hands ready. But Dr Vasilev holds us apart. Introductions are not to be rushed. On his left '. . . a great English friend!' who's going to grow into a fine little doctor. On his right '. . . two great Bulgarian friends!' engineers by profession. He allows us to shake hands. I like their faces!

Dr Vasilev puts glasses in our hands and sits us down. The table's been laid with a cloth, and with all Vasileva's specialities, her yoghurt soup, stuffed peppers, tomato salad, fried chicken. I take one of her beautiful chips. She's keeping the oil hot, she says, there'll be plenty more. Then, beside the bottle in the centre of the table, I spy an envelope with my name on it. 'Oh-ho!' cries Dr Vasilev. I can't match his own excitement as I open it. Inside, there are three photographs. Calie and Vasileva, me and Dr Vasilev, in front of the giant green rushes; me and Dr Vasilev again, on the bonnet of the Peugeot 404.

On the back of each one, he's written in pencil: 'Dellys, Algérie, 1970'.

The bottle in the centre of the table is not Mascara, nor Martini, nor anything like that. It has no label and the liquid inside is brown. It looks powerful stuff, corrosive and explosive, inside its extra-thick glass. 'Our whisky!' announces Dr Vasilev. It's Bulgarian national brandy, a whole litre of it, 'the oldest and finest', says the pleasanter of the two pleasant engineers, and imported from Sofia this morning. Dr Vasilev pours us a glassful each. They coach me in pronouncing its name, the way people do at goodwill gatherings, toasting each other's national differences. They show me how to drink it: 'Pam!' I begin to sweat, and Dr Vasilev's reminded of our first evening together, when Vasileva had given me a towel for my face and we'd examined the thermometer together: '36°!'

But now to more serious things. 'Politics!' exclaims Dr Vasilev, 'po – li – TICS!' That is what men talk about, round the brandy bottle in Bulgaria. Vasileva politely smiles. She's not keen, and nor am I. I'm happy as it is, digesting the alcohol and enjoying her food. But Dr Vasilev's not to be dissuaded. The brandy's making short work of him, drunk as he already is on the company, and undermined by too little food and too many cigarettes. He invites me to ask his friends all my questions on Bulgaria. I say that I don't really have any. He insists, so I ask the pleasanter engineer if he's a member of the Communist Party. He says he is. 'Me too!' cries Dr Vasilev tipsily. I ask them why. Dr Vasilev can't give a reason. The engineer takes over, explaining that the Party is the only force in Bulgaria that's able to build a workers' state.

I must look unconvinced, because he then asks me, coming from a capitalist country as I do, to say 'sincerely' what I think about their country. He insists on the 'sincerely'. Dr Vasilev raises his glass over our confrontation, an unsteady matchmaker. I don't know where to begin, not on my last night. I try to say that their communism isn't what it says it is, that it's not even a social democracy, that it's a lie, a so-called workers' state with a bureaucracy more oppressive and alienating than capitalism. And so on, but only a few sentences. There seems to be no point going on, no one has the slightest idea what I'm saying. Dr Vasilev's smile hasn't left his face, the engineer seems pleased too, they haven't even understood that what I'm saying could be offensive. I should have kept to the brandy and the food.

But I've set Dr Vasilev going. 'Me', he cries, 'I was in the . . .' – he pronounces a word that sounds like 'goof'. 'The G – U – F!', he says, spelling the letters for me. I'm no wiser. He's well drunk by this time, and he goes on to tell me the wretched fact that during the five years he spent studying medicine in Padua before the second world war, he was in the 'Gruppo Universitario Fascista'. It used to be known by its initials as 'the GUF'. 'Hey!', cries Dr Vasilev nostalgically, 'the GUF!' He was actually its representative abroad. Why did he join? 'With my GUF card', he says, 'I used to get a reduction on public transport of 50 per cent!' Did he ever manage to see Mussolini? 'Of course!' He tells me of a big conference he helped to organize for all the Axis youth movements. They had 'young people from Germany . . . Japan . . . and Italy, naturally!' The GUF organized it all in Padua. Hitler came too, says Dr Vasilev, and as a GUF representative he was able to get close and take all the photographs he wanted. He's got a special album commemorating the occasion, that he'll show me when I come to visit him in Bulgaria.

Did it make things difficult for joining the Communist Party in Bulgaria after the war? 'Not at all!' cries Dr Vasilev, and the pleasanter engineer leans forward to explain: 'The Doctor admitted his mistakes.'

The word's odd. Nothing Dr Vasilev's said has given any indication that he thinks a mistake was made. On the contrary, fascism was his youth, the time when he was alive. I feel resentment and anger. I want to get up and go. But I realize I'm wrong. Even as a fascist – above all, as a fascist – he must have been pathetic. What can his body have looked like in boots and a blackshirt? Who could have called to him for help in a beer-house brawl, who could have relied on Dr Vasilev to kick a communist to death? And what sort of fascist is it who takes Hitler's picture because he's keen on photography? He must have scandalized the German delegates. Only the Italian party could have admitted such a member to its ranks.

There follows an insane moment in which Dr Vasilev throws his right arm in the air. I could bring it down with a single finger, but why bother now. He raises his glass and invites us to drink to Mussolini's 'Per Noi! – For Us!' The others join in, saluting too, and they all drink to the toast again.

That's the climax. The glow leaves the evening and Dr Vasilev becomes tiny and hunched once more. 'All that,' he tells me, 'it was just politics.' Vasileva comes back from the kitchen, to brake his progress downhill. He rambles on incoherently about the price of gas in Bulgaria and Algeria, with his hand on my arm, and he's too drunk to see his wife pouring away half of each glass before he touches it, he's too drunk to sense the total lack of respect being shown 'the great Doctor', as the others had called him when the brandy bottle was still full, despised by his friends, despised by his staff, universally pathetic. He complains that I'm leaving. Vasileva's long-suffering face as she sees me to the door.

They all came to the garage to see me off. Dr Kostov seemed moved, not just by the thought I was driving to sterling country. Dr Vasilev lifted his thin arms in a peculiar triumphant salute, vestige of his Paduan days, as I actually drove away. If only they'd known I'd been a spy all the time. Dr Kostov would have hauled me off my horse, he'd have kicked and punched and called me a prostate. Dr Vasilev couldn't have said I was very sympathetic. One of his betrayed 'Ahhhs!'

PIMLICO

PAUL SCOTT   A Life by Hilary Spurling

'Must rate as one of the best biographies written since the War. It is a brilliant and disturbing study of a gifted writer whose engaging manner and apparent normality concealed a violent and obsessive nature.' Selina Hastings, *Harpers & Queen*

SURVIVING THE HOLOCAUST   The Kovno Ghetto Diary by Avraham Tory; edited and introduced by Martin Gilbert

'We have here a record of what it is like to live through seasons in Hell . . . Remarkable and unforgettable, I cannot commend this book too highly to anyone who seeks to understand these terrible times.' Allan Massie, *Sunday Telegraph*

BATTLES OF THE ENGLISH CIVIL WAR by Austin Woolrych

'An excellent book . . . It covers the three decisive engagements which sealed the fate of King Charles I: Marston Moor [July 1644] which lost him the North, Naseby [June 1645] which lost him most of his army, and Preston [August 1648] which lost him his head . . . It most skilfully indicates all the essential connections between the Civil War's political, social and military aspects.' C.V. Wedgwood, *Daily Telegraph*

THE ENGLISHMAN'S FOOD   Five Centuries of English Diet by J.C. Drummond and Anne Wilbraham; introduction by Tom Jaine

'The achievement of this pioneering book is very great. It remains a remarkable contribution to the study of eating habits and health in society.' Derek Cooper

BADEN-POWELL by Tim Jeal

'In an age of good biographies, here is one that deserves to be called great . . . a magnificent book.' Piers Brendon, *Mail on Sunday*

BRITANNIA   A History of Roman Britain by Sheppard Frere

'Brilliant . . . An integrated commentary and comprehensive judgement on the whole Romano-British scene.' *The Times Literary Supplement*

WEEK-END WODEHOUSE Introduction by Hilaire Belloc

'A peerless collection.' Max Hastings, *Sunday Times*

THE FACE OF BATTLE by John Keegan

'This without any doubt is one of the half-dozen best books on warfare to appear in the English language since the end of the Second World War.' Michael Howard, *Sunday Times*

ALAN MOOREHEAD by Tom Pocock

'Pocock's biography is excellent . . . it would be difficult to think of a better guide to the life of a Second World War correspondent.' Frank McLynn, *Sunday Telegraph*

THE CONTROL OF NATURE by John McPhee

'This splendid book describes three monumental acts of defiance against Mother Nature . . . The human drama is almost as breathtaking as the scale of these enterprises.' *Observer*

ARIEL   A Shelley Romance by André Maurois

'An historic landmark in modern literary biography, as fine as any miniature produced by Lytton Strachey or Harold Nicolson.' Richard Holmes

COMPLETE VERSE by Hilaire Belloc; introduction by A. N. Wilson

'The verses sing a multitude of memories. The wonder is, in finding them all collected, how profuse and pure a genius is here displayed.' Evelyn Waugh, *Spectator*

CROSSMAN   The Pursuit of Power by Anthony Howard

'Written from a background of great political knowledge and with shafts of penetrating insight . . . I doubt if it will be quickly, if ever, superseded.' Roy Jenkins, *Sunday Times*

GEORGIAN LONDON by John Summerson; a new illustrated and revised edition

'The scintillating text of this provocative classic was never matched by worthy pictures. Now, with a complete, handsome revamp, and with an Epilogue bringing the story up to date, the whole fine book at last truly reflects the perfection of the buildings.' Graham Hughes, *Arts Review*

SELF PORTRAIT WITH FRIENDS   The Selected Diaries of Cecil Beaton Edited by Richard Buckle

'His book shows him to be sharper and more sardonic with his pen than with his camera – no less talented a portraitist, but an exacter and sometimes a crueller one. What this gifted, witty, sensitive creature writes best about is people. This is a minor masterpiece of wit and observation.' Cyril Ray, *Daily Mail*

F.E. SMITH   First Earl of Birkenhead by John Campbell

'A triumph of scholarship, judgement, lucidity and art . . . Like its subject, John Campbell's book is leisurely, feline and very, very clever.' Roy Foster, *Guardian*

A VERY CLOSE CONSPIRACY   Vanessa Bell and Virginia Woolf by Jane Dunn

'This is not only an important book in its own field, the triumphant outcome of years of loving concentration, but a book of rare discernment and imagination. It is one of the few books which allows me to believe that the author actually knew both my mother and my aunt, and I welcome it as deepening my understanding both of them and their relation to Bloomsbury.' Angelica Garnett

THE POUND ERA by Hugh Kenner

'Not so much a book as a library, or better, a new kind of book in which biography, history and the analysis of literature are harmoniously articulated . . . For the student of modern letters it is a treasure, for the general reader it is one of the most interesting books he will ever pick up in a lifetime of reading.' Guy Davenport, *National Review*